CHILTON'S
REPAIR & TUNE-UP GUIDE

GM
A-BODY
1982-83

Chevrolet CELEBRITY • Buick CENTURY
Oldsmobile CUTLASS CIERA • Pontiac 6000

Vice President and General Manager JOHN P. KUSHNERICK
Managing Editor KERRY A. FREEMAN, S.A.E.
Senior Editor RICHARD J. RIVELE, S.A.E.
Editor CARL CANFIELD, S.A.E.

CHILTON BOOK COMPANY
Radnor, Pennsylvania
19089

SAFETY NOTICE

Proper service and repair procedures are vital to the safe, reliable operation of all motor vehicles, as well as the personal safety of those performing repairs. This book outlines procedures for servicing and repairing vehicles using safe, effective methods. The procedures contain many NOTES, CAUTIONS and WARNINGS which should be followed along with standard safety procedures to eliminate the possibility of personal injury or improper service which could damage the vehicle or compromise its safety.

It is important to note that repair procedures and techniques, tools and parts for servicing motor vehicles, as well as the skill and experience of the individual performing the work vary widely. It is not possible to anticipate all of the conceivable ways or conditions under which vehicles may be serviced, or to provide cautions as to all of the possible hazards that may result. Standard and accepted safety precautions and equipment should be used when handling toxic or flammable fluids, and safety goggles or other protection should be used during cutting, grinding, chiseling, prying, or any other process that can cause material removal or projectiles.

Some procedures require the use of tools specially designed for a specific purpose. Before substituting another tool or procedure, you must be completely satisfied that neither your personal safety, nor the performance of the vehicle will be endangered.

Although information in this guide is based on industry sources and is as complete as possible at the time of publication, the possibility exists that the manufacturer made later changes which could not be included here. While striving for total accuracy, Chilton Book Company cannot assume responsibility for any errors, changes, or omissions that may occur in the compilation of this data.

PART NUMBERS

Part numbers listed in this reference are not recommendations by Chilton for any product by brand name. They are references that can be used with interchange manuals and aftermarket supplier catalogs to locate each brand supplier's discrete part number.

ACKNOWLEDGMENTS

The Chilton Book Company expresses its appreciation to the General Motors Corporation, Detroit, Michigan for their generous assistance.

Information has been selected from shop manuals, owners manuals, service bulletins and technical training manuals.

Copyright © 1983 by Chilton Book Company
All Rights Reserved
Published in Radnor, Pennsylvania 19089, by Chilton Book Company
and simultaneously in Canada by Fleet Publishers,
a Division of International Thomson Limited,
1410 Birchmount Road, Scarborough, Ontario MIP 2E7

Manufactured in the United States of America
1234567890   0219876543

Chilton's Repair & Tune-Up Guide: GM A-Body 1982–83
ISBN 0-8019-7309-0 pbk.
Library of Congress Catalog Card No. 82-72931

CONTENTS

Quick Reference Specifications For Your Vehicle

Fill in this chart with the most commonly used specifications for your vehicle. Specifications can be found in Chapters 1 through 3 or on the tune-up decal under the hood of the vehicle.

Tune-Up

Firing Order_____

Spark Plugs:

   Type_____

   Gap (in.)_____

Point Gap (in.)_____

Dwell Angle (°)_____

Ignition Timing (°)_____

   Vacuum (Connected/Disconnected)_____

Valve Clearance (in.)

   Intake_____   **Exhaust**_____

Capacities

Engine Oil (qts)

   With Filter Change_____

   Without Filter Change_____

Cooling System (qts)_____

Manual Transmission (pts)_____

   Type_____

Automatic Transmission (pts)_____

   Type_____

Front Differential (pts)_____

   Type_____

Rear Differential (pts)_____

   Type_____

Transfer Case (pts)_____

   Type_____

FREQUENTLY REPLACED PARTS

Use these spaces to record the part numbers of frequently replaced parts.

PCV VALVE

Manufacturer_____

Part No._____

OIL FILTER

Manufacturer_____

Part No._____

AIR FILTER

Manufacturer_____

Part No._____

General Information and Maintenance

HOW TO USE THIS BOOK

Chilton's Repair and Tune-Up Guide for the GM A-Body is designed to teach you some of the operating principles of your car, and guide you through maintenance and repair operations. You can perform many repairs yourself, as long as you have the time, initiative, patience, and an assortment of basic tools.

A secondary purpose of this book is a reference for owners who want to understand their car and/or their mechanics better. In this case, no tools at all are required.

Chapters 1 and 2 will probably be the most frequently used in the book. The first chapter contains all the information that may be required at a moment's notice—information such as the location of the various serial numbers and the proper towing instructions. It also contains all the information on basic day-to-day maintenance that you will need to ensure good performance and long component life. Chapter 2 covers tune-up procedures which will assist you not only in keeping the engine running properly and at peak performance levels, but also in restoring some of the more delicate components to operating condition in the event of a failure. Chapters 3 through 11 cover repairs (rather than maintenance) for various portions of the car, with each chapter covering either one system or two related systems. The appendix then lists general information which may be useful in rebuilding the engine or performing some other operation on any car.

In using the Table of Contents, refer to the bold listings for the beginning of the chapter. See the smaller listings or the index for information on a particular component or specifications.

Before removing any bolts, read through the entire procedure. This will give you the overall view of what tools and supplies will be required. There is nothing more frustrating than having to walk to the bus stop on Monday morning because you were short one bolt on Sunday afternoon. So read ahead and plan ahead. Each operation should be approached logically and all procedures thoroughly understood before attempting any work.

Cautions and notes will be provided where appropriate to help prevent you from injuring yourself or damaging your car. Therefore, you should read through the entire procedure before beginning the work, and make sure that you are aware of the warnings. Since no number of warnings could cover every possible situation, you should work slowly and try to envision what is going to happen in each operation ahead of time.

When it comes to tightening things, there is generally a slim area between too loose to properly seal or resist vibration and so tight as to risk damage or warping. When dealing with major engine parts, or with any aluminum component, it pays to procure a torque wrench and go by the recommended figures.

When reference is made in this book to the "right side" or "left side" of the car, it should be understood that the positions are always to be viewed from the front seat. Thus, the left side of the car is always the driver's side and the right side is always the passenger's side, even when facing the car, as when working on the engine.

We have attempted to eliminate the use of special tools whenever possible, substituting more readily available hand tools. However, in some cases the special tools are necessary. These can be purchased from your General Motors dealer, or an automotive parts store.

Always be conscious of the need for safety in your work. Never get under the car unless it is firmly supported by jackstands or ramps. Never smoke near or allow flame to get near the battery or the fuel system. Keep your

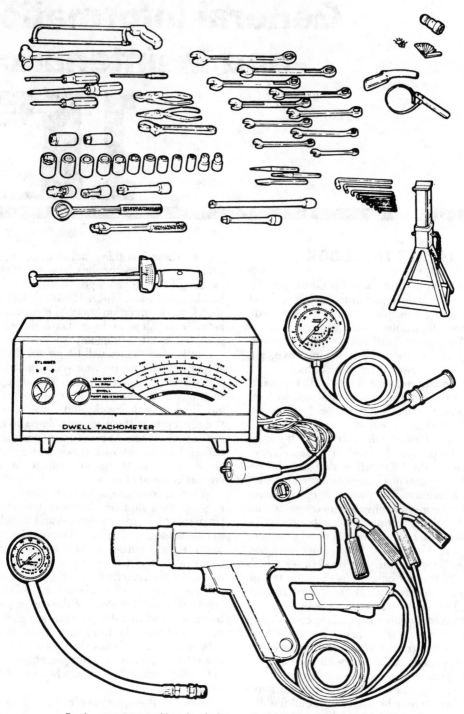

Basic assortment of handtools for most maintenance and repair jobs

clothing, hands and hair clear of the fan and pulleys when working near the engine, if it is running. Most importantly, try to be patient; even in the midst of an argument with a stubborn bolt, reaching for the largest hammer in the garage is usually a cause for later regret and more extensive repair. As you gain confidence and experience, working on your car will become a source of pride and satisfaction.

When repair is not considered practical, we tell you how to remove the part and then how to install the new or rebuilt replacement. In this way, you at least save the labor costs. This book will not explain such things as rebuilding the differential for the simple reason that the expertise required and the investment in special tools make this task uneconomical.

TOOLS AND EQUIPMENT

It would be impossible to catalog each and every tool that you may need to perform all the operations included in this book. It would also not be wise for the amateur to rush out and buy an expensive set of tools on the theory that he may need one of them at some time. The best approach is to proceed slowly, gathering together a good quality set of those tools that are used most frequently. Don't be misled by the low cost of bargain tools. It is far better to spend a little more for quality, name brand tools. Forged wrenches, 12 point sockets and fine-tooth ratchets are a better investment than their less expensive counterparts. As any good mechanic can tell you, there are few worse experiences than trying to work on a car or truck with bad tools. Your monetary savings will be far outweighed by frustration and mangled knuckles.

Begin accumulating those tools that are used most frequently: those associated with routine maintenance and tune-up. In addition to the normal assortment of screwdrivers and pliers, you should have the following tools for routine maintenance jobs:

1. SAE (or Metric) or SAE/Metric wrenches—sockets and combination open end/box end wrenches in sizes from ⅛ in. (3 mm) to ¾ in. (19 mm) and a spark plug socket (⅝ in.).

If possible, buy various length socket drive extensions. One break in this department is that the metric sockets available in the U.S. will all fit the ratchet handles and extensions you may already have (¼, ⅜, and ½ in. drive);

2. Jackstands—for support;
3. Oil filter wrench;
4. Oil filler spout—for pouring oil;
5. Grease gun—for chassis lubrication;
6. A container for draining oil;
7. Many rags for wiping up the inevitable mess.

In addition to the above items there are several others that are not absolutely necessary, but handy to have around. These include "oil dry" (oil-absorbent), a transmission funnel and the usual supply of lubricants, antifreeze and fluids, although these can be purchased as needed. This is a basic list for routine maintenance, but only your personal needs and desire can accurately determine your list of tools.

A more advanced set of tools, suitable for tune-up work, can be drawn up easily. While the tools are slightly more sophisticated, they need not be outrageously expensive. The key to these purchases is to make them with an eye towards adaptability and wide range. A basic list of tune-up tools could include:

1. Tachometer;
2. Spark plug gauge and gapping tool;
3. Feeler gauges;
4. Timing light.

The choice of a timing light should be made carefully. A light which works on the DC current supplied by the car battery is the best choice; it should have a xenon tube for brightness. Since all A-Body cars have an electronic ignition system, the timing light should have an inductive pickup which clamps around the No. 1 spark plug cable (the timing light illustrated has one of these pickups).

In addition to these basic tools, there are several other tools and gauges which, though not particularly necessary for basic tune-up work, you may find to be quite useful. These include:

1. A compression gauge. The screw-in type seals easily and eliminates the need for a remote starting switch during compression testing.
2. A manifold vacuum gauge;
3. A 12 VDC test light;
4. A combination volt/ohmmeter;
5. An induction meter, used to determine whether or not there is current flowing through a wire.

Finally, you will find a torque wrench necessary for all but the most basic of work. The beam-type models are perfectly adequate. The newer click-type (breakaway) and digital torque wrenches are more accurate, but are also much more expensive and must be periodically recalibrated.

Special Tools

Most of the jobs covered in this guide can be accomplished with commonly available hand tools. However, in some cases special tools are required. Your General Motors dealer can probably supply the necessary tools, or they can be ordered from:

Kent-Moore Corporation
1501 South Jackson St.
Jackson, MI. 49203

SERVICING YOUR CAR SAFELY

It is virtually impossible to anticipate all of the hazards involved with automotive maintenance and service, but care and common sense will prevent most accidents.

The rules of safety for mechanics range from "don't smoke around gasoline," to "use the proper tool for the job." The trick to avoiding injuries is to develop safe work habits and take every possible precaution.

Do's

• Do keep a fire extinguisher and first aid kit within easy reach.

• Do wear safety glasses or goggles when cutting, drilling, grinding or prying, even if you have 20-20 vision. If you wear glasses for the sake of vision, then they should be made of hardened glass that can serve also as safety glasses, or wear safety goggles over your regular glasses.

• Do shield your eyes whenever you work around the battery. Batteries contain sulphuric acid; in case of contact with the eyes or skin, flush the area with water or a mixture of water and baking soda and get medical attention immediately.

• Do use safety stands for any undercar service. Jacks are for raising vehicles; safety stands are for making sure the vehicle stays raised until you want it to come down. Whenever the vehicle is raised, block the wheels remaining on the ground and set the parking brake.

• Do use adequate ventilation when working with any chemicals. Like carbon monoxide, the asbestos dust resulting from brake lining wear can be poisonous in sufficient quantities.

• Do disconnect the negative battery cable when working on the electrical system. The secondary ignition system can contain up to 40,000 volts.

• Do follow manufacturer's directions whenever working with potentially hazardous materials. Both brake fluid and antifreeze are poisonous if taken internally.

• Do properly maintain your tools. Loose hammerheads, mushroomed punches and

chisels, frayed or poorly grounded electrical cords, excessively worn screwdrivers, spread wrenches (open end), cracked sockets, slipping ratchets, or faulty droplight sockets can cause accidents.

• Do use the proper size and type of tool for the job being done.

• Do when possible, pull on a wrench handle rather than push on it, and adjust your stance to prevent a fall.

• Do be sure that adjustable wrenches are tightly adjusted on the nut or bolt and pulled so that the face is on the side of the fixed jaw.

• Do select a wrench or socket that fits the nut or bolt. The wrench or socket should sit straight, not cocked.

• Do strike squarely with a hammer—avoid glancing blows.

• Do set the parking brake and block the drive wheels if the work requires that the engine be running.

Dont's

• Don't run an engine in a garage or anywhere else without proper ventilation—EVER! Carbon monoxide is poisonous; it takes a long time to leave the human body and you can build up a deadly supply of it in your system by simply breathing in a little every day. You may not realize you are slowly poisoning yourself. Always use power vents, windows, fans or open the garage doors.

• Don't work around moving parts while wearing a necktie or other loose clothing. Short sleeves are much safer than long, loose sleeves and hard-toed shoes with neoprene soles protect your toes and give a better grip on slippery surfaces. Jewelry such as watches, fancy belt buckles, beads or body adornment of any kind is not safe working around a car. Long hair should be hidden under a hat or cap.

• Don't use pockets for toolboxes. A fall or bump can drive a screwdriver deep into your body. Even a wiping cloth hanging from the back pocket can wrap around a spinning shaft or fan.

• Don't smoke when working around gasoline, cleaning solvent or other flammable material.

• Don't smoke when working around the battery. When the battery is being charged, it gives off explosive hydrogen gas.

• Don't use gasoline to wash your hands; there are excellent soaps available. Gasoline may contain lead, and lead can enter the body through a cut, accummulating in the body until you are very ill. Gasoline also removes all the natural oils from the skin so that bone dry hands will suck up oil and grease.

Always support the car on jackstands when working underneath it

• Don't service the air conditioning system unless you are equipped with the necessary tools and training. The refrigerant, R-12, is extremely cold and when exposed to the air, will instantly freeze any surface it comes in contact with, including your eyes. Although the refrigerant is normally non-toxic, R-12 becomes a deadly poisonous gas in the presence of an open flame. One good whiff of the vapors from burning refrigerant can be fatal.

SERIAL NUMBER IDENTIFICATION

Vehicle

The vehicle identification number (V.I.N.) is a seventeen digit alpha-numeric sequence stamped on a plate which is located at the top, left-hand side of the instrument panel.

As far as the car owner is concerned, many of the digits in the V.I.N. are of little or no value. At certain times, it may be necessary to refer to the V.I.N. to interpret certain information, such as when ordering replacement parts or determining if your vehicle is involved in a factory service campaign (recall). In either of these instances, the following information may be helpful:

• 1ST DIGIT—Indicates the place of manufacture. A "1" designates the U.S.A.; "2" designates Canada.

• 8TH DIGIT—Indicates the type and the manufacturer of the original engine which was installed in the vehicle (see "engine").

• 10TH DIGIT—Indicates the model year of the vehicle. "C" designates a 1982 model, "D" is for 1983, and so on.

• 11TH DIGIT—Indicates the specific plant at which the vehicle was assembled.

• 12TH–17TH DIGITS—This is the plant sequential number, which identifies the specific number of each vehicle within a production run. In the event or engineering change of a recall involving only a certain quantity of vehicles within a production run, the affected vehicles can be identified.

Body

An identification plate for body-related items is attached to the front tie bar, just behind the passenger side headlamp. Information on the body identification plate would rarely be useful to the owner. An illustration of the plate is provided.

Engine

The engine identification code will sometimes be required to order replacement engine parts. The code is stamped in different locations, depending upon the size of the engine. Refer to the accompanying illustrations to determine the code location for your engine.

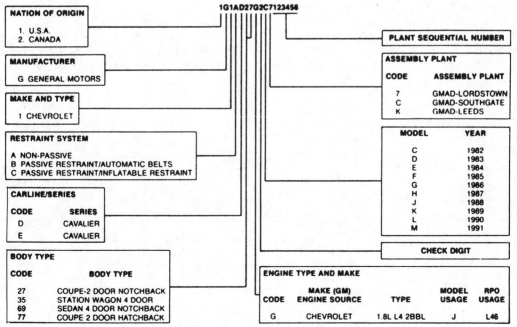

Vehicle Identification Numbers

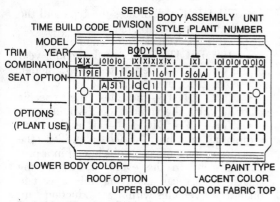

Body identification plate

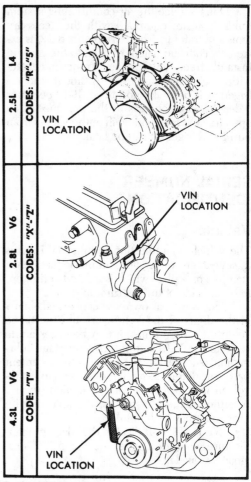

Engine VIN locations

Transaxle

The transaxle code serves the same purpose as the engine identification code. Transaxle code locations may be determined by referring to the accompanying illustration.

ROUTINE MAINTENANCE

Proper maintenance of any vehicle is the key to long and trouble-free vehicle life. As a conscientious car owner, set aside a Saturday morning, say once a month, to check or replace items which could cause major problems later. Keep your own personal log to jot down which services you performed, how much parts cost you, the date, and the exact odometer reading at the time. Keep all receipts for such items as engine oil and filters, so that they may be referred to in case of related problems or to determine operating expenses. As a do-it-yourselfer, these receipts are the only proof you have that the required maintenance was performed. In the event of a warranty problem, these receipts will be invaluable.

The literature provided with your car when it was originally delivered includes the fac-

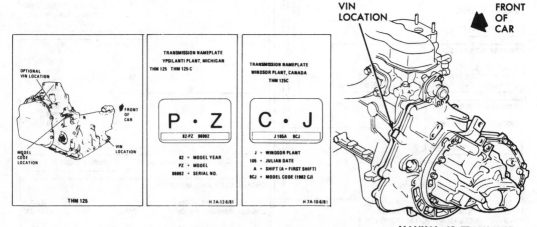

Transaxle identification number location

Engine Identification

8th Digit of V.I.N.	Option Code	Engine Displacement Cu. In. (L)	Engine Manufacturer	Fuel Delivery System
R	LR8	151 (2.5)	Pontiac	T.B.I.
5	LW9	151 (2.5)	Pontiac	2 bbl. carb.
X①	LE2	173 (2.8)	Chevrolet	2 bbl. carb.
Z②	LH7	173 (2.8)	Chevrolet	2 bbl. carb.
E	LK9	183 (3.0)	Buick	2 bbl. carb.
T	LT7	263 (4.3)	Oldsmobile	Diesel-F.I.

① Standard performance engine
② High performance engine
bbl. carb.—barrel carburetor

F.I.—Fuel injection
T.B.I.—Throttle body (fuel injection); Sometimes referred to as E.F.I. (electronic fuel injection).

tory-recommended maintenance schedule. If you do not have the factory schedule, we have provided a "mirror image" of the GM schedule which should be used. No matter which schedule is used, follow it to the letter. Even if your A-Body was previously owned, it is important that the maintenance be performed. The effects of poor maintenance can at least be halted by initiating a regular maintenance program.

Air Cleaner

Regular air cleaner element replacement is a must, since a partially clogged element will cause a performance loss, decreased fuel mileage, and engine damage if enough dirt gets into the cylinders and contaminates the engine oil.

The air cleaner element must be checked periodically. Replacement of the element is simply a matter of removing the wing nut(s) from the air cleaner lid, lifting off the lid, and removing the old filter element. Wipe the inside of the housing with a damp cloth before placing the new element into the housing. When tightening the wing nut(s), just snug it down with moderate finger pressure. Excessive tightening of the wing nut(s) will damage components.

NOTE: *Never attempt to clean or soak the element in gasoline, oil, or cleaning solvent. The element is designed to be a throw-away item.*

PCV Valve

The Positive Crankcase Ventilation (PCV) valve regulates crankcase ventilation during various engine running conditions. At high vacuum

Lift the old filter element out

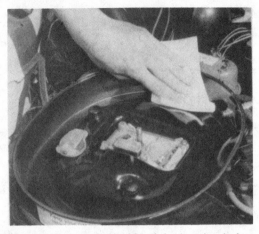

Always wipe out the inside of the housing before installing a new element

2. Slide back the filter retaining clip and remove the old filter.

3. Install the new filter, replace the retaining clip and replace the housing lid.

Evaporative Emissions System

Check the fuel vapor lines and the vacuum hoses for proper connections and correct routing, as well as condition. Replace clogged, damaged or deteriorated parts as necessary.

For more details on the evaporative emissions system, please refer to Chapter Four.

Battery

The single battery used in models equipped with gasoline engines is located at the drivers side front corner of the engine compartment. Because of the added cranking loads, diesel models use two batteries; one in each front corner of the engine compartment. All models use a Delco Freedom II® battery. Though this battery is considered to be maintenance-free due to the fact that it will never need water added, the battery should be given some attention once in a while.

The major cause of slow engine cranking or a "no-start" condition is battery terminals

(idle speed and partial load range) it will open slightly and at low vacuum (full throttle) it will open fully. This causes vapors to be drawn from the crankcase by engine vacuum and then sucked into the combustion chamber where they are dissipated.

The PCV valve must be replaced every 30,000 miles. Details on the PCV system, including system tests, are given in Chapter Four.

The valve is located in a rubber grommet in the valve cover, connected to the air cleaner housing by a large diameter rubber hose. To replace the valve:

1. Pull the valve (with the hose attached) from the rubber grommet in the valve cover.

2. Remove the valve from the hose.

3. Install a new valve into the hose.

4. Press the valve back into the rubber grommet in the valve cover.

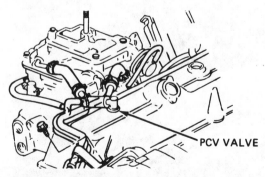

PCV valve

PCV FILTER

The PCV filter is located in the air cleaner housing and must be replaced every 50,000 miles.

1. Remove the air cleaner housing lid.

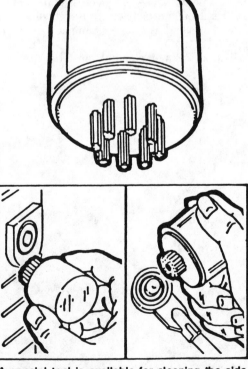

A special tool is available for cleaning the side terminals and clamps

which are loose, dirty, or corroded. Every 3 months or so, disconnect the battery and clean the terminals of both the battery and the cables. Cleaning tools for this purpose are available at most any auto parts store. When you buy a cleaning tool, be sure to specify whether you have a top terminal or side terminal battery, as the type of tool differs depending upon the style of battery.

CAUTION: *When loosening or tightening the positive battery cable screw(s) at the battery, DO NOT touch the wrench to any metal surface. Personal injury and/or component damage will result.*

NOTE: *To use a terminal cleaning tool on the battery(s), it will probably be necessary to remove the windshield washer bottle (all models) or the coolant recovery tank (diesel only) to gain the necessary clearance.*

Check the battery cables for signs of wear or chafing. If corrosion is present on the cable or if the cable is visible through the cable jacket, the cable assembly should be replaced. If cable replacement is necessary, it is best to purchase a high-quality cable that has the cable jacket sealed to the terminal ends.

Batteries themselves can be cleaned using a solution of baking soda and water. Surface coatings on battery cases can actually conduct electricity which will cause a slight voltage drain, so make sure the battery case is clean. To remove the battery(s):

1. Raise the hood and remove the front end diagonal brace(s) from above the battery(s).

2. Disconnect the battery cables from the battery(s). It may be necessary to use a small box end wrench or a ¼" drive ratchet to sneak in between the battery and the windshield washer (or coolant recovery) tank. Avoid using an open-end wrench for the cable bolts. See the previous "CAUTION".

3. Loosen and remove the battery hold-down bolt and block. The use of a long extension which places the ratchet above the battery makes it very easy to get to the hold-down bolt.

4. Carefully lift the battery from the engine compartment. It may be necessary to remove the air cleaner intake duct (except 4 cyl.) or the intake resonator (4 cyl. only) for clearance.

5. Clean the battery and the battery tray thoroughly with the baking soda/water solution. Don't allow the solution to get into the small vent holes of the battery.

6. Rinse the battery with clear water and wipe it dry with a couple of clean paper towels. Don't use the towels for anything else— they probably have traces of sulfuric acid on them. Dispose of the paper towels.

7. Thoroughly flush the battery tray and the surrounding area with clear water. Using a wire brush, remove any rust which may be on the tray. Clear away the rust and dry the tray.

8. Coat the battery tray liberally with anti-rust paint. Thoroughly clean the battery and cable terminals BEFORE installing the battery.

9. Install the battery in the reverse of steps 1–4. Tighten the hold-down bolt snugly—don't overtighten it.

After you clean the terminals and reconnect the battery, apply a corrosion inhibitor to the terminals. Stay away from using any substance which is not meant specifically for this purpose. Do not apply the corrosion inhibitor to the mating surfaces of the terminals unless specified by the chemical manufacturer.

Any time the engine won't crank, check the color of the battery condition indicator (which is actually a built-in hydrometer). If the indicator is green, the battery is sufficiently charged and in good condition. A complete check of the starter and related wiring should be performed. If the indicator is darkened, the battery is discharged. In this case, the reason for the discharge should be determined (e.g.— low alternator output, voltage draw, etc.) then the battery itself should be tested and recharged. If the indicator is light without a green dot visible or if it is yellow in color, the battery must be replaced—DO NOT attempt to test or recharge a battery with this indicator condition. Test the electrical system after the battery has been replaced.

Drive Belts

BELT TENSION

Every 12 months or 15,000 miles (every 5000 miles on diesel engines, not dependent upon a period in months), check the drive belts for proper tension. Also look for signs of wear, fraying, separation, glazing and so on, and replace the belts as required.

Belt tension should be checked with a gauge made for the purpose. If a gauge is not available, tension can be checked with moderate thumb pressure applied to the belt at its longest span midway between pulleys. If the belt has a free span less than twelve inches, it should deflect approximately ⅛–¼ inch. If the span is longer than twelve inches, deflection can range between ⅛ and ⅜ inches.

NOTE: *Models with diesel engines use a serpentine belt which is automatically adjusted by a spring loaded belt tensioner. Adjustments are not normally required.*

1. Loosen the driven accessory's pivot and mounting bolts.

2. Move the accessory toward or away from

HOW TO SPOT WORN V-BELTS

V-Belts are vital to efficient engine operation—they drive the fan, water pump and other accessories. They require little maintenance (occasional tightening) but they will not last forever. Slipping or failure of the V-belt will lead to overheating. If your V-belt looks like any of these, it should be replaced.

Cracking or weathering

This belt has deep cracks, which cause it to flex. Too much flexing leads to heat build-up and premature failure. These cracks can be caused by using the belt on a pulley that is too small. Notched belts are available for small diameter pulleys.

Softening (grease and oil)

Oil and grease on a belt can cause the belt's rubber compounds to soften and separate from the reinforcing cords that hold the belt together. The belt will first slip, then finally fail altogether.

Glazing

Glazing is caused by a belt that is slipping. A slipping belt can cause a run-down battery, erratic power steering, overheating or poor accessory performance. The more the belt slips, the more glazing will be built up on the surface of the belt. The more the belt is glazed, the more it will slip. If the glazing is light, tighten the belt.

Worn cover

The cover of this belt is worn off and is peeling away. The reinforcing cords will begin to wear and the belt will shortly break. When the belt cover wears in spots or has a rough jagged appearance, check the pulley grooves for roughness.

Separation

This belt is on the verge of breaking and leaving you stranded. The layers of the belt are separating and the reinforcing cords are exposed. It's just a matter of time before it breaks completely.

the engine until the tension is correct. You can use a wooden hammer handle or a broomstick as a lever, but do not use anything metallic.

3. Tighten the bolts and recheck the tension. If new belts have been installed, run the engine for a few minutes, then recheck and readjust as necessary.

It is better to have belts too loose than too tight, because overtight belts will lead to bearing failure, particularly in the water pump and alternator. However, loose belts place an extremely high impact load on the driven component due to the whipping action of the belt.

Cooling System

Every 12 months or 15,000 miles, the following services should be performed:

1. Wash and inspect the radiator cap and the filler neck.

2. Check the coolant level and the degree of freezing protection.

3. If a pressure tester is available, pressure test the system and the radiator cap.

4. Inspect the hoses of the cooling system (expect to replace the hoses at 24 months/30,000 miles).

5. Check the fins of the radiator (or air conditioning condenser, if equipped as such) for blockage.

RADIATOR CAP

Before removing the cap, squeeze the upper radiator hose. If it compresses easily (indicating little or no pressure in the system), the cap may be removed by turning it counterclockwise until it reaches the stop. If any hissing is noted at this point (indicating the release of pressure), wait until the hissing stops before you remove the cap. To completely remove the cap, press downward and turn it counterclockwise.

CAUTION: *To avoid personal injury, DO NOT ATTEMPT to remove the radiator cap while the engine is hot.*

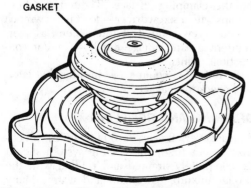

Check the condition of the radiator cap gasket

If the upper radiator hose is hard, pressure is indicated within the system. In this case, a greater degree of caution should be used in removing the cap. Cover the radiator cap with a thick cloth, and while wearing a heavy glove, carefully turn the cap to the stop. This will allow the pressure to be relieved from the system. After the hissing stops, completely remove the cap (press and turn counterclockwise).

Check the condition of the radiator cap gasket and the seal inside of the cap. The radiator cap is designed to seal the cooling system under normal operating conditions which allows the system to build-up a certain amount of pressure (this pressure rating is stamped or printed on the cap). The pressure in the system raises the boiling point of the coolant to help prevent overheating. If the radiator cap does not seal, the boiling point of the coolant is lowered and overheating will occur. If the cap must be replaced, purchase the new cap according to the pressure rating which is specified for your vehicle.

Prior to installing the cap, inspect and clean the radiator filler neck. If you are reusing the old cap, clean it thoroughly with clear water. After turning the cap on, make sure that the arrows on the cap align with the overflow hose.

CHECKING THE COOLANT

Any time the hood is raised, check the level of the coolant in the "see-through" plastic coolant recovery tank. With the engine cold, the coolant level should be near the "ADD" mark on the tank. At normal engine operating temperature, the level should be at the "FULL" mark on the bottle. If coolant must be added to the tank, use a 50/50 mix of coolant/water to adjust the fluid level on models with gasoline engines. On models with diesel engines, use straight, undiluted coolant to adjust the level

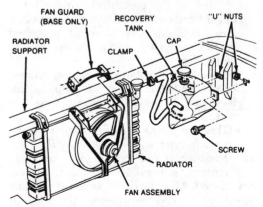

The coolant recovery tank is at the right front of the engine compartment

You can use an inexpensive tester to check anti-freeze protection

in the tank. See "Coolant Requirements" for additional information.

An inexpensive tester may be purchased to test the freezing protection of the coolant. Follow the instructions provided with the tester. The coolant used in models with gasoline engines should protect to −37°F; diesels must have protection to −75°F.

COOLANT REQUIREMENTS

The coolant used in any General Motors engine must:

a. be a high-quality ethylene glycol-based solution. Do not use alcohol or methanol-based solutions at any time.

b. have "built-in" rust inhibitors

c. be designed for year-round use

d. offer complete protection for a minimum of 2 years/30,000 miles, without replacement, as long as the proper concentration is maintained.

e. meet G.M. specification 1825-M (as specified on the container). This point is critical for diesel engines; coolant meeting other specifications could result in cooling system damage and engine damage due to overheating.

f. be mixed in the proper proportions: 50% coolant/50% water for gasoline engines; 64% coolant/36% water for diesel engines.

NOTE: *On diesels, this proportion can be accurately attained only when refilling the system entirely.* See Draining and Refilling.

The use of "self-sealing" coolants is not recommended. Also, the use of a coolant meeting the above requirements negates the need for supplemental additives. Use of such supplemental products is an unnecessary expense and

may cause less than optimum cooling system performance.

HOSES

The upper and lower radiator hoses and the heater hoses should be checked periodically for deterioration, leaks, and loose clamps. G.M. recommends that this be done every 12 months or 15,000 miles. For your own peace of mind, it may be wise to check these items at least every spring and fall, since the summer and winter months wreak the most havoc with your cooling system. Expect to replace the hoses about every 24 months or 30,000 miles. To replace the hoses:

1. Drain the cooling system.

2. Loosen the hose clamps at each end of the hose to be removed. If the clamps are of the type which have a screw positioned vertically in relation to the hose, loosen the screw and gently tap the head of the screw towards the hose. Repeat this until the clamp is loose enough. If corrosion on the clamp prevents loosening in this manner, carefully cut the clamp off with cutters and replace the clamp with a new one.

3. Once the clamps are out of the way, grasp the hose and twist it off of the tube connection using only moderate force. If the hose won't break loose, DON'T use excessive force—doing so can easily damage the heater core and/or radiator tubes. Using a razor blade, carefully slit the portion of the hose which covers the connection point, peel the hose off of the connection and disconnect the hose.

4. If so equipped, disconnect the hose routing clamps from the hose.

5. Remove the hose and clean the hose connection points.

6. Slip the (loosened) hose clamps onto the hose ends and install the new hose, being careful to position the hose so that no interference is encountered.

7. Position the clamps at the ends of the hoses, beyond the sealing bead, and centered on the clamping surface. Tighten the hose clamps with a screwdriver—don't use a wrench on the screw heads to tighten them, as over-tightening can damage the hose and/or connections points.

8. Refill the cooling system (detailed later) and check for leakage.

DRAINING AND REFILLING

At least every 2 years or 30,000 miles (whichever comes first), the cooling system should be completely drained and refilled with the proper mixture of coolant and water. Many mechanics recommend that this be done once

HOW TO SPOT BAD HOSES

Both the upper and lower radiator hoses are called upon to perform difficult jobs in an inhospitable environment. They are subject to nearly 18 psi at under hood temperatures often over 280°F., and must circulate nearly 7500 gallons of coolant an hour—3 good reasons to have good hoses.

A good test for any hose is to feel it for soft or spongy spots. Frequently these will appear as swollen areas of the hose. The most likely cause is oil soaking. This hose could burst at any time, when hot or under pressure.

Swollen hose

Cracked hoses can usually be seen but feel the hoses to be sure they have not hardened; a prime cause of cracking. This hose has cracked down to the reinforcing cords and could split at any of the cracks.

Cracked hose

Weakened clamps frequently are the cause of hose and cooling system failure. The connection between the pipe and hose has deteriorated enough to allow coolant to escape when the engine is hot.

Frayed hose end (due to weak clamp)

Debris, rust and scale in the cooling system can cause the inside of a hose to weaken. This can usually be felt on the outside of the hose as soft or thinner areas.

Debris in cooling system

a year for extra protection against corrosion and subsequent overheating.

Though most coolants are labeled "permanent," this only means that the coolant will retain its anti-freezing characteristics. The required rust inhibitors and other chemicals which were added to the coolant during its manufacture will become less effective over a period of time. The following procedure covers the factory-recommended procedure for draining and refilling the system.

NOTE: *If you are only replacing the hoses, perform steps 1–3, and 11–16 as required.*

1. Remove the radiator cap.

2. Raise the front of the vehicle and support it safely with jackstands.

3. Open the radiator drain fitting (located at the bottom of the radiator) by turning it counterclockwise. It may be wise to coat the fitting with penetrating lubricant before you attempt to turn it. Allow the coolant to drain from the radiator.

4. Remove the drain plug(s) from the engine block (located on the engine block, above the engine oil pan) and allow the coolant to drain.

5. Close the radiator drain fitting and reinstall the engine block plugs.

6. Add clear water to the system until it is filled.

7. Start the engine and repeat steps 3–6 until the drained water is almost colorless. Turn the engine Off.

8. Allow the system to drain completely and repeat step 5. Remove the cap from the coolant recovery tank, leaving the hoses connected to the cap.

9. Unbolt and remove the coolant recovery tank, drain it, and flush it with clear water. Reinstall the tank.

10. Fill the radiator to the base of the radiator filler neck with a 50/50 mixture of coolant/water. Remember, on diesel-equipped models, add a gallon of undiluted coolant first, then add the 50/50 solution.

NOTE: *If only the radiator was drained, use a 50/50 solution to refill it, then check the freezing protection after the level stabilizes.*

11. Fill the coolant recovery tank to the "FULL" mark with the 50/50 solution.

12. With the radiator cap still removed, start the engine and allow it to idle until the upper radiator hose becomes hot, indicating that the thermostat has opened.

13. With the engine still idling, fill the radiator to the base of the filler neck with the 50/50 solution.

14. Install the radiator cap, being sure to align the arrows on the cap with the overflow tube.

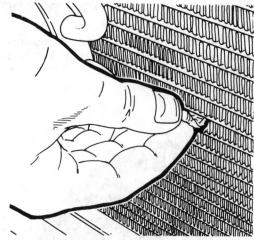

Clean the front of the radiator as part of the yearly cooling system service

15. Turn the engine Off, check for leakage, and double-check that the radiator drain is closed and the drain plug(s) is tight.

CLEAN RADIATOR OF DEBRIS

Periodically clean any debris—leaves, paper, insects, etc.—from the radiator fins. Pick the large pieces off by hand. The smaller pieces can be washed away with water pressure from a hose.

Carefully straighten any bent radiator fins with a pair of needle nose pliers. Be careful—the fins are very soft. Don't wiggle the fins back and forth too much. Straighten them once and try not to move them again.

Air Conditioning System

The air conditioning system requires no routine maintenance, except for periodic belt tension adjustment, as outlined previously. The air conditioning system should be operated for about five minutes each week, even in winter. This will circulate lubricating oil within the system to prevent the various seals from drying out.

The factory-installed air conditioning unit has no sight glass for system checks. It is recommended that all air conditioning service work be entrusted to a qualified mechanic. The system is a potentially hazardous one.

CAUTION: *Do not attempt to charge or discharge the refrigerant system unless you are thoroughly familiar with its operation and the hazards involved. The compressed refrigerant used in the air conditioning system expands and evaporates (boils) into the atmosphere at a temperature of $-21.7°F$ ($-29.8°C$) or less. This will freeze any surface that it contacts, including your eyes. In* addition, *the refrigerant decomposes into a poisonous gas in the presence of flame.*

Windshield Wipers

Each exposed windshield wiper is divided basically into four segments:

1. Wiper arm—connected to the pivot at the base of the windshield.

2. Wiper blade—connected at the opposite end of the wiper arm and holds the yokes.

3. Wiper yokes—hold the element in a manner which distributes the pressure load across the element.

4. Wiper element—flexible rubber element which contacts the windshield glass and actually performs the cleaning function.

For maximum effectiveness and longest life, the windshield and wiper elements should be kept clean. Dirt, tree sap, road tar, etc., will cause streaking, smearing, and wiper element deterioration. Hardening of the elements will cause the elements to chatter as they wipe the windshield. Wash the windshield thoroughly with a glass cleaner at least once a month. Wipe off the rubber element with a wet rag afterwards.

Obviously, the item most frequently requiring replacement is the element. It is very rarely necessary to replace the blade or arm unless they become accidentally bent or damaged in some other manner.

Your A-Body can use one of three types of elements: the first type is commonly referred to as the Anco® style; the second type is the Trico® style; and the third is the plastic style which uses a plastic blade assembly. Replacement of any element type is very simple and requires only a few minutes to do.

TO REPLACE THE ANCO® STYLE ELEMENT

1. Locate the red release button at the top of one of the yokes (free yoke), push the button, and separate the free yoke from the blade.

2. Pull the element out of the other yoke (attached yoke).

3. Transfer the free yoke to the new element, being sure to engage the element into all of the yoke jaws.

4. Feed the other end of the element into the attached yoke, again being sure that the element is fully engaged.

5. Push the button and snap the free yoke

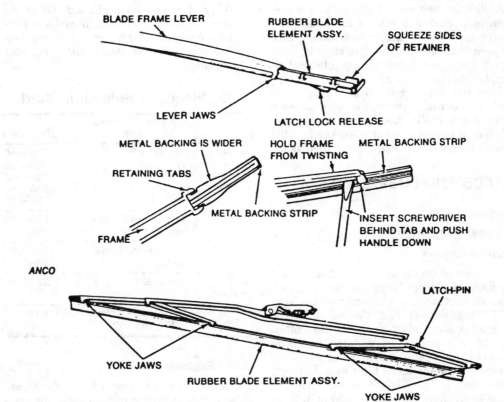

TRICO

BLADE FRAME LEVER

RUBBER BLADE ELEMENT ASSY.

SQUEEZE SIDES OF RETAINER

LEVER JAWS

LATCH LOCK RELEASE

METAL BACKING IS WIDER

HOLD FRAME FROM TWISTING

METAL BACKING STRIP

RETAINING TABS

METAL BACKING STRIP

FRAME

INSERT SCREWDRIVER BEHIND TAB AND PUSH HANDLE DOWN

ANCO

LATCH-PIN

YOKE JAWS

RUBBER BLADE ELEMENT ASSY.

YOKE JAWS

The rubber element can be changed without replacing the entire blade assembly; your car may have either one of these types of blades

into place on the blade. Release the button and double-check that the element is fully engaged into all of the yoke jaws.

TO REPLACE THE TRICO® STYLE ELEMENT

1. Squeeze the sides of the element retainer (located on only one side of the element) and pull the element out of the blade/yoke assembly.

2. To install the new element, guide the new element into all of the blade/yoke jaws. The element must be positioned in the same manner as the one which was removed. When the retainer comes in contact with the end of the blade, make sure that each side of the retainer is positioned on the inside of the jaws, then snap the element into place.

3. Check that the element is fully engaged to all of the jaws before operating the wipers.

TO REPLACE THE ELEMENT USED WITH THE PLASTIC BLADE

1. Remove the wiper blade and element assembly from the wiper arm.

2. Pull the wiper blade and the element apart, then pull the element downward. This will disengage the element from the retaining tabs.

3. Pull the element out, guide the new element into place, and release the hand pressure on the blade to engage the retaining tabs. Be sure that the element is completely engaged. Snap the wiper blade and element assembly into place on the arm.

Two different wiper blade attachment methods are used. Refer to the accompanying illustration to replace the blades.

Wiper arm replacement is covered in the Chassis Electrical chapter, later in this book.

FLUIDS AND LUBRICANTS

Engine Oil
RECOMMENDATIONS
Gasoline Engines

Under normal conditions, the engine oil and the filter should be changed at the first 7500 miles or once a year, whichever comes first. G.M. recommends that the oil filter be changed at every other oil change thereafter. For the small price of an oil filter, it's cheap insurance to replace the filter at every oil change. One of the larger filter manufacturers points out in its advertisements that not changing the filter leaves one quart of dirty oil in the engine. This claim is true and should be kept in mind when changing your oil.

Under severe conditions, such as: a) driving in dusty areas b) trailer towing c) frequent idling or idling for extended periods, or d) frequently driving short distances (4 miles or so) in freezing weather, the engine oil and filter should be changed every 3 months or 3000 miles, whichever comes first. If dust storms are ever encountered in your area, change the oil and filter as soon as possible after the storm.

The A.P.I. (American Petroleum Institute) designation (printed on the oil container) indicates the classification of engine oil for use under certain operating conditions. Oils having an A.P.I. service designation of SF should be used in your A-Body. The SF rating designates the highest quality oil meant for passenger car usage. It is okay to use an SF oil having a combination rating such as SF/CC or SF/CD for gasoline powered engines. In addition, G.M. recommends the use of SF/Energy Conserving oil. Oils labeled "Energy Conserving (or Saving)"; "Fuel (Gas or Gasoline) Saving, etc., are recommended due to their superior lubricating qualities (less friction = easier and more efficient engine operation) and fuel saving characteristics. Use of engine oil additives is not recommended, because if the correct oil is purchased to begin with, the additives will be of no value.

NOTE: *Use of engine oils without an SF rating, or failing to change the oil and filter at the recommended intervals will cause excessive engine wear and could affect your warranty.*

Oil Viscosity Selection Chart

	Anticipated Temperature Range	SAE Viscosity
Multi-grade	Above 32°F	10W—40 10W—50 20W—40 20W—50 10W—30
	May be used as low as −10°F	10W—30 10W—40
	Consistently below 10°F	5W—20 5W—30
Single-grade	Above 32°F	30
	Temperature between +32°F and −10°F	10W

Diesel Engines

The engine oil requirements for diesel engines are more stringent than those for gasoline engines, since contaminant build-up in the engine oil occurs much faster in the diesel engine. Also, the diesel contaminants are more damaging to the engine oil.

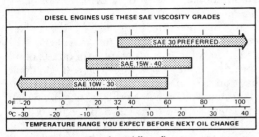

DIESEL ENGINES USE THESE SAE VISCOSITY GRADES

SAE 30 PREFERRED

SAE 15W - 40

SAE 10W - 30

| °F | -20 | | 0 | | 20 | 32 | 40 | | 60 | | 80 | | 100 |
| °C | -30 | | -20 | | -10 | | 0 | | 10 | | 20 | 30 | | 40 |

TEMPERATURE RANGE YOU EXPECT BEFORE NEXT OIL CHANGE

Engine oil viscosity chart (diesel)

Under normal operating conditions, the engine oil and filter MUST be changed every 5000 miles, regardless of the time period involved.

Under severe operating conditions, such as those mentioned previously under "Gasoline Engines", the oil and filter must be changed every 2500 miles or 3 months, whichever comes first.

In the diesel equipped A-Body, ONLY an engine oil having one of the two following A.P.I. designations should be used: SF/CC or SF/CD. Period! Don't use any other type of oil.

CAUTION: *Failure to use an SF/CC or SF/CD oil will result in excessive engine wear and will probably void the engine warranty. Failure to change the oil and filter at the recommended intervals will have the same results.*

In diesel engines, the use of oil in regard to its viscosity is limited. With a diesel, you only have three choices: 10W-30, 15W-40, or straight 30W. Refer to the accompanying chart to choose the engine oil viscosity according to the expected outside air temperature.

Oil dipstick location—typical

CHECKING THE OIL LEVEL

The engine oil level may be checked either when the engine is cold or warm, though the latter is preferred. If you check the level while the engine is cold, DO NOT start the engine first, since the cold oil won't drain back to the engine oil pan fast enough to give an accurate reading. Even when the engine is warm, wait a couple of minutes after turning it off to let the oil drain back to the pan.

1. Raise the hood, pull the dipstick out and wipe it clean.

2. Reinsert the dipstick, being sure that you push it back in completely.

3. Pull the dipstick back out, hold it horizontally, and check the level at the end of the dipstick. Some dipsticks are marked with "ADD" and "FULL" lines, others with "ADD 1 QT" and "OPERATING RANGE". In either

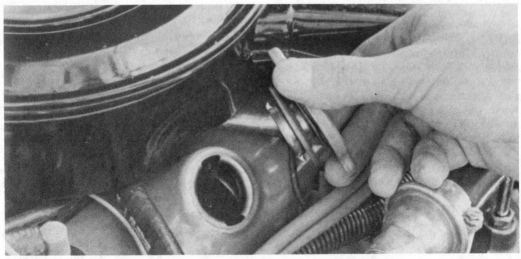

Add oil through the capped filler hole in the valve cover

case, the level must be above the "ADD" line. Reinsert the dipstick completely.

4. If oil must be added, it can be poured in through the rocker (valve) cover after removing the filler cap on the cover. Recheck the level a few minutes after adding oil.

5. Be sure that the dipstick and oil filler cap are installed before closing the hood.

CHANGING THE ENGINE OIL

1. Drive the car until the engine is at normal operating temperature. A run to the parts store for oil and a filter should accomplish this. If the engine is not hot when the oil is changed, most of the acids and contaminants will remain inside the engine.

2. Shut off the engine, and slide a pan of at least six quarts capacity under the oil pan.

3. Remove the drain plug from the engine oil pan, after wiping the plug area clean. The drain plug is the bolt inserted at an angle into the lowest point of the oil pan.

4. The oil from the engine will be HOT. It will probably not be possible to hold onto the drain plug. You may have to let it fall into the pan and fish it out later. Allow all the oil to drain completely. This will take a few minutes.

5. Wipe off the drain plug, removing any traces of metal particles. Check the condition of the plastic drain plug gasket. If it is cracked or distorted in any way, replace it. Reinstall the drain plug and gasket. Tighten the drain plug snugly.

6. The oil filter for the V6 gasoline engine is right up front, just behind the radiator. The four cylinder oil filter is at the back of the engine. It is impossible to reach from above, and almost as inaccessible from below. It may be easiest to remove the right front wheel and reach through the fender opening to get at the four cylinder oil filter. The oil filter of the diesel V6 engine is located on the passenger side face of the engine block. Use an oil filter strap wrench to loosen the oil filter; these are available at auto parts stores. It is recommended that you purchase one with as thin a strap as possible, to get into tight areas. Place the drain pan on the ground, under the filter. Unscrew and discard the old filter. It will be VERY HOT, so be careful.

7. If the oil filter is on so tightly that it collapses under pressure from the wrench, drive a long punch or a nail through it, across the diameter and as close to the base as possible, and use this as a lever to unscrew it. Make sure you are turning it counterclockwise.

8. Clean off the oil filter mounting surface with a rag. Apply a thin film of clean engine oil to the filter gasket.

9. Screw the filter on by hand until the gasket makes contact. Then tighten it by hand an additional ½ to ¾ of a turn. *Do not overtighten.*

10. Remove the filler cap on the rocker (valve) cover, after wiping the area clean.

11. Add the correct number of quarts of oil specified in the "Capacities" chart. If you don't have an oil can spout, you will need a funnel. Be certain you do not overfill the engine, which can cause serious damage. Replace the cap.

12. Check the oil level on the dipstick. It is normal for the level to be a bit above the full mark. Start the engine and allow it to idle for a few minutes.

CAUTION: *Do not run the engine above idle speed until it has built up oil pressure, indicated when the oil light goes out.*

Check around the filter and drain plug for any leaks.

13. Shut off the engine, allow the oil to drain for a minute, and check the oil level.

After completing this job, you will have several quarts of filthy oil to dispose of. The best thing to do with it is to funnel it into old plastic milk containers or bleach bottles. Then, you can either pour it into the recycling barrel at the gas station (if you're on good terms with the attendant), or put the containers into the trash.

Manual Transaxle Lubricant
RECOMMENDATIONS

Under normal conditions, the lubricant used in the manual transaxle does not require periodic changing. The fluid level in the transaxle should be checked every 12 months or 7500 miles, whichever comes first. The manual transaxle is designed for use with Dexron® II automatic transmission. Don't use standard manual transmission lubricant in the A-Body transaxle.

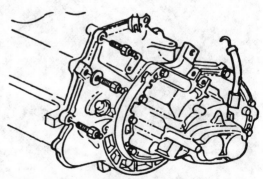

Some models use a dipstick to check the level of the manual transaxle lubricant

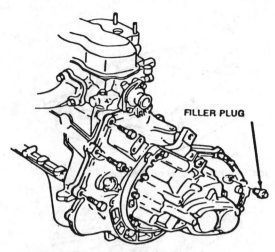

FILLER PLUG

Some models use a filler plug to check the level of the manual transaxle lubricant

CHECKING THE FLUID LEVEL

1. Park the car on a level surface. Before proceeding, the transaxle case must be cool to the touch. Due to the expansion characteristics of the Dexron® II fluid, it will be above the level of the filler plug when the transmission is hot.

2. Slowly remove the filler plug from the drivers side of the transaxle (see the illustration). The lubricant level should be right at the bottom of the filler plug hole. If the fluid trickles out as the plug is removed, or if you can just touch the fluid through the filler plug hole, the level is correct.

3. If you cannot feel the fluid level with your finger through the filler plug hole, add Dexron® II automatic trans through the hole until the fluid begins to trickle out of the hole.

4. When the level is correct, install the filler plug and tighten it snugly.

Automatic Transaxle Fluid
RECOMMENDATIONS

Under normal operating conditions, the automatic transmission fluid only needs to be changed every 100,000 miles, according to G.M. If one or more of the following driving conditions is encountered, the fluid and filter should be changed every 15,000 miles: a) driving in heavy city traffic when the outside temperature regularly reaches 90°F, b) driving regularly in hilly or mountainous areas, c) towing a trailer, or d) using the vehicle as a taxi or police car, or for delivery purposes.

Remember, these are the factory recommendations, and in this case are considered to be the minimum. You must determine a change interval which fits your driving habits. If your vehicle is never subjected to these conditions, a 100,000 mile change interval is adequate. If you are a normal driver, a two-year/30,000 mile interval will be more than sufficient to maintain the long life for which your automatic transaxle was designed.

When replacing or adding fluid, use only fluid labeled Dexron® II. Use of other fluids could cause erratic shifting and transmission damage.

CHECKING THE FLUID LEVEL

The fluid level may be checked with the transaxle cold, warm, or hot, as this is accounted for on the dipstick graduations.

NOTE: *If the vehicle has just been driven in extreme conditions, allow the fluid to cool for about 30 minutes.*

1. Park the car on a level surface and set the parking brake.

2. Start the engine, apply the regular brakes, and move the shift lever through all of the gear ranges, ending up in Park.

3. Let the engine idle for at least 5 minutes with the transaxle in Park.

4. The dipstick is located on the drivers side of the engine compartment, ahead of the engine.

5. Raise the hood, pull the dipstick out and wipe it off with a clean cloth.

6. Reinsert the dipstick, being sure that it is fully seated.

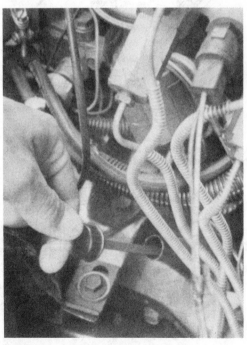

Automatic transaxle fluid dipstick and filler tube location

7. Again, remove the dipstick. Hold it horizontally and read the fluid level. Touch the fluid—if it feels cold or warm, the level should be between the dimples above the "FULL HOT" mark. If the fluid feels hot, the level should be in the hatched area, between the "ADD 1 PT" and "FULL HOT" marks.

8. If required, add just enough Dexron® II automatic transmission fluid to bring the level to where it should be. One pint of fluid will raise the level from "ADD" to "FULL" when the transaxle is hot. Recheck the level.

9. Reinsert the dipstick, again making sure that it is fully seated. Lower the hood.

CAUTION: *NEVER overfill the transaxle, as fluid foaming and subsequent transaxle damage will occur.*

CHANGING THE FLUID AND FILTER

NOTE: *Some transaxles use RTV sealer in place of a gasket. Do not attempt to replace the sealer with a gasket.*

1. Jack up the front of your vehicle and support it with jackstands.

2. Remove the front and side pan bolts.

3. Loosen the rear bolts about 4 turns.

4. Carefully pry the oil pan loose, allowing the fluid to drain.

5. Remove the remaining bolts, the pan, and the gasket or RTV. Discard the gasket.

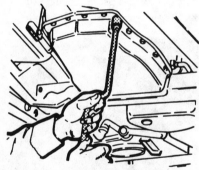

Loosen the pan bolts and allow one corner of the pan to tilt slightly to drain the fluid

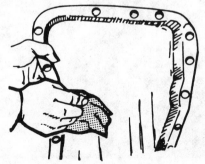

Clean the pan thoroughly with solvent and allow it to air dry completely

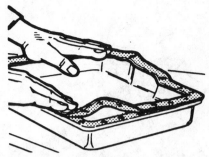

Install a new gasket on the pan

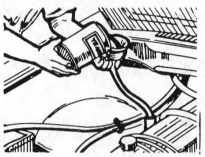

Fill the transaxle with the required amount of fluid. Do not overfill. Check the fluid level and add fluid if necessary

6. Clean the pan with solvent and dry thoroughly, with compressed air.

7. Remove the strainer and "O" ring seal.

8. Install new strainer and new "O" ring seal locating the strainer against the dipstick stop.

9. Install a new gasket or RTV. Tighten the pan bolts to 12 ft. lbs.

10. Lower the car. Add about 4 quarts of Dexron® II transmission fluid.

11. Start the engine; let it idle. Block the wheels and apply the parking brake.

12. Move the shift lever through the ranges.

13. With the lever in park check the fluid level. Add fluid if necessary.

NOTE: *Always replace the filter with a new one—don't attempt to clean the old one.*

NOTE: *The transmission fluid currently being used may appear to be darker and have a strong odor. This is normal and not a sign of required maintenance or transmission failure.*

Brake Master Cylinder
RECOMMENDATIONS

Only extra-heavy duty fluid meeting D.O.T.-3 specifications must be used. Using an inferior fluid will result in component damage and reduced braking capabilities.

CHECKING

About once a month, the fluid level in the master cylinder should be checked.

1. Park the car on a level surface, turn it off and raise the hood.

2. Wipe off the master cylinder cover before you remove it, to prevent contaminating the fluid with dirt.

NOTE: *On most models, a "see-through" reservoir is used, eliminating the need of removing the cylinder cover.*

3. The cover is snapped into place on the master cylinder. To remove the cover, just press up on the two tabs on the side of the cover, tilt it, then remove it. Be careful not to damage the rubber seal under the cover.

CAUTION: *If you value the paint on your car, don't spill brake fluid on the finish. Brake fluid destroys paint.*

NOTE: *Don't leave the cover off of the master cylinder or the cap off of the brake fluid container any longer than necessary.*

4. The fluid level in each master cylinder reservoir should be ¼ in. below the lowest edge of the filler opening. Use fresh brake fluid to adjust the level if necessary.

It is normal for the master cylinder fluid level to drop as the brake linings wear (⅛ in. drop about every 10,000 miles). If the fluid level is constantly low, the system should be checked for leaks.

5. Carefully seat the cover seal into the cover, then snap the cover into place on the master cylinder. Be sure that all four snaps latch completely.

Power Steering Fluid

RECOMMENDATIONS

When adding power steering fluid use G.M. part #1050017 or its equal. Dexron® II automatic transmission fluid is an acceptable substitute.

CHECKING

The power steering fluid level should be checked at every oil change. On models with gasoline engines, the power steering pump and reservoir are integrated into one unit bolted to the front of the engine. On diesel-engined models, the pump is mounted on the engine, and a separate, translucent reservoir is attached to the firewall in the engine compartment.

To check the fluid level, run the engine until it reaches normal operating temperature, then turn the engine off. Remove the reservoir filler cap and check the oil level on the dipstick. The fluid level must be between the HOT and COLD marks on the filler cap indicator. Add power steering fluid as required then reinstall the cap.

Coolant

Coolant level checks are covered earlier in this chapter under "Cooling System". Check the coolant level once a month.

Battery

All A-Body cars have a maintenance-free battery which does not require periodic additions of water.

Windshield Washer Fluid

Check the fluid level in the windshield washer tank at every engine oil level check. The fluid may be mixed in a 50% solution with water, if desired, as long as temperatures remain above freezing. Below freezing, the fluid should be used full strength, or as specified by the manufacturer. Never add engine coolant antifreeze to the windshield washer system—it will streak the windshield terribly and damage the painted finish.

TIRES

Tires should be checked weekly for proper air pressure. A chart, located at the left front door edge, gives the recommended inflation pressures. Maximum fuel economy and tire life will result if the pressure is maintained at the highest figure given on the chart. The tires should be checked before driving since pressure can increase as much as six pounds per square inch (psi) due to heat buildup. It is a good idea to have your own accurate pressure gauge, because not all gauges on service station air pumps can be trusted. When checking pressures, do not neglect the spare tire. Note that some spare tires require pressures considerably higher than those used in the other tires.

While you are about the task of checking air pressure, inspect the tire treads for cuts, bruises, and other damage. Check the air valves to be sure that they are tight. Replace any missing valve caps.

Check the tires for uneven wear that might indicate the need for front end alignment or tire rotation. Tires should be replaced when a tread wear indicator appears as a solid band across the tread.

When buying new tires, give some thought to the following points, especially if you are

Maintenance Intervals

Perform	Check	Change	Service	Gasoline-fueled	Diesel-fueled
X			Chassis lubrication	12 mo./7500 mi.	12 mo./5000 mi.
	X		Fluid levels	12 mo./7500 mi.	12 mo./5000 mi.
		X	Engine oil	12 mo./7500 mi.②	5000 mi.②
		X	Engine oil filter	①	every oil change
X	X		Clutch adjustment	③	③
	X		Engine drive belts	12 mo./15,000 mi.	5000 mi.
	X		Front suspension	12 mo./7500 mi.	12 mo./10,000 mi.
	X		Exhaust system	12 mo./7500 mi.	④
X	X		Rotate tires and wheels	⑤	④
	X		Disc Brakes	⑤	12 mo./10,000 mi.
	X		Brake lines	12 mo./7500 mi.	12 mo./10,000 mi.
	X		Drum and parking brakes	12 mo./15,000 mi.	12 mo./15,000 mi.
	X		Throttle linkage	12 mo./15,000 mi.	12 mo./15,000 mi.
	X		Cooling system	12 mo./15,000 mi.	12 mo./15,000 mi.
X			Cooling system drain & refill	24 mo./30,000 mi.	24 mo./30,000 mi.
	X		Manual transaxle fluid level	12 mo./7500 mi.	12 mo./7500 mi.
	X		Auto. transaxle fluid/filter	see text	see text
		X	Auto. transaxle fluid/filter	see text	see text

① See the text for recommendations
② Under normal conditions. See the text for additional information.
③ Adjust every 5000 miles or less. See chapter 6 for information.
④ 1st 5000 miles, then every 15,000 thereafter.
⑤ 1st 7500 miles, then every 15,000 thereafter.

Capacities

Year	Engine Displacement Cu. In. (Liters)	Crankcase Quarts (Liters) w/filter	wo/filter	Transaxle Pints (Liters) 4-Speed	5-Speed	Auto.	Gas Tank Gal. (Liters)	Cooling Systems Quarts (Liters) wo/A.C.	w/A.C.	w/H.D.
1982– 83	151 (2.5)	3 (2.8)	3 (2.8)	5.9 (2.8)	—	9.7 (4.6)	15.7 (59.4)	9.4 (9.9)	9.7 (10.25)	12.1 (12.8)
	173 (2.8)	4 (3.8)	4 (3.8)	5.9 (2.8)	—	9.7 (4.6)	16.4 (62.1)	11.3 (11.9)	11.7 (12.4)	12.1 (12.7)
	183 (3.0)	4 (3.8)	4 (3.8)	5.9 (2.8)	—	9.7 (4.6)	16 (60)	14.4 (15.2)	13.6 (14.3)	14.0 (14.8)
	263 (4.3)	6 (5.7)	6 (5.7)	5.9 (2.8)	—	9.7 (4.6)	16.6 (62.8)	13.2 (13.9)	13.9 (14.7)	13.9 (14.7)

considering a switch to larger tires or a different profile series:

1. All four tires should be of the same construction type. Radial, bias, or bias-belted tires must not be mixed.

2. The wheels must be the correct width for the tire. Tire dealers have charts of tire and wheel rim compatibility. A mismatch can cause sloppy handling and rapid tread wear. The tread width should match the rim width (inside bead to inside bead) within an inch. For radial tires, the rim width should be 80% or less of the tire (not tread) width.

3. The height (mounted diameter) of the new tires can change speedometer accuracy, engine speed per given road speed, fuel mileage, acceleration, and ground clearance. Tire manufacturers furnish full measurement specifications.

4. The spare tire should be usable, at least for low speed operation, with the new tires.

5. There shouldn't be any body interference when the car is loaded, on bumps or in turning.

All of these problems can be avoided by replacing the tires with new ones of the same type and size. The P-metric radials installed as standard equipment on the A-cars are particularly fuel-efficient; you can expect some reduction on fuel mileage if, when they wear out, they are replaced with conventional radials, or tires of other construction types. One other thing to remember when buying new tires: always have the dealer install new valve stems.

Few things are more aggravating than having a new tire go flat because of an old, leaky valve stem.

TIRE ROTATION

Tire rotation, is recommended every 7,500 miles or so, to obtain maximum tire wear. The pattern you use depends on whether or not your car has a usable spare. Radial tires should not be cross-switched (from one side of the car to the other); they last longer if their direction of rotation is not changed. Snow tires sometimes have directional arrows molded into the side of the carcass; the arrow shows the direction of rotation. They will wear very rapidly if their rotation is reversed. Studded tires will lose their studs if their rotational direction is reversed. Mark the wheel position or direction of rotation on radial tires or studded snow tires before removing them to avoid these problems.

FUEL SYSTEM

Gasoline Engines

FUEL RECOMMENDATIONS

All G.M. A-Body cars must use unleaded fuel. The use of leaded fuel will plug the catalyst rendering it inoperative, and will increase the exhaust back pressure to the point where engine output will be severely reduced. The minimum octane for all engines is 91 RON. All unleaded fuels sold in the U.S. are required to meet this minimum octane rating.

Use of a fuel too low in octane (a measurement of anti-knock quality) will result in spark knock. Since many factors affect operating efficiency, such as altitude, terrain, and air temperature and humidity, knocking may result even though the recommended fuel is being used. If persistent knocking occurs, it may be necessary to switch to a slightly higher grade of unleaded gasoline. Continuous or heavy knocking may result in serious engine damage, for which the manufacturer is not responsible.

NOTE: *Your car's engine fuel requirement can change with time, due to carbon buildup, which changes the compression ratio. If your car's engine knocks, pings, or runs on, switch to a higher grade of fuel, if possible, and check the ignition timing. Sometimes changing brands of gasoline will cure the problem. If it is necessary to retard timing from specifications, don't change it more than a few degrees. Retarded timing will reduce power output and fuel mileage, and will increase engine temperature.*

Diesel Engines

FUEL RECOMMENDATIONS

CAUTION: *Failure to use fuels specified below will result in engine damage for which the manufacturer is not responsible. Use of fuel system additives is NOT recommended.*

At any outside temperature above 20°F., Number 2-D diesel fuel should be used, since it will give better fuel economy than Number 1-D. When the outside temperature is below 20°F., use either Number 1-D fuel (preferred if available) or a blended Number 2-D. The blended Number 2-D has 1-D fuel in it, but will usually be called just Number 2-D. Check with the service station operator to be sure you get the proper fuel.

NOTE: *Diesel fuel may foam during filling, which is normal. The foam may cause the automatic pump nozzle to turn off before the tank is actually filled. The foaming effect can be reduced by slowing the fill rate.*

OPERATING IN COLD WEATHER

All types of diesel fuel have a certain parrafin content. The parrafin components are high in energy content and help to improve fuel economy. Below about 20°F., the trouble with parrafin begins. At this temperature, the parrafin components begin turning to wax flakes. Depending upon the temperature, the wax flakes can block either or both of the two fuel filters (tank or engine) and stop fuel from reaching the engine.

Since Number 2-D fuel has more parrafin components than Number 1-D (or blended Number 2-D), Number 2-D would be more apt to cause "waxing" problems (See "Fuel Recommendations").

If the fuel tank filter plugs due to waxing, a check valve inside of the fuel tank will open and allow fuel to flow to the engine. Because of the check valve location, not all of the fuel in the tank can be used if the filter remains clogged (check valve open). About 4 gallons of fuel will remain in the tank when you run out of fuel. When driving in temperatures below 20°F., be sure to keep the tank more than ¼ full to help prevent running out of fuel if the filter plugs.

If equipped, the fuel line heater should be used when temperatures are expected to be below 10°F and you have Number 2-D fuel in the tank.

WATER IN THE FUEL

Diesel fuel should be purchased from a reputable dealer, since the majority of the water found in a diesel fuel system gets into the system during refueling. Water can cause extensive (and expensive) damage to the diesel fuel system.

The A-Bodies have a water separator system in the fuel tank and a "Water-In-Fuel" indicator on the instrument panel. The indicator is designed to illuminate when starting the engine (as a bulb check), or when water is detected in the tank. If the light comes on at any other time, there is probably a fault in the detector circuit. If the engine loses power and begins to run rough without the detector light on, there is probably water in the system. Both the fuel system and the detector circuit should be checked.

If the indicator light comes on immediately after refueling, a large amount of water was pumped into the tank—DON'T run the engine; the fuel system must be purged right away.

If the indicator lights after braking, cornering, etc., a moderate amount of water is in the system. In this case, the water should be removed within one or two days.

PURGING THE FUEL SYSTEM

Please refer to Chapter 4 for this information.
   CAUTION: *Use the same safety precautions when working around diesel fuel as you would when working around gasoline (No smoking; No sparks; No trouble lamps in the area, etc.).*

CHASSIS AND BODY LUBRICATION

Front Suspension and Steering Linkage

These parts should be greased every 12 months or 7,500 miles (12,000 Km.) with an EP grease meeting G.M. specification 6031M.

If you choose to do this job yourself, you will need to purchase a hand operated grease gun, if you do not own one already, and a long flexible extension hose to reach the various grease fittings. You will also need a cartridge of the appropriate grease.

Press the fitting on the grease gun hose onto the grease fitting on the suspension or steering linkage component. Pump a few shots of grease into the fitting, until the rubber boot on the joint begins to expand, indicating that the joint is full. Remove the gun from the fitting. Be careful not to overfill the joints, which will rupture the rubber boots, allowing the entry of dirt. You can keep the grease fittings clean by covering them with a small square of tin foil.

TRANSAXLE SHIFT LINKAGE

Lubricate the manual transaxle shift linkage contact points with the EP grease used for chassis greasing, which should meet G.M. specification 6031M. The automatic transaxle linkage should be lubricated with clean engine oil.

HOOD LATCH AND HINGES

Clean the latch surfaces and apply clean engine oil to the latch pilot bolts and the spring anchor. Use the engine oil to lubricate the hood hinges as well. Use a chassis grease to lubricate all the pivot points in the latch release mechanism.

DOOR HINGES

The gas tank filler door, car door, and rear hatch or trunk lid hinges should be wiped clean and lubricated with clean engine oil. Silicone spray also works well on these parts, but must be applied more often. Use engine oil to lubricate the trunk or hatch lock mechanism and the lock bolt and striker. The door lock cylinders can be lubricated easily with a shot of silicone spray or one of the many dry penetrating lubricants commercially available.

PARKING BRAKE LINKAGE

Use chassis grease on the parking brake cable where it contacts the guides, links, levers, and pulleys. The grease should be a water resistant one for durability under the car.

ACCELERATOR LINKAGE

Lubricate the carburetor stud, carburetor lever, and the accelerator pedal lever at the support inside the car with clean engine oil.

PUSHING AND TOWING

DO NOT attempt to start your A-Body by pushing or towing—damage to the catalytic convertor or other components may result. If the battery is weak, the vehicle may be jump started, using the procedure found after this section.

As long as the driveline and steering are normally operable, your A-Body may be towed on all four wheels. If this is done, don't exceed 35 mph or travel further than 50 miles. The steering wheel must be unlocked, the transaxle in Neutral, and the parking brake released. Never attach towing equipment to the bumpers or bumper brackets—the equipment must be attached to the main structural members of the car.

   NOTE: *Remember that there will be no power assist for brakes and steering with the*

JUMP STARTING A DEAD BATTERY

The chemical reaction in a battery produces explosive hydrogen gas. This is the safe way to jump start a dead battery, reducing the chances of an accidental spark that could cause an explosion.

Jump Starting Precautions

1. Be sure both batteries are of the same voltage.
2. Be sure both batteries are of the same polarity (have the same grounded terminal).
3. Be sure the vehicles are not touching.
4. Be sure the vent cap holes are not obstructed.
5. Do not smoke or allow sparks around the battery.
6. In cold weather, check for frozen electrolyte in the battery.
7. Do not allow electrolyte on your skin or clothing.
8. Be sure the electrolyte is not frozen.

Jump Starting Procedure

1. Determine voltages of the two batteries; they must be the same.
2. Bring the starting vehicle close (they must not touch) so that the batteries can be reached easily.
3. Turn off all accessories and both engines. Put both cars in Neutral or Park and set the handbrake.
4. Cover the cell caps with a rag—do not cover terminals.
5. If the terminals on the run-down battery are heavily corroded, clean them.
6. Identify the positive and negative posts on both batteries and connect the cables in the order shown.
7. Start the engine of the starting vehicle and run it at fast idle. Try to start the car with the dead battery. Crank it for no more than 10 seconds at a time and let it cool off for 20 seconds in between tries.
8. If it doesn't start in 3 tries, there is something else wrong.
9. Disconnect the cables in the reverse order.
10. Replace the cell covers and dispose of the rags.

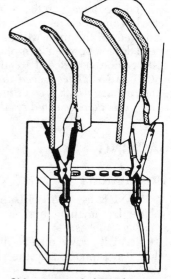

Side terminal batteries occasionally pose a problem when connecting jumper cables. There frequently isn't enough room to clamp the cables without touching sheet metal. Side terminal adaptors are available to alleviate this problem and should be removed after use. On models with diesel engines, make the jumper cable connections to the battery on the passenger side of the engine compartment.

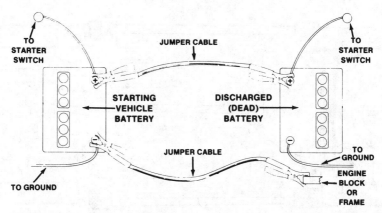

Hook-up for negative ground cars only. Make certain vehicles do not touch

engine Off. Also, be sure to check into state and local towing laws before flat-towing your vehicle.

If the car is to be towed by a wrecker, instructions supplied by the wrecker manufacturer should be followed. Because of the front wheel drive, towing on the rear wheels is preferred. If absolutely necessary, the A-Body may be towed on the front wheels as long as the speed does not exceed 25 mph and the towing distance does not exceed 10 miles.

CAUTION: *Don't exceed the speed or distance limits which are outlined here. Severe transaxle damage could result.*

JACKING

Precautions

• **NEVER** use the jack supplied with the vehicle for anything but changing tire and wheel assemblies.

• **NEVER** crawl underneath the vehicle while it is supported by the factory-supplied jack.

• **NEVER** start or run the engine while the car is supported by only a jack.

• **ALWAYS** resecure the spare tire, jack, etc., to prevent loose parts from causing personal injury during hard braking.

Instructions (Factory-supplied Jack Only)

Please refer to the accompanying illustrations for detailed jacking instructions and spare tire/jack stowage instructions.

HOISTING

NOTE: *Hoisting locations mentioned here may also be used when lifting the vehicle*

with a jack or supporting the vehicle with jackstands.

CAUTION: *Be especially careful not to damage the catalytic convertor when jacking from the floor side rails.*

The accompanying illustrations depict the preferred hoisting points underneath the vehicle. When using a floor jack, either the center of the engine cradle crossmember or the center of the rear axle bar can be used as jacking points in addition to the previous hoisting points.

HOW TO BUY A USED CAR

Many people believe that a two or three year old used car is a better buy than a new car. This may be true; the new car suffers the heaviest depreciation in the first two years, but is not old enough to present a lot of costly repair problems. Whatever the age of the used car you might want to buy, this section and a little patience will help you select one that should be safe and dependable.

TIPS

1. First decide what model you want, and how much you want to spend.

2. Check the used car lots and your local newspaper ads. Privately owned cars are usually less expensive, however you will not get a warranty that, in most cases, comes with a used car purchased from a lot.

3. Never shop at night. The glare of the lights make it easy to miss faults on the body caused by accident or rust repair.

4. Try to get the name and phone number of the previous owner. Contact him/her and ask about the car. If the owner of the lot refuses this information, look for a car somewhere else.

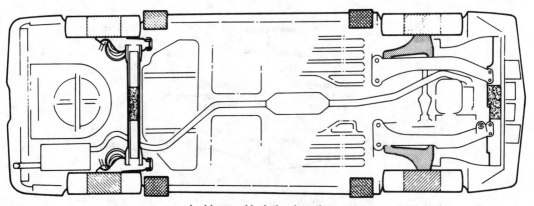

Jacking and hoisting locations

A private seller can tell you about the car and maintenance. Remember, however, there's no law requiring honesty from private citizens selling used cars. There is a law that forbids the tampering with or turning back the odometer mileage. This includes both the private citizen and the lot owner. The law also requires that the seller or anyone transferring ownership of the car must provide the buyer with a signed statement indicating the mileage on the odometer at the time of transfer.

5. Write down the year, model and serial number before you buy any used car. Then dial 1-800-424-9393, the toll free number of the National Highway Traffic Safety Administration, and ask if the car has ever been included on any manufacturer's recall list. If so, make sure the needed repairs were made.

6. Use the "Used Car Checklist" in this section and check all the items on the used car you are considering. Some items are more important than others. You know how much money you can afford for repairs, and, depending on the price of the car, may consider doing any needed work yourself. Beware, however, of trouble in areas that will affect operation, safety or emission. Problems in the "Used Car Checklist" break down as follows:

1-8: Two or more problems in these areas indicate a lack of maintenance. You should beware.

9-13: Indicates a lack of proper care, however, these can usually be corrected with a tune-up or relatively simple parts replacement.

14-17: Problems in the engine or transmission can be very expensive. Walk away from any car with problems in both of these areas.

7. If you are satisfied with the apparent condition of the car, take it to an independent diagnostic center or mechanic for a complete check. If you have a state inspection program, have it inspected immediately before purchase, or specify on the bill of sale that the sale is conditional on passing state inspection.

8. Road test the car—refer to the "Road Test Checklist" in this section. If your original evaluation and the road test agree—the rest is up to you.

USED CAR CHECKLIST

NOTE: *The numbers on the illustrations refer to the numbers on this checklist.*

1. *Mileage:* Average mileage is about 12,000 miles per year. More than average mileage may indicate hard usage. 1975 and later catalytic converter equipped models may need converter service at 50,000 miles.

2. *Paint:* Check around the tailpipe, molding and windows for overspray indicating that the car has been repainted.

3. *Rust:* Check fenders, doors, rocker panels, window moldings, wheelwells, floorboards, under floormats, and in the trunk for signs of rust. Any rust at all will be a problem. There is no way to check the spread of rust, except to replace the part or panel.

4. *Body appearance:* Check the moldings, bumpers, grille, vinyl roof, glass, doors, trunk lid and body panels for general overall condition. Check for misalignment, loose holdown clips, ripples, scratches in glass, rips or patches in the top. Mismatched paint, welding in the trunk, severe misalignment of body panels or ripples may indicate crash work.

5. *Leaks:* Get down and look under the car. There are no normal "leaks", other than water from the air conditioning condenser.

6. *Tires;* Check the tire air pressure. A common trick is to pump the tire pressure up to make the car roll easier. Check the tread wear, open the trunk and check the spare too. Uneven wear is a clue that the front end needs alignment. See the troubleshooting chapter for clues to the causes of tire wear.

7. *Shock absorbers:* Check the shock absorbers by forcing downward sharply on each corner of the car. Good shocks will not allow the car to bounce more than twice after you let go.

8. *Interior:* Check the entire interior. You're looking for an interior condition that agrees with the overall condition of the car. Reasonable wear is expected, but be suspicious of new seatcovers on sagging seats, new pedal pads, and worn armrests. These indicate an attempt to cover up hard use. Pull back the carpets and look for evidence of water leaks or flooding. Look for missing hardware, door handles, control knobs etc. Check lights and signal operations. Make sure all accessories (air conditioner, heater, radio etc.) work. Check windshield wiper operation.

9. *Belts and Hoses:* Open the hood and check all belts and hoses for wear, cracks or weak spots.

10. *Battery:* Low electrolyte level, cor-

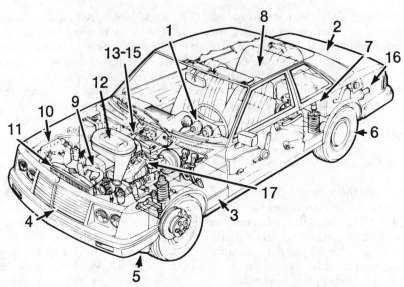

You should check these points when buying a used car. The "Used Car Checklist" gives an explanation of the numbered items

roded terminals and/or cracked case indicate a lack of maintenance.

11. *Radiator:* Look for corrosion or rust in the coolant indicating a lack of maintenance.

12. *Air filter:* A dirty air filter usually means a lack of maintenance.

13. *Ignition Wires:* Check the ignition wires for cracks, burned spots, or wear. Worn wires will have to be replaced.

14. *Oil level:* If the oil level is low, chances are the engine uses oil or leaks. Beware of water in the oil (cracked block), excessively thick oil (used to quiet a noisy engine), or thin, dirty oil with a distinct gasoline smell (internal engine problems).

15. *Automatic Transmission:* Pull the transmission dipstick out when the engine is running. The level should read "Full", and the fluid should be clear or bright red. Dark brown or black fluid that has distinct burnt odor, signals a transmission in need of repair or overhaul.

16. *Exhaust:* Check the color of the exhaust smoke. Blue smoke indicates, among other problems, worn rings; black smoke can indicate burnt valves or carburetor problems. Check the exhaust system for leaks; it can be expensive to replace.

17. *Spark Plugs:* Remove one of the spark plugs (the most accessible will do). An engine in good condition will show plugs with a light tan or gray deposit on the firing tip. See the color Tune-Up tips section for spark plug conditions.

ROAD TEST CHECK LIST

1. *Engine Performance:* The car should be peppy whether cold or warm, with adequate power and good pickup. It should respond smoothly through the gears.

2. *Brakes:* They should provide quick, firm stops with no noise, pulling or brake fade.

3. *Steering:* Sure control with no binding, harshness, or looseness and no shimmy in the wheel should be expected. Noise or vibration from the steering wheel when turning the car means trouble.

4. *Clutch (Manual Transmission):* Clutch action should give quick, smooth response with easy shifting. The clutch pedal should have about 1–1½ inches of free-play before it disengages the clutch. Start the engine, set the parking brake, put the transmission in first gear and slowly release the clutch pedal. The engine should begin to stall when the pedal is one-half to three-quarters of the way up.

5. *Automatic Transmission:* The transmission should shift rapidly and smoothly, with no noise, hesitation, or slipping.

6. *Differential:* No noise or thumps should be present. Differentials have no "normal" leaks.

7. *Driveshaft, Universal Joints:* Vibration and noise could mean driveshaft problems. Clicking at low speed or coast conditions means worn U-joints.

8. *Suspension:* Try hitting bumps at different speeds. A car that bounces has weak shock absorbers. Clunks mean worn bushings or ball joints.

9. *Frame:* Wet the tires and drive in a straight line. Tracks should show two straight lines, not four. Four tire tracks indicate a frame bent by collision damage. If the tires can't be wet for this purpose, have a friend drive along behind you and see if the car appears to be traveling in a straight line.

Tune-Up and Performance Maintenance

T2

TUNE-UP PROCEDURES

In order to extract the full measure of performance and economy from your car's engine it is essential that it be properly tuned at regular intervals. Although the tune-up intervals for the A-Body have been stretched to limits which would have been thought impossible a few years ago, periodic maintenance is still required. A regularly schedule tune-up will keep your car's engine running smoothly and will prevent the annoying minor breakdowns and poor performance associated with an untuned engine.

A complete tune-up should be performed at the interval specified in the "Maintenance Intervals" chart in Chapter One. This interval should be havled if the car is operated under severe conditions, such as trailer towing, prolonged idling, continual stop-and-start driving, or if starting and running problems are noticed. It is assumed that the routine maintenance described in the first chapter has been kept up, as this will have a decided effect on the results of a tune-up. All of the applicable steps should be followed in order, as the result is a cumulative one.

If the specifications on the tune-up label in the engine compartment of your A-Body disagree with the "Tune-Up Specifications" chart in this chapter, the figures on the sticker must be used. The label often reflects changes made during the production run.

Spark Plugs

Spark plugs ignite the air and fuel mixture in the cylinder as the piston reaches the top of the compression stroke. The controlled explosion that results forces the piston down, turning the crankshaft and the rest of the drive train.

The average life of a spark plug in a A-Body is 30,000 miles. Part of the reason for this extraordinarily long life is the exclusive use of unleaded fuel, which reduces the amount of deposits within the combustion chamber and on the spark plug electrodes themselves, compared with the deposits left by the leaded gasoline used in the past. An additional contribution to long life is made by the HEI (High Energy Ignition) System, which fires the spark plugs with over 35,000 volts of electricity. The high voltage serves to keep the electrodes clear, and because it is a "cleaner" blast of electricity than that produced by conventional breaker-points ignitions, the electrodes suffer less pitting and wear.

Nevertheless, the life of a spark plug is dependent on a number of factors, including the mechanical condition of the engine, driving conditions, and the driver's habits.

When you remove the plugs, check the condition of the electrodes; they are a good indicator of the internal state of the engine. Since the spark plug wires must be checked every 15,000 miles, the spark plugs can be removed and examined at the same time. This will allow you to keep an eye on the mechanical status of the engine.

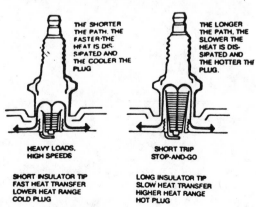

THE SHORTER THE PATH, THE FASTER THE HEAT IS DISSIPATED AND THE COOLER THE PLUG

THE LONGER THE PATH, THE SLOWER THE HEAT IS DISSIPATED AND THE HOTTER THE PLUG.

HEAVY LOADS, HIGH SPEEDS

SHORT TRIP STOP-AND-GO

SHORT INSULATOR TIP FAST HEAT TRANSFER LOWER HEAT RANGE COLD PLUG

LONG INSULATOR TIP SLOW HEAT TRANSFER HIGHER HEAT RANGE HOT PLUG

Spark plug heat range

A small deposit of light tan or rust-red material on a spark plug that has been used for any period of time is to be considered normal. Any other color, or abnormal amounts of wear or deposits, indicates that there is something amiss in the engine.

The gap between the center electrode and the side or ground electrode can be expected to increase not more than 0.001 in. every 1,000 miles under normal conditions.

When a spark plug is functioning normally or, more accurately, when the plug is installed in an engine that is functioning properly, the plugs can be taken out, cleaned, regapped, and reinstalled in the engine without doing the engine any harm.

When, and if, a plug fouls and begins to misfire, you will have to investigate, correct the cause of the fouling, and either clean or replace the plug.

There are several reasons why a spark plug will foul and you can learn which is at fault by just looking at the plug. A few of the most common reasons for plug fouling, and a description of the fouled plug's appearance, are listed in Chapter Ten, which also offers solutions to the problems. Also see the "Color Insert" section of Chapter Four.

Spark plugs suitable for use in your car's engine are offered in a number of different heat ranges. The amount of heat which the plug absorbs is determined by the length of the lower insulator. The longer the insulator, the hotter the plug will operate; the shorter the insulator, the cooler it will operate. A spark plug that absorbs (or retains) little heat and remains too cool will accumulate deposits of oil and carbon, because it is not hot enough to burn them off. This leads to fouling and consequent misfiring. A spark plug that absorbs too much heat will have no deposits, but the electrodes will burn away quickly and, in some cases, preignition may result. Preignition occurs when the spark plug tips get so hot that they ignite the fuel/mixture before the actual spark fires. This premature ignition will usually cause a pinging sound under conditions of low speed and heavy load. In severe cases, the heat may become high enough to start the fuel/air mixture burning throughout the combustion chamber rather than just to the front of the plug. In this case, the resultant explosion (detonation) will be strong enough to damage pistons, rings, and valves.

In most cases the factory recommended heat range is correct; it is chosen to perform well under a wide range of operating conditions. However, if most of your driving is long distance, high speed travel, you may want to install a spark plug one range colder than stan-

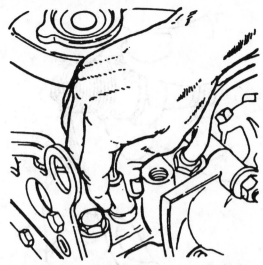

Twist and pull on the rubber boot to remove the spark plug wires; never pull on the wire itself

dard. If most of your driving is of the short trip variety, when the engine may not always reach operating temperature, a hotter plug may help burn off the deposits normally accumulated under those conditions.

REMOVAL

1. Number the wires with pieces of adhesive tape so that you won't cross them when you replace them.

2. The spark plug boots have large grips to aid in removal. Grasp the wire by the rubber boot and twist the boot ½ turn in either direction to break the tight seal between the boot and the plug. Then twist and pull on the boot to remove the wire from the spark plug. Do not pull on the wire itself or you will damage the carbon cord conductor.

3. Use a ⅝ inch spark plug socket to loosen all of the plugs about two turns. A universal joint installed at the socket end of the extension will ease the process.

If removal of the plugs is difficult, apply a few drops of penetrating oil or silicone spray to the area around the base of the plug, and allow it a few minutes to work.

4. If compressed air is available, apply it to the area around the spark plug holes. Otherwise, use a rag or a brush to clean the area. Be careful not to allow any foreign material to drop into the spark plug holes.

5. Remove the plugs by unscrewing them the rest of the way.

INSPECTION

Check the plugs for deposits and wear. If they are not going to be replaced, clean the plugs thoroughly. Remember that any kind of de-

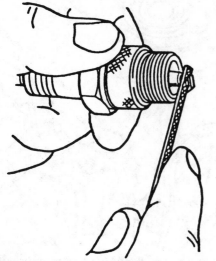

Plugs that are in good condition can be filed and reused

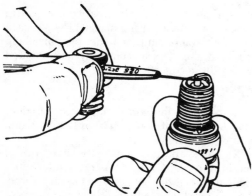

Always use a wire gauge to check the electrode gap

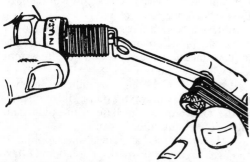

Adjust the electrode gap by bending the side electrode

posit will decrease the efficiency of the plug. Plugs can be cleaned on a spark plug cleaning machine, which can sometimes be found in service stations, or you can do an acceptable job of cleaning with a stiff brush. If the plugs are cleaned, the electrodes must be filed flat. Use an ignition points file, not an emery board

or the like, which will leave deposits. The electrodes must be filed perfectly flat with sharp edges; rounded edges reduce the spark plug voltage by as much as 50%.

Check the spark plug gap before installation. The ground electrode must be parallel to the center electrode and the specified size wire gauge should pass through the gap with a slight drag. Always check the gap on new plugs, too; they are not always correctly set at the factory. Do not use a flat feeler gauge when measuring the gap, because the reading will be inaccurate. Wire gapping tools usually have a bending tool attached. Use that to adjust the side electrode until the proper distance is obtained. Also, be careful not to bend the side electrode too far or too often; it may weaken and break off within the engine, requiring removal of the cylinder head to retrieve it.

INSTALLATION

1. Lubricate the threads of the spark plugs with a drop of oil or a shot of silicone spray. Install the plugs and tighten them handtight. Take care not to crossthread them.

2. Tighten the spark plugs with the socket. Do not apply the same amount of force you would use for a bolt; just snug them in. These spark plugs do not use gaskets, and over-tightening will make future removal difficult. If a torque wrench is available, tighten to 7–15 ft. lbs.

NOTE: *While over-tightening the spark plug is to be avoided, under-tightening is just as bad. If combustion gases leak past the threads, the spark plug will overheat and rapid electrode wear will result.*

3. Install the wires on their respective plugs. Make sure the wires are firmly connected. You will be able to feel them click into place. Spark plug wiring diagrams are in Chapter Three if you get into trouble.

CHECKING AND REPLACING SPARK PLUG WIRES

Every 15,000 miles, inspect the spark plug wires for burns, cuts, or breaks in the insulation. Check the boots and the nipples on the distributor cap. Replace any damaged wiring.

Every 45,000 miles or so, the resistance of the wires should be checked with an ohmmeter. Wires with excessive resistance will cause misfiring, and may make the engine difficult to start in damp weather. Generally, the useful life of the cables is 45,000–60,000 miles.

To check resistance, remove the distributor cap, leaving the wires in place. Connect one lead of an ohmmeter to an electrode within the cap; connect the other lead to the corresponding spark plug terminal (remove it from

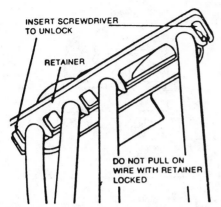

INSERT SCREWDRIVER TO UNLOCK

RETAINER

DO NOT PULL ON WIRE WITH RETAINER LOCKED

Unlock the plastic retainers to replace the spark plug wires

the spark plug for this test). Replace any wire which shows a resistance over 30,000 ohms. The following chart gives resistance values as a function of length. Generally speaking, however, resistance should not be considered the outer limit of acceptability.

- 0–15 inches—3,000–10,000 Ω;
- 15–25 inches—4,000–15,000 Ω;
- 25–35 inches—6,000–20,000 Ω;
- Over 35 inches—25,000 Ω.

It should be remembered that resistance is also a function of length; the longer the wire, the greater the resistance. Thus, if the wires on your car are longer than the factory originals, resistance will be higher, quite possibly outside these limits.

When installing new wires, replace them one at a time to avoid mixups. Start by replacing the longest one first. Install the boot firmly over the spark plug. Route the wire over the same path as the original. Insert the nipple firmly onto the tower on the distributor cap, then install the cap cover and latches to secure the wires.

Ignition System

The General Motors High Energy Ignition (H.E.I.) system is virtually maintenance-free, since it is electronic and, therefore uses no breaker points. The only required service for the H.E.I. distributor is to check the distributor cap and rotor for cracks, carbon tracking, and corrosion every 30,000 miles.

Please refer to the Engine Electrical section of Chapter 3 for further H.E.I. information.

Ignition Timing

Ignition timing is the point at which each spark plug fires in relation to its respective piston, during the compression stroke of the engine.

As far as ignition timing is concerned, the position of the piston can be related (in degrees) to the following reference terms: Top Dead Center (TDC), After Top Dead Center (ATDC), and Before Top Dead Center (BTDC). The movement of the piston is expressed in degrees due to the rotation of the crankshaft. Even though the crankshaft turns 720° to complete one entire four-stroke cycle, all we're concerned about here is the compression stroke, since this is when the ignition of the air/fuel mixture takes place (or more accurately, *should* take place).

Because it takes a fraction of a second for the spark (at the spark plug) to ignite the air fuel mixture and for the mixture to burn completely, the spark should ideally occur just before the piston reaches TDC. If the spark didn't occur until exactly TDC or ATDC, the piston would already be on its way down before the mixture ignited and began to burn properly. In this case, the mixture explosion would not exert as much downward force on the piston as it would if the ignition timing was properly set. The result of this would be reduced power and fuel economy.

Should ignition of the air/fuel mixture occur too far BTDC (advanced), the mixture explosion will try to force the piston downward before it can mechanically do so. This contest between the explosion forcing the piston downward and the crankshaft forcing the piston upward will result in a "pinging" sound if you're lucky; severe engine damage if you're not so lucky. If you experience pinging, check with a trusted mechanic to determine if the pinging is mild or severe. Only a trained ear can safely determine this.

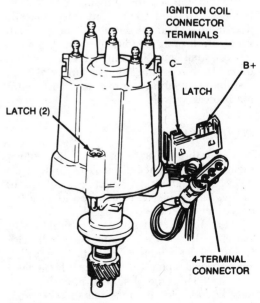

IGNITION COIL CONNECTOR TERMINALS

C−   B+

LATCH

LATCH (2)

4-TERMINAL CONNECTOR

HEI EST distributor

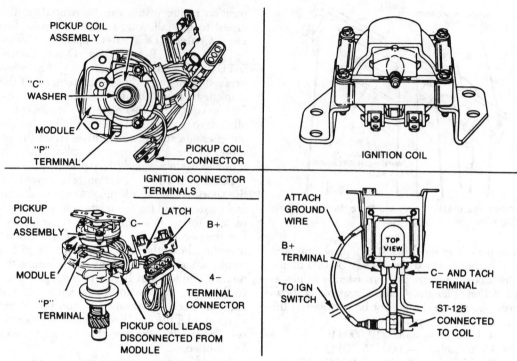

Distributor and ignition coil components

NOTE: *Pinging can also be caused by inferior gasoline, since lower octane gas burns at a faster, more uncontrolled rate than a higher octane fuel. In order to compensate for low quality gas, the ignition timing may be retarded a couple of degrees, though this is not recommended since performance and fuel economy will suffer.*

On United States engines, after the initial (base) timing is set, the emission control computer and related components electronically determine and adjust the degree of spark advance under all conditions. On Canadian models, total ignition timing advance is determined by three things: initial timing setting, distributor vacuum control and distributor mechanical control.

ADJUSTMENT

To check the timing before and after adjustment, a timing light is used. The timing light will visually show you a) when the spark is sent to the spark plug, and b) the position of the crankshaft when the spark occurs.

There are three basic types of timing light available. The first is a simple neon bulb with two wire connections (one for the spark plug and one for the plug wire, connecting the light in series). This type of light is quite dim, and must be held closely to the marks to be seen, but it is quite inexpensive. The second type of light operates from the car's battery. Two alligator clips connect to the battery terminals, while a third wire connects to the spark plug with an adapter. This type of light is more expensive, but the xenon bulb provides a nice bright flash which can even be seen in sunlight. The third type replaces the battery source with 110 volt house current. Some timing lights have other functions built into them, such as dwell meters, tachometers, or remote starting switches. These are convenient, in that they reduce the tangle of wires under the hood, but may duplicate the functions of tools you already have.

Because your car has electronic ignition, you should use a timing light which has an inductive pick-up. This type of pick-up merely clamps around the No. 1 spark plug wire, eliminating any kind of adapter. Other types of timing lights may cause false timing readings when used with H.E.I. systems.

CAUTION: *NEVER use a timing light which requires piercing of the spark plug wire.*

To adjust the ignition timing:

1. Refer to the instructions listed on the emission control label inside the engine compartment. *Follow all instructions on the label.*

2. Locate the timing marks on the front of the engine and on the crankshaft balancer.

3. Clean off the marks so that they are readable. Chalk or white paint on the balancer mark (line) and at the correct point on the tim-

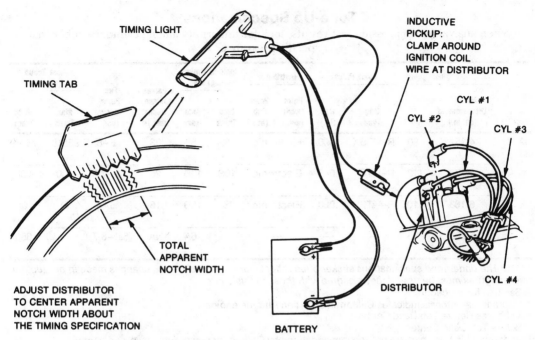

TIMING LIGHT

INDUCTIVE
PICKUP:
CLAMP AROUND
IGNITION COIL
WIRE AT DISTRIBUTOR

TIMING TAB

CYL #1

CYL #2

CYL #3

TOTAL
APPARENT
NOTCH WIDTH

ADJUST DISTRIBUTOR
TO CENTER APPARENT
NOTCH WIDTH ABOUT
THE TIMING SPECIFICATION

CYL #4

DISTRIBUTOR

BATTERY

Ignition timing is accomplished using the averaging method

ing scale will make the marks much easier to accurately align.

4. If specified on the emissions label, attach a tachometer to the engine according to the tachometer manufacturers instructions.

NOTE: *On four cylinder engines, the TACH terminal is at the brown wire connection at the ignition coil; on V6's, it is next to the BAT connector on the distributor cap.*

5. Attach a timing light according to the timing light manufacturers instructions. Remember that the inductive pick-up is clamped around the No. 1 spark plug wire.

6. Check that all wiring is clear of the fan, then start the engine. Allow the engine to reach normal operating temperature.

7. Aim the timing light at the timing marks. The line on the crankshaft balancer will line up at a timing mark. If the line is within one degree of where it should be, no adjustment is necessary.

8. If adjustment is necessary, loosen the distributor hold-down bolt slightly. Slowly rotate the distributor until the proper setting is attained.

9. Tighten the hold-down bolt, recheck the timing and readjust if required.

10. Turn the engine off and disconnect the timing light (and tachometer, if in use).

NOTE: *Disregard the short tube which may be integral with the timing scale on some engines. This tube is used to connect magnetic timing equipment which is marketed to professional shops.*

Valve Adjustment

All models utilize an hydraulic valve lifter system to obtain zero lash. No adjustment is necessary. An initial adjustment is required anytime that the lifters are removed or the valve train is disturbed, this procedure is covered in Chapter 3.

Idle Speed and Mixture Adjustment

U.S. FUEL INJECTED MODELS

Adjustments to gasoline or diesel fuel injection units are to be performed only in the case of parts replacement on the injection unit.

U.S. CARBURETED MODELS

No periodic idle adjustments are required on these models. All U.S. carburetors have an idle speed control (I.S.C.) motor which is controlled by the vehicles' on-board emissions computer (electronic control module/ E.C.M.).

Various idle speeds are programmed into the E.C.M. so that it can signal the I.S.C. to provide optimum idle speed according to specific situations. The only time the idle speed needs adjustment is if the I.S.C. has been replaced.

Idle mixture screws in all models are concealed by hardened, steel plugs. Adjustments to the idle mixture system are not considered to be part of a normal tune-up, due to strict emissions standards. Access to and adjustment

Tune-Up Specifications

When analyzing compression test results, look for uniformity among cylinders rather than specific pressures.

	Engine		Spark Plugs		Distributor		Ignition Timing (deg) ▲●		Valves Intake Opens (deg.)■	Fuel Pump Pressure (psi)	Idle Speed (rpm) ▲●	
Year	No. Cyl. Displacement (cu. in.)	hp	Orig Type	Gap (in.)	Point Dwell (deg)	Point Gap (in.)	Man Trans	Auto Trans			Man Trans	Auto Trans
82–83	4-151	90	R-44TSX	.060	Electronic		8B	8B	33	6–8	950①	750②
	6-173	112	R-43TS	.045	Electronic		10B	10B	25	6–7.5	800	600
	6-183	110	R-44TS8	.080	Electronic		③	15B	16	6–8	③	③
	6-263	85	—	—	—			6A	NA	5.8–8.7	—	650

NOTE: *The underhood specifications sticker often reflects tune-up specification changes made in production. Sticker figures must be used if they disagree with those in this chart.*
▲ See text for procedure
● Figure in parenthesis indicates California and High Altitude engine
■ All figures Before Top Dead Center
B Before Top Dead Center
Part numbers in this chart are not recommendations by Chilton for any product by brand name.
① Without air conditioning: 850
② Without air conditioning: 680
③ See underhood sticker
NA: not available

of the screws is possible but we strongly recommend that mixture adjustments be referred to a qualified, professional technician.

CANADIAN MODELS

The idle speed may be adjusted on Canadian models, though this is not part of a normal tune-up. Be sure to follow the instructions on the underhood emissions label to the letter in order to properly perform this adjustment.

As on U.S. models, the idle mixture screws are concealed under hardened plugs and mixture adjustments are not normally required. Since carburetor removal is necessary in order to gain access to the screws, the plug removal and adjustment procedures are covered in Chapter 4. The mixture adjustment procedures for U.S. and Canadian models are different. Be sure to follow the proper procedure.

Engine and Engine Rebuilding

3

UNDERSTANDING THE ENGINE ELECTRICAL SYSTEM

The engine electrical system can be broken down into three separate and distinct systems—(1) the starting system; (2) the charging system; (3) the ignition system.

Battery and Starting System

The battery is the first link in the chain of mechanisms which work together to provide cranking of the automobile engine. In most modern cars, the battery is a lead-acid electrochemical device consisting of six two-volt (2 V) subsections connected in series so the unit is capable of producing approximately 12 V of electrical pressure. Each subsection, or cell, consists of a series of positive and negative plates held a short distance apart in a solution of sulfuric acid and water. The two types of plates are of dissimilar metals. This causes a chemical reaction to be set up, and it is this reaction which produces current flow from the battery when its positive and negative terminals are connected to an electrical appliance such as a lamp or motor. The continued transfer of electrons would eventually convert the sulfuric acid in the electrolyte to water, and make the two plates identical in chemical composition. As electrical energy is removed from the battery, its voltage output tends to drop. Thus, measuring battery voltage and battery electrolyte composition are two ways of checking the ability of the unit to supply power. During the starting of the engine, electrical energy is removed from the battery. However, if the charging circuit is in good condition and the operating conditions are normal, the power removed from the battery will be replaced by the generator (or alternator) which will force electrons back through the battery, reversing the normal flow, and restoring the battery to its original chemical state.

The battery and starting motor are linked by very heavy electrical cables designed to minimize resistance to the flow of current. The major power supply cable that leaves the battery goes directly to the starter, while other electrical system needs are supplied by a smaller cable. During the starter operation, power flows from the battery to the starter and is grounded through the car's frame and the battery's negative ground strap.

The starting motor is a specially designed, direct current electric motor capable of producing a very great amount of power for its size. One thing that allows the motor to produce a great deal of power is its tremendous rotating speed. It drives the engine through a tiny pinion gear (attached to the starter's armature), which drives the very large flywheel ring gear at a greatly reduced speed. Another factor allowing it to produce so much power is that only intermittent operation is required of it. Thus, little allowance for air circulation is required, and the windings can be built into a very small space.

The starter solenoid is a magnetic device which employs the small current supplied by the starting switch circuit of the ignition switch. This magnetic action moves a plunger which mechanically engages the starter and electrically closes the heavy switch which connects it to the battery. The starting switch circuit consists of the starting switch contained within the ignition switch, a transmission neutral safety switch or clutch pedal switch, and the wiring necessary to connect these with the starter solenoid or relay.

A pinion, which is a small gear, is mounted to a one-way drive clutch. This clutch is splined to the starter armature shaft. When the ignition switch is moved to the "start" position, the solenoid plunger slides the pinion toward the flywheel ring gear via a collar and spring.

If the teeth on the pinion and flywheel match properly, the pinion will engage the flywheel immediately. If the gear teeth butt one another, the spring will be compressed and will force the gears to mesh as soon as the starter turns far enough to allow them to do so. As the solenoid plunger reaches the end of its travel, it closes the contacts that connect the battery and starter and then the engine is cranked.

As soon as the engine starts, the flywheel ring gear begins turning fast enough to drive the pinion at an extremely high rate of speed. At this point, the one-way clutch begins allowing the pinion to spin faster than the starter shaft so that the starter will not operate at excessive speed. When the ignition switch is released from the starter position, the solenoid is de-energized, and a spring contained within the solenoid assembly pulls the gear out of mesh and interrupts the current flow to the starter.

The Charging System

The automobile charging system provides electrical power for operation of the vehicle's ignition and starting systems and all the electrical accessories. The battery serves as an electrical surge or storage tank, storing (in chemical form) the energy originally produced by the engine-driven A.C. (alternator). The system also provides a means of regulating alternator output to protect the battery from being overcharged and to avoid excessive voltage to the accessories.

The storage battery is a chemical device incorporating parallel lead plates in a tank containing a sulfuric acid-water solution. Adjacen plates are slightly dissimilar, and the chemical reaction of the two dissimilar plates produces electrical energy when the battery is connected to a load such as the starter motor. The chemical reaction is reversible, so that when the alternator is producing a voltage (electrical pressure) greater than that produced by the battery, electricity is forced into the battery, and the battery is returned to its fully charged state.

The vehicle's alternator is driven mechanically, through belts, by the engine crankshaft. It consists of two coils of fine wire, one stationary (the "stator"), and one movable (the "rotor"). The rotor may also be known as the "armature," and consists of fine wire wrapped around an iron core which is mounted on a shaft. The electricity which flows through the two coils of wire (provided initially by the battery in some cases) creates in intense magnetic field around both rotor and stator, and the interaction between the two fields creates voltage, allowing the generator to power the accessories and charge the battery.

Newer automobiles, including your A-Body, use alternating current alternators because they are efficient, can be rotated at high speeds, and have few brush problems. In an alternator, the field rotates while all the current produced passes only through the stator windings. The brushes bear against continuous slip rings rather than a commutator. This causes the current produced to periodically reverse the direction of its flow. Diodes (electrical one-way switches) block the flow of current from traveling in the wrong direction. A series of diodies is wired together to permit the alternating flow of the stator to be converted to a pulsating, but unidirectional flow at the alternator output. The alternator's field is wired in series with the the voltage regulator. Alternators are self-limiting as far as maximum current is concerned.

SAFETY PRECAUTIONS

Observing these precautions will ensure safe handling of the electrical system components, and will avoid damage to the vehicle's electrical system:

a. Be *absolutely* sure of the polarity of a booster battery before making connections. Connect the cables positive to positive, and negative to negative. Connect positive cables first and then make the last connection to a ground on the body of the booster vehicle so that arcing cannot ignite hydrogen gas that may have accumulated near the battery. Even momentary connection of a booster battery with the polarity reserved will damage alternator diodes.

b. Disconnect both vehicle battery cables before attempting to charge a battery.

c. Never ground the alternator output or battery terminal. Be cautious when using metal tools around a battery to avoid creating a short circuit between the terminals.

d. Never run an alternator or generator without load unless the field circuit is disconnected.

e. Never attempt to polarize an alternator.

ENGINE ELECTRICAL

Distributor

REMOVAL

Four Cylinder Engines

1. Disconnect the negative battery cable.
2. Raise the front of the vehicle and sup-

port it safely with jackstands. DO NOT place the jackstands under the engine cradle.

3. Place a jack under the engine cradle then extend the jack so that it just touches the cradle. The jack must not block any of the engine cradle bolts.

4. Remove the two rear engine cradle attaching bolts and lower the cradle just enough to gain access to the distributor.

5. Remove the five screws which attach the brake line support to the floorpan.

6. Remove the coil wire from the distributor.

7. Remove the distributor cap.

8. Mark the position of the rotor firing tip on the distributor body, then mark the relationship between the distributor body and some point on the engine.

CAUTION: *DO NOT attempt to crank the engine while the distributor is removed.*

9. Loosen the distributor hold-down clamp bolt and slide the hold-down clamp aside to clear the distributor body.

10. Lift the distributor out of the engine and mark the point at which the rotor stops turning while you're pulling upward. The rotor will have to be positioned at this same spot in order to install the distributor correctly.

V6 Engines

1. Disconnect the negative battery cable at the battery.

2. Release the distributor and ignition coil electrical connections at the distributor cap.

3. Follow steps 8 through 10 of the previous proceudre to complete the removal of the distributor.

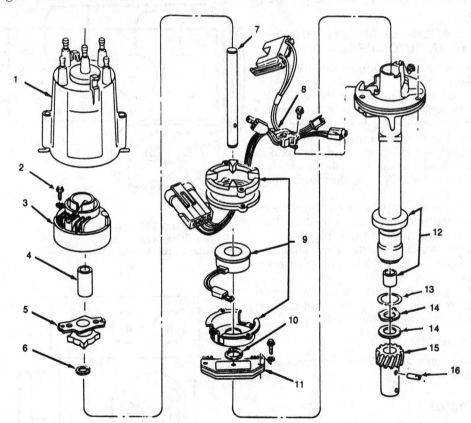

1. Distributor cap	9. Pole piece and plate assy. (pick-up coil)
2. Screw	10. Seal
3. Rotor	11. Module
4. Bushing	12. Housing assembly
5. Distributor shaft	13. O-ring
6. Retainer	14. Washer
7. Distributor shaft	15. Distributor gear
8. Wiring harness	16. Pin

Exploded view of the distributor

INSTALLATION—ENGINE NOT DISTURBED

1. Align the ignition rotor with the mark made during the previous step 10.

2. Install the distributor into the engine, noting that the marks made during the previous step 8 must align. If they don't line up the first time, remove the distributor and try again.

3. Re-position the hold-down clamp on the distributor body and tighten the bolt until the distributor is snug, but can be moved with a little effort.

4. Connect all wiring to the distributor, and on four cylinder models, jack the engine cradle back into place, install the engine cradle bolts and the brake line support bolts.

5. Connect the battery cable and lower the vehicle if necessary.

6. Adjust the ignition timing as previously outlined.

INSTALLATION—ENGINE DISTURBED WITH DISTRIBUTOR REMOVED

1. Remove the spark plug from the No. 1 cylinder.

2. Place your thumb over the spark plug hole and turn the crankshaft by hand with a wrench until pressure is felt at the plug hole.

3. Look at the timing marks on the front of the engine and check to see if the balancer slash is aligned with the "0" on the timing scale. If necessary, turn the crankshaft until it does align.

4. On the four cylinder engine, turn the rotor until the rotor firing tip is positioned between the Nos. 1 and 3 spark splug towers of the distributor cap. On the V6, position the firing tip between the Nos. 1 and 6 towers of the cap.

5. Install the distributor and follow steps 3 through 6 of the first (previous) installation procedure to complete the installation.

FIRING ORDER

To avoid confusion, replace the spark plug wires one at a time.

Alternator

Two models of the SI series alternator are used on A-cars. The 10 SI and 15 SI are of similar construction; the 15 SI is slightly larger, uses different stator windings, and produces more current.

PRECAUTIONS

1. When installing a battery, make sure that the positive and negative cables are not reversed.

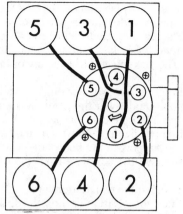

GM (Buick) 183 V6 (3.0L) Engine firing order: 1-6-5-4-3-2 Distributor rotation: clockwise

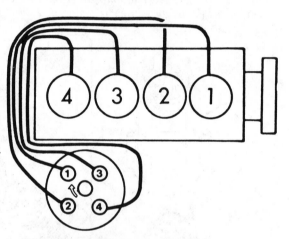

GM (Pontiac) 151-4
Engine firing order: 1-3-4-2
Distributor rotation: clockwise

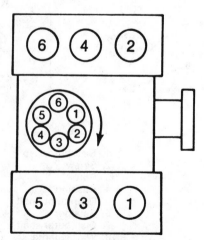

GM (Chevrolet) 173 V6 (2.8 L)
Engine firing order: 1-2-3-4-5-6
Distributor rotation: clockwise

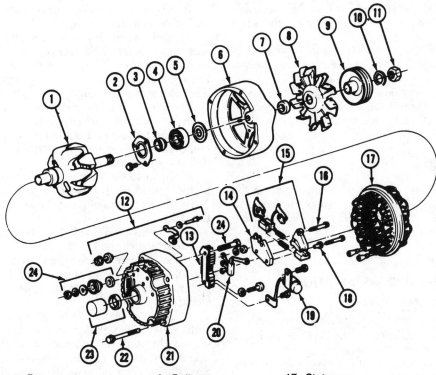

1. Rotor
2. Front bearing retainer
3. Inner collar
4. Bearing
5. Washer
6. Front housing
7. Outer collar
8. Fan
9. Pulley
10. Lockwasher
11. Pulley nut
12. Terminal assembly
13. Rectifier bridge
14. Regulator
15. Brush assembly
16. Screw
17. Stator
18. Insulating washer
19. Capacitor
20. Diode trio
21. Rear housing
22. Through bolt
23. Bearing and seal assembly
24. Terminal assembly

Exploded view of the 10SI alternator (15SI similar)

2. When jump-starting the car, be sure that like terminals are connected. This also applies to using a battery charger. Reversed polarity will burn out the alternator and regulator in a matter of seconds.

3. Never operate the alternator with the battery disconnected or on an otherwise uncontrolled open circuit.

4. Do not short across or ground any alternator or regulator terminals.

5. Do not try to polarize the alternator.

6. Do not apply full battery voltage to the field (brown) connector.

7. Always disconnect the battery ground cable before disconnecting the alternator lead.

8. Always disconnect the battery (negative cable first) when charging it.

9. Never subject the alternator to excessive heat or dampness. If you are steamcleaning the engine, cover the alternator.

10. Never use arc-welding equipment on the car with the alternator connected.

REMOVAL AND INSTALLATION

1. Disconnect the negative battery cable.

2. Remove the two-terminal plug and the battery leads from the rear of the alternator.

3. Remove the adjusting bolt from the alternator on gasoline-engined models. The adjusting bolt is the one within the slotted hole.

4. On diesel-equipped models, fit the end of a ratchet extension into the square hole of the belt tensioner bracket, then attach a ratchet to the extension. Lever the tensioner towards the firewall side of the engine compartment and remove the serpentine drive belt from the alternator.

5. On gasoline-engined models, move the alternator to loosen the drive belt, then remove the belt.

6. On four cylinder models, remove the upper alternator bracket.

7. On diesel models, remove the alternator brace bolt from the rear of the alternator.

8. On gasoline-engined models, remove the alternator pivot bolt and remove the alternator.

9. On diesel models, remove both alternator attaching bolts and remove the alternator.

10. Installation is the reverse of removal. Be sure to adjust the tension of the drive belt properly, then tighten the adjusting bolt(s) (on gasoline-engined models).

Regulator

A solid state regulator is mounted within the alternator. All regulator components are enclosed in a solid mold. The regulator is non-adjustable and requires no maintenance.

Starter

REMOVAL AND INSTALLATION

Except Diesel Engines

1. Disconnect the negative battery cable.
2. Raise the front of the vehicle and support it safely with jackstands.
3. From underneath the vehicle, remove the two starter motor-to-engine bolts and carefully lower the starter. Note the location of shims (if so equipped).
4. On the four cylinder engine, remove the nut that holds the starter bracket to the rear of the starter.
5. Mark and disconnect all wiring at the starter.
6. Installation is the reverse of removal.

Diesel Engine

1. Disconnect the negative battery cable(s).
2. Raise the front of the vehicle and support it safely with jackstands.
3. Remove the lower starter shield nut and flex the starter shield for access during removal.
4. Mark and disconnect the wires from the starter.
5. Remove the front starter attaching bolt.
6. Loosen the rear starter attaching bolt and remove the starter assembly, leaving the rear bolt in the starter housing.
7. Installation is the reverse of removal.

STARTER OVERHAUL—GASOLINE ENGINES

Drive Replacement

1. Disconnect the field coil straps from the solenoid.
2. Remove the thru-bolts, and separate the commutator end frame, field frame assembly, drive housing, and armature assembly from each other.

3. Slide the two piece thrust collar off the end of the armature shaft.

4. Slide a suitably sized metal cylinder, such as a standard half-inch pipe coupling, or an old pinion, on the shaft so that the end of the coupling or pinion butts up against the edge of the pinion retainer.

5. Support the lower end of the armature securely on a soft surface, such as a wooden block, and tap the end of the coupling or pinion, driving the retainer towards the armature end of the snap ring.

6. Remove the snap ring from the groove in the armature shaft with a pair of pliers. Then, slide the retainer and starter drive from the shaft.

7. To reassemble, lubricate the drive end of the armature shaft with silicone lubricant, and then slide the starter drive onto the shaft with the pinion facing outward. Slide the retainer onto the shaft with the cupped surface facing outward.

8. Again support the armature on a soft surface, with the pinion at the upper end. Center the snap ring on the top of the shaft (use a new snap ring if the original was damaged during removal). Gently place a block of wood flat on top of the snap ring so as not to move it from a centered position. Tap the wooden block with a hammer in order to force the snap ring around the shaft. Then, slide the ring down into the snap ring groove.

9. Lay the armature down flat on the surface you're working on. Slide the retainer close up on to the shaft and position it and the thrust collar next to the snap ring. Using two pairs of pliers on opposite sides of the shaft, squeeze the thrust collar and the retainer together until the snap ring is forced into the retainer.

10. Lube the drive housing bushing with a silicone lubricant. Then, install the armature and clutch assembly into the drive housing, engaging the solenoid shift lever with the clutch, and positioning the front end of armature shaft into the bushing.

11. Apply a sealing compound approved for this application onto the drive housing; then position the field frame around the armature shaft and against the drive housing. Work slowly and carefully to prevent damaging the starter brushes.

12. Lubricate the bushing in the commutator end frame with a silicone lubricant, place the leather brake washer onto the armature shaft, and then slide the commutator end frame over the shaft and into position against the field frame. Line up the bolt holes, and then install and tighten the thrubolts.

13. Reconnect the field coil straps to the "motor" terminal of the solenoid.

NOTE: *If replacement of the starter drive*

fails to cure the improper engagement of the starter pinion to the flywheel, there are probably defective parts in the solenoid and/or shift lever. The best procedure would probably be to take the assembly to a shop where a pinion clearance check can be made by energizing the solenoid on a test bench. If the pinion clearance is incorrect, disassemble the solenoid and the shift lever, inspect, and replace worn parts.

Brush Replacement

1. After removing the starter from the engine, disconnect the field coil from the motor solenoid terminal.

2. Remove the starter thru-bolts and remove the commutator end frame and washer.

3. Remove the field frame and the armature assembly from the drive housing.

4. Remove the brush holder pivot pin which positions one insulated and one grounded brush.

5. Remove the brush springs.

6. Remove the brushes.

7. Installation is in the reverse order of removal.

STARTER OVERHAUL—DIESEL TYPE ONE

NOTE: *The Type One diesel starter is identified by having a cast iron housing, whereas the Type Two unit covered later, has an aluminum housing.*

Drive Replacement

1. Remove the starter from the vehicle as previously outlined.

2. Remove the screw from the field coil connector strap at the solenoid.

3. Separate the field frame assembly from the drive gear assembly.

4. Remove the solenoid mounting screws, turn the solenoid 90° and remove the solenoid.

5. Remove the shift lever shaft retaining ring, lever shaft, and the housing through-bolts in order to separate the drive assembly, drive housing and gear housing.

6. Remove the thrust washer or collar from the drive shaft, in front of the drive assembly.

7. Slide a ⅝" deep socket (or a piece of suitably sized pipe) over the shaft and against the retainer.

8. Tap the socket (or pipe) to move the retainer off the snap ring.

9. Remove the snap ring from the groove in the shaft. If the ring becomes distorted during removal, it must be replaced with a new ring during assembly.

10. Remove the starter drive assembly from the shaft.

11. Slide the new drive assembly onto the drive shaft, then place the snap ring retainer over the shaft with the cupped side of the retainer facing away from the gear of the drive unit.

12. Position the armature upright (drive unit facing upward), resting the lower end on a block of wood.

13. Center the snap ring on the top of the shaft. Remember that a new ring should be used if the old one was damaged during removal.

14. Carefully place a block of wood on the ring then tap on the block of wood (using a light hammer) to force the ring onto the shaft. Slide the ring down into the snap ring groove.

15. Place the thrust collar onto the drive shaft, then squeeze the thrust collar and retainer together, which will force the retainer over the snap ring.

16. Assemble the plunger and shift lever into the drive housing with the lever shaft and the retaining ring.

17. Place the drive shaft washer over the drive shaft on the side of the gear opposite the drive assembly. Lubricate the gear teeth with G.M. #1960954 lubricant or its equivalent.

18. Assemble the gear housing with the attaching screws.

19. Assemble the solenoid to the drive housing.

20. Lubricate the bushing in the commutator end frame with the same lubricant mentioned previously.

21. Assemble the armature, field frame and the commutator end frame to the gear housing with the through-bolts.

22. Attach the field coil connector to the solenoid terminal. Install the starter assembly as previously outlined.

Brush Replacement

1. Please follow steps 1–5 of the last Drive Replacement procedure in order to separate the field coil and frame assembly from the armature.

2. Remove the commutator end frame in order to gain access to the brushes.

3. Remove the brush holder pivot pin which positions one insulated and one grounded brush.

4. Remove the brush spring.

5. Replace the brushes as required, then reinstall the brush spring and the pivot pin.

6. Repeat steps 3, 4, and 5 for the remaining pair of brushes.

7. Reassemble the remaining starter components in the reverse of removal.

STARTER OVERHAUL—DIESEL TYPE TWO

NOTE: *The Type Two diesel starter is identified by having an aluminum housing.*

Drive and Brush Replacement

NOTE: *G.M. special tool #J-22888 and a dial indicator will be needed to properly assemble the starter.*

1. Remove the starter assembly from the vehicle as previously outlined.

2. Remove the nut from the field coil connector at the solenoid.

3. Remove the two solenoid mounting screws then remove the solenoid by pulling it upward and forward.

NOTE: *In some cases, shims will be present between the solenoid and the drive end housing. These shims are used to set the drive pinion position.*

4. Remove the two through bolts and the two brush holder retaining screws. Remove the commutator end frame from the armature and bearing assembly.

5. Remove the field frame assembly and the armature from the center housing.

6. Carefully pry each brush spring back so that each brush can be backed away from the armature about ¼″. Release the spring to hold the brushes in the backed out position, then remove the armature from the field frame and brush holder.

7. Remove the cover retaining screws, cover, C-washer and plate from the armature side of the center housing.

8. Remove the two center housing bolts, the center housing and the shim thrust washers.

9. Remove the reduction gear, spring holder and two lever springs.

10. Slide a ⅝″ socket or suitably sized piece of pipe over the nose of the pinion shaft, against the drive pinion stopper.

11. Tap on the socket (or pipe) to drive the stopper off of the snap ring. Using a pair of snap ring pliers, remove the drive pinion snap ring from the groove in the pinion shaft.

NOTE: *If the ring becomes distorted during removal, it must be replaced with a new ring during assembly.*

12. Remove the stopper, drive pinion gear and spring.

13. Remove the pinion shaft/overrunning clutch from the drive end housing.

To replace the brushes:

14. Remove the brush holder and the negative brush assembly from the field frame by removing the positive brushes from the brush holder.

15. Cut the old positive brush leads from the field coil bar as close to the brush connection point as possible; cut the negative brush leads from the brush holder plate.

16. Connection tangs are provided for installation of new brushes. Clean the connection tangs then solder the new brush leads on the tangs. Use only high temperature solder to connect the new brushes, and make sure that the positive brush connections are made properly in order to prevent grounding of the brush connection.

17. Reinstall the positive and the negative brushes in the brush holder assembly. Position the brushes in the backed-out position as described earlier.

To assemble the starter:

NOTE: *The lubricant mentioned during assembly should be G.M. #1960954 or its equivalent.*

18. Lubricate the splines and bearing surfaces of the pinion shaft/overrunning clutch, the nylon lever holders and both ends of the lever.

19. Install the lever assembly on the overrunning clutch (see the accompanying illustration). The lever MUST be installed as shown; if not, the clutch mechanism could lock during operation.

20. Install the pinion shaft/overrunning clutch and lever assembly into the drive end housing.

21. Slide the spring, drive pinion and stopper (in that order) over the pinion shaft, making sure that the cupped side of the stopper faces the end of the shaft.

22. Press the drive pinion and stopper towards the drive end housing and install the snap ring into the groove of the pinion shaft.

23. Using tool J-22888, force the drive pinion towards the end of the pinion shaft, which will force the stopper over the snap ring. It may be necessary to tap the ring with a drift pin to seat the ring in the groove of the stopper.

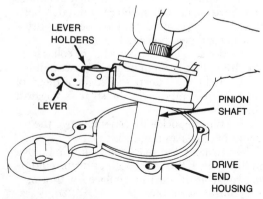

LEVER HOLDERS

LEVER

PINION SHAFT

DRIVE END HOUSING

Aluminum starter

24. Install the two lever springs and the spring holder into the drive end housing.

25. Lubricate the reduction gear teeth, then install the gear and shim thrust washer(s) onto the pinion shaft assembly.

26. Position the center housing to the drive end housing and install the two attaching bolts.

27. Check the end-play of the pinion shaft as follows:

a. Install the plate and the C-shaped washer onto the pinion shaft.

b. With the drive end housing suitably supported, insert an appropriately sized feeler gauge between the C-washer and the cover plate. Using a screwdriver, move the pinion shaft axially to determine the total end play. Try different sized feeler gauges until the thickest gauge fits the clearance. Total end-play should be 0.004–0.020″. Replace or remove the shim thrust washers as required to bring the clearance within specification.

c. Remove the cover plate (if it is not already removed) and fill the cover ½ full with lubricant.

d. Reinstall the cover and install and tighten the two cover bolts.

28. Install the armature by carefully engaging the splines of the shaft with the reduction gear.

29. Position the field frame and brush holder assembly on the center housing, noting that the rubber grommet for the field coil lead must align with the locating ribs of the center housing.

30. Pry the brush spring back, which will allow the brushes to seat against the commutator bars of the armature.

31. Position the commutator end frame onto the field frame, aligning the marks made during disassembly.

32. Install and tighten the two brush holder screws, then the through bolts.

33. Install the solenoid switch and shims onto the drive end housing. Make sure that the slot of the solenoid plunger engages with the top of the lever. Install and tighten the solenoid retaining bolts.

34. Connect the field coil connector to the solenoid switch terminal.

35. Because the starter has been disassembled, it is necessary to check the pinion position as follows:

a. Connect one 12V lead of a battery to the terminal marked "S" on the solenoid. Momentarily touch the other 12V lead to the starter frame. This action will shift the drive pinion into its cranking position until one of the battery leads is disconnected. DO NOT

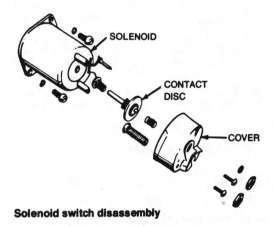

Solenoid switch disassembly

leave the pinion in the cranking position for more than 30 seconds at a time.

b. With the pinion in the cranking position, set up a dial indicator as shown, then "zero" the indicator needle.

c. Push the pinion shaft back by hand and record the amount of movement indicated by the indicator needle. Detach one of the battery leads to bring the drive pinion back to its off position.

d. The indicator reading should have been between 0.020 and 0.080″. The clearance is adjusted by adding or removing shims between the solenoid and the front bracket. Shims are available in 0.010″ and 0.020″ thicknesses.

e. If a shim thickness adjustment was required, reinstall the solenoid with the new shims and repeat the clearance check.

STARTER SOLENOID REMOVAL AND INSTALLATION

Except Diesel Aluminum Starter

1. Remove the starter and solenoid assembly as previously outlined.

2. Remove the screw and washer from the motor connector strap terminal.

3. Remove the two screws which retain the solenoid housing to the end frame assembly.

4. Twist the solenoid clockwise to remove the flange key from the keyway slot in the housing.

5. Remove the solenoid assembly.

6. With the solenoid return spring installed on the plunger, position the solenoid body on the drive housing and turn it counterclockwise to engage the flange key in the keyway slot.

7. Install the two screws which retain the solenoid housing to the end frame.

Diesel Aluminum Starter (Type 2)

After the field coil connector nut and the two solenoid attaching screws are removed, pull the solenoid upward and forward to remove it. Installation is simply a matter of bolting the solenoid into place, fastening the field coil connector and reinstalling the starter. It is recommended by G.M., however, to check the pinion position as previously outlined (Step 35a–35e of the Diesel Type 2 assembly procedure).

ENGINE MECHANICAL

Engine

REMOVAL AND INSTALLATION

4-151 with Manual Transaxle

NOTE: *Relieve the pressure in the fuel system as described under Fuel Pump.*

1. Disconnect battery cables at battery.
2. Hoist car.
3. Remove front mount-to-cradle nuts.
4. Remove forward exhaust pipe.
5. Remove starter assembly (wires attached and swing to side).
6. Remove flywheel inspection cover.
7. Lower car.
8. Remove air cleaner.
9. Remove all bell housing bolts.
10. Remove forward torque reaction rod from engine and core support.
11. If equipped with A/C, remove A/C belt and compressor and swing to side.
12. Remove emission hoses at canister.
13. Remove power steering hose (if so equipped).
14. Remove vacuum hoses and electrical connectors at solenoid.
15. Remove heater blower motor.
16. Disconnect throttle cable.
17. Drain cooling system.
18. Disconnect heater hose.
19. Disconnect radiator hose.
20. Disconnect engine harness at bulkhead connector.
21. With engine lifting tool, hoist engine (remove heater hose at intake manifold and disconnect fuel line).
22. Installation is the reverse of removal.

4-151 with Automatic Transaxle

NOTE: *Relieve the pressure in the fuel system as described under Fuel Pump.*

1. Disconnect battery cables at battery.
2. Drain cooling system.
3. Remove air cleaner and pre-heat tube.
4. Disconnect engine harness connector.
5. Disconnect all external vacuum hose connections.
6. Remove throttle and transaxle linkage at E.F.I. assembly and intake manifold.

7. Remove upper radiator hose.
8. If equipped with air conditioning, remove A/C compressor from mounting brackets and set aside. Do not disconnect hoses.
9. Remove fron engine strut assembly.
10. Disconnect heater hose at intake manifold.
11. Remove transaxle to engine bolts leaving the upper two bolts in place.
12. Remove front mount-to-cradle nuts.
13. Remove forward exhaust pipe.
14. Remove flywheel inspection cover and remove starter motor.
15. Remove torque converter to flywheel bolts.
16. Remove P/S pump and bracket and move to one side.
17. Remove heater hose and lower radiator hose.
18. Remove two rear transaxle support bracket bolts.
19. Remove fuel supply line at fuel filter.
20. Using a floor jack and a block of wood placed under the transaxle, raise engine and transaxle until engine front mount studs clear cradle.
21. Connect engine lift equipment and put tension on engine.
22. Remove two remaining transaxle bolts.
23. Slide engine forward and lift from car. Install engine on stand.
24. Installation is the reverse of removal. Do not completely lower the engine with a jack supporting the transaxle.

6-173 with Manual Transaxle

1. Disconnect cables from battery.
2. Remove air cleaner.
3. Drain cooling system.
4. Disconnect vacuum hosing to all non-engine mounted components.
5. Disconnect accelerator linkage from carburetor.
6. Disconnect engine harness connector.
7. Disconnect radiator hoses from radiator.
8. Disconnect heater hoses from engine.
9. If equipped, remove power steering pump and bracket assembly from engine.
10. Disconnect clutch cable from transaxle.
11. Disconnect shift linkage from transaxle shift levers. Remove cables from transaxle bosses.
12. Disconnect speedometer cable from transaxle.
13. Install engine support fixture. Raise engine until weight is relieved from mount assemblies.
14. Remove exhaust crossover.

15. Remove all but one of the transaxle to engine retaining bolts.

16. Remove side and crossmember assembly.

17. Disconnect exhaust pipe.

18. Remove all powertrain mount to cradle attachments.

19. Using tool J-28468 or J-33008, pull both axle drive shafts from transaxle assembly.

20. Lower vehicle.

21. Lower left side of engine/transaxle assembly by loosening tool J-22825.

22. Place jack under transaxle.

23. Remove the final transaxle to engine attaching bolt and separate transaxle from engine and lower.

24. Lower vehicle.

25. Install engine lifting fixture.

26. If A/C equipped, remove compressor from mounting bracket and swing aside.

27. Disconnect forward strut bracket from radiator support. Swing aside.

28. Lift engine out of vehicle.

29. Installation is the reverse of removal.

6-173 with Automatic Transaxle

1. Disconnect battery cables from battery.

2. Remove air cleaner.

3. Drain cooling system.

4. Disconnect vacuum hosing to all non-engine mounted components.

5. Disconnect detent cable from carburetor lever.

6. Disconnect accelerator linkage.

7. Disconnect engine harness connector.

8. Disconnect ground strap from engine at engine forward strut.

9. Disconnect radiator hoses from radiator.

10. Disconnect heater hoses from engine.

11. Remove power steering pump and bracket assembly from engine, if equipped.

12. Raise vehicle.

13. Disconnect exhaust pipe.

14. Disconnect fuel lines at rubber hose connections at right side of engine.

15. Remove engine front mount to cradle retaining nuts (right side of vehicle).

16. Disconnect battery cables from engine (Starter and transaxle housing bolt).

17. Remove flex plate cover and disconnect torque convertor from flex plate.

18. Remove transaxle case to cylinder case support bracket bolts.

19. Lower vehicle. Place a support under the transaxle rear extension.

20. Remove engine strut bracket from radiator support and swing rearward.

21. Remove exhaust crossover pipe.

22. Remove transaxle to cylinder case re-taining bolts. Make note of ground stud location.

23. If A/C equipped, remove compressor from mounting bracket and lay aside.

24. Install lift fixture to engine and remove engine from vehicle.

25. Installation is the reverse of removal.

6-183

1. Disconnect battery cables from battery.

2. Remove air cleaner.

3. Drain cooling system.

4. Disconnect vacuum hosing to all non-engine mounted components.

5. Disconnect detent cable from carburetor lever.

6. Disconnect accelerator linkage.

7. Disconnect engine harness connector.

8. Disconnect ground strap from engine at engine forward strut.

9. Disconnect radiator hoses from radiator.

10. Disconnect heater hoses from engine.

11. Remove power steering pump and bracket assembly from engine.

12. Raise vehicle.

13. Disconnect exhaust pipe at manifold.

14. Disconnect fuel lines at rubber hose connections.

15. Remove engine front mount to cradle retaining nuts (right side of vehicle).

16. Disconnect battery cables from engine (Starter and transaxle housing bolt).

17. Remove flex plate cover and disconnect torque converter from flex plate.

18. Remove transaxle case to cylinder case support bracket bolts.

19. Lower vehicle. Place a support under the transaxle rear extension.

20. Remove engine strut bracket from radiator support and swing rearward.

21. Remove transaxle to cylinder case retaining bolts. Make note of ground stud location.

22. If A/C equipped, remove compressor from mounting bracket and lay aside.

23. Install lift fixture to engine and remove engine from vehicle.

24. Installation is the reverse of removal.

6-263 Diesel

1. Drain the cooling system. Remove the serpentine drive belt (and vacuum pump drive belt, if A/C equipped).

2. Remove air cleaner and install cover J-26996.

3. Disconnect battery negative cable(s) at batteries and ground wires at inner fender panel. Disconnect engine ground strap, rear (right) head to cowl.

ENGINE OVERHAUL

Most engine overhaul procedures are fairly standard. In addition to specific parts replacement procedures and complete specifications for your individual engine, this chapter also is a guide to accepted rebuilding procedures. Examples of standard rebuilding practice are shown and should be used along with specific details concerning your particular engine.

Competent and accurate machine shop services will ensure maximum performance, reliability and engine life. Procedures marked with the symbol shown above should be performed by a competent machine shop, and are provided so that you will be familiar with the procedures necessary to a successful overhaul.

In most instances it is more profitable for the do-it-yourself mechanic to remove, clean and inspect the component, buy the necessary parts and deliver these to a shop for actual machine work.

On the other hand, much of the rebuilding work (crankshaft, block, bearings, pistons, rods, and other components) is well within the scope of the do-it-yourself mechanic.

Tools

The tools required for an engine overhaul or parts replacement will depend on the depth of your involvement. With a few exceptions, they will be the tools found in a mechanic's tool kit (see Chapter 1). More in-depth work will require any or all of the following:
• a dial indicator (reading in thousandths) mounted on a universal base
• micrometers and telescope gauges
• jaw and screw-type pullers
• scraper
• valve spring compressor
• ring groove cleaner
• piston ring expander and compressor
• ridge reamer
• cylinder hone or glaze breaker

• Plastigage®
• engine stand
Use of most of these tools is illustrated in this chapter. Many can be rented for a one-time use from a local parts jobber or tool supply house specializing in automotive work.

Occasionally, the use of special tools is called for. See the information on Special Tools and the Safety Notice in the front of this book before substituting another tool.

Inspection Techniques

Procedures and specifications are given in this chapter for inspecting, cleaning and assessing the wear limits of most major components. Other procedures such as Magnaflux and Zyglo can be used to locate material flaws and stress cracks. Magnaflux is a magnetic process applicable only to ferrous materials. The Zyglo process coats the material with a flourescent dye penetrant and can be used on any material. Check for suspected surface cracks can be more readily made using spot check dye. The dye is sprayed onto the suspected area, wiped off and the area sprayed with a developer. Cracks will show up brightly.

Overhaul Tips

Aluminum has become extremely popular for use in engines, due to its low weight. Observe the following precautions when handling aluminum parts:
• Never hot tank aluminum parts (the caustic hot-tank solution will eat the aluminum)
• Remove all aluminum parts (identification tag, etc.) from engine parts prior to hot-tanking.
• Always coat threads lightly with engine oil or anti-seize compounds before installation, to prevent seizure.
• Never over-torque bolts or spark plugs, especially in aluminum threads.
Stripped threads in any component can be repaired using any of several commercial repair kits (Heli-Coil, Microdot, Keenserts, etc.)

When assembling the engine, any parts that will be in frictional contact must be prelubed to provide lubrication at initial start-up. Any product specifically formulated for this purpose can be used, but engine oil is not recommended as a pre-lube.

When semi-permanent (locked, but removable) installation of bolts or nuts is desired, threads should be cleaned and coated with Loctite® or other similar, commercial non-hardening sealant.

Repairing Damaged Threads

Several methods of repairing damaged threads are available. Heli-Coil® (shown here), Keenserts® and Microdot® are among the most widely used. All involve basically the same principle—drilling out stripped threads, tapping the hole and installing a prewound insert—making welding, plugging and oversize fasteners unnecessary.

Two types of thread repair inserts are usually supplied—a standard type for most Inch Coarse, Inch Fine, Metric Coarse and Metric Fine thread sizes and a spark plug type to fit most spark plug port sizes. Consult the individual manufacturer's catalog to determine exact applications. Typical thread repair kits will contain a selection of prewound threaded inserts, a tap (corresponding to the outside diameter threads of the insert) and an installation tool. Spark plug inserts usually differ because they require a tap equipped with pilot threads and a combined reamer/tap section. Most manufacturers also supply blister-packed thread repair inserts separately in addition to a master kit containing a variety of taps and inserts plus installation tools.

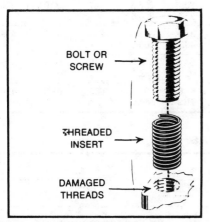

Damaged bolt holes can be repaired with thread repair inserts

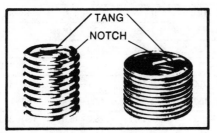

Standard thread repair insert (left) and spark plug thread insert (right)

Before effecting a repair to a threaded hole, remove any snapped, broken or damaged bolts or studs. Penetrating oil can be used to free frozen threads; the offending item can be removed with locking pliers or with a screw or stud extractor. After the hole is clear, the thread can be repaired, as follows:

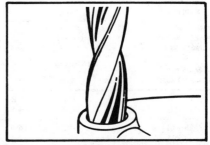

Drill out the damaged threads with specified drill. Drill completely through the hole or to the bottom of a blind hole

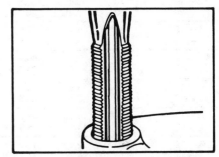

With the tap supplied, tap the hole to receive the thread insert. Keep the tap well oiled and back it out frequently to avoid clogging the threads

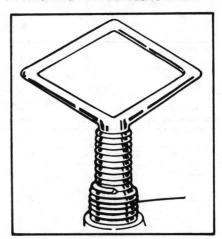

Screw the threaded insert onto the installation tool until the tang engages the slot. Screw the insert into the tapped hole until it is ¼–½ turn below the top surface, After installation break off the tang with a hammer and punch

Standard Torque Specifications and Fastener Markings

In the absence of specific torques, the following chart can be used as a guide to the maximum safe torque of a particular size/grade of fastener.

- There is no torque difference for fine or coarse threads.
- Torque values are based on clean, dry threads. Reduce the value by 10% if threads are oiled prior to assembly.
- The torque required for aluminum components or fasteners is considerably less.

U.S. Bolts

SAE Grade Number	1 or 2			5			6 or 7		
Number of lines always 2 less than the grade number.									
Bolt Size (Inches)—(Thread)	Maximum Torque			Maximum Torque			Maximum Torque		
	Ft./Lbs.	Kgm	Nm	Ft./Lbs.	Kgm	Nm	Ft./Lbs.	Kgm	Nm
¼ — 20	5	0.7	6.8	8	1.1	10.8	10	1.4	13.5
— 28	6	0.8	8.1	10	1.4	13.6			
⁵/₁₆ — 18	11	1.5	14.9	17	2.3	23.0	19	2.6	25.8
— 24	13	1.8	17.6	19	2.6	25.7			
⅜ — 16	18	2.5	24.4	31	4.3	42.0	34	4.7	46.0
— 24	20	2.75	27.1	35	4.8	47.5			
⁷/₁₆ — 14	28	3.8	37.0	49	6.8	66.4	55	7.6	74.5
— 20	30	4.2	40.7	55	7.6	74.5			
½ — 13	39	5.4	52.8	75	10.4	101.7	85	11.75	115.2
— 20	41	5.7	55.6	85	11.7	115.2			
⁹/₁₆ — 12	51	7.0	69.2	110	15.2	149.1	120	16.6	162.7
— 18	55	7.6	74.5	120	16.6	162.7			
⅝ — 11	83	11.5	112.5	150	20.7	203.3	167	23.0	226.5
— 18	95	13.1	128.8	170	23.5	230.5			
¾ — 10	105	14.5	142.3	270	37.3	366.0	280	38.7	379.6
— 16	115	15.9	155.9	295	40.8	400.0			
⅞ — 9	160	22.1	216.9	395	54.6	535.5	440	60.9	596.5
— 14	175	24.2	237.2	435	60.1	589.7			
1 — 8	236	32.5	318.6	590	81.6	799.9	660	91.3	894.8
— 14	250	34.6	338.9	660	91.3	849.8			

Metric Bolts

Relative Strength Marking	4.6, 4.8			8.8		
Bolt Markings						
Bolt Size Thread Size x Pitch (mm)	Maximum Torque			Maximum Torque		
	Ft./Lbs.	Kgm	Nm	Ft./Lbs.	Kgm	Nm
6 x 1.0	2–3	.2–.4	3–4	3–6	.4–.8	5–8
8 x 1.25	6–8	.8–1	8–12	9–14	1.2–1.9	13–19
10 x 1.25	12–17	1.5–2.3	16–23	20–29	2.7–4.0	27–39
12 x 1.25	21–32	2.9–4.4	29–43	35–53	4.8–7.3	47–72
14 x 1.5	35–52	4.8–7.1	48–70	57–85	7.8–11.7	77–110
16 x 1.5	51–77	7.0–10.6	67–100	90–120	12.4–16.5	130–160
18 x 1.5	74–110	10.2–15.1	100–150	130–170	17.9–23.4	180–230
20 x 1.5	110–140	15.1–19.3	150–190	190–240	26.2–46.9	160–320
22 x 1.5	150–190	22.0–26.2	200–260	250–320	34.5–44.1	340–430
24 x 1.5	190–240	26.2–46.9	260–320	310–410	42.7–56.5	420–550

4. Hoist car.

5. Remove the flywheel cover.

6. Remove the flywheel to torque converter bolts.

7. Disconnect the exhaust pipe from the rear exhaust manifold.

8. Remove the engine to transaxle brace.

9. Remove the engine mount to cradle retaining nuts and washers.

10. Disconnect the leads to the starter motor, #2 cylinder glow plugs and battery ground cable at transaxle to engine bolt.

11. Disconnect the lower oil cooler hose and cap the openings.

12. Remove the accessible power steering pump bracket fasteners.

13. Lower the car.

14. Remove the remaining power steering pump bracket/brace fasteners and lower the power steering pump with hoses out of the way.

15. Remove heater water return pipe.

16. Disconnect all remaining glow plug leads at the glow plugs.

17. Disconnect all other leads at the engine, disconnect the engine harness at the cowl connector and body mounted relays and position the engine harness aside.

18. If A/C equipped, disconnect the compressor with brackets and lines attached and position aside.

19. Disconnect the fuel and vacuum hoses, cap all fuel line openings.

20. Disconnect the throttle and T.V. cables at the injection pump and cable bracket. Position cables aside.

21. Disconnect the upper oil cooler hose and cap the openings.

22. Remove the exhaust crossover pipe heat shield.

23. Disconnect and move aside the transaxle filler tube.

24. Remove the exhaust crossover pipe.

25. Remove the engine mounting strut and strut brackets.

26. Install a suitable engine lifting device. Make certain that when installing chains to the cylinder heads that washers are used under the chains and bolt heads and that the bolts are torqued to 20 ft. lbs.

CAUTION: *Failure to properly secure the engine lift to the aluminum cylinder heads can result in personal injury.*

27. Position a support under the transaxle rear extension. *It may be necessary to raise the support as the engine is being removed.*

28. Remove the engine to transaxle bolts and remove the engine.

29. Installation is the reverse of removal. NOTE the following:

a. Before installing the flex plate-to-converter bolts, make sure that the weld nuts on the converter are flush with the flex plate, and the converter rotates freely by hand.

b. Use only new O-rings at all connections.

c. Adjust the throttle valve cable as outlined in the Automatic Transmission Unit Repair section.

Valve Cover(s)
REMOVAL AND INSTALLATION
4-151 Engine

1. Remove the air cleaner assembly, being sure to tag all disconnected hoses for reassembly purposes.

2. Remove the P.C.V. valve and hose from the valve cover grommet.

3. Remove the valve cover retaining bolts.

4. Remove the spark plug wires from the spark plugs and the locating clips. Be sure to tag the wires so that they may be reattached properly.

5. Remove the cover retaining bolts, then the valve cover by tapping it with a rubber mallet. This must be done to break the R.T.V. seal. DON'T attempt to pry the cover off, as it is easily damaged.

6. Clean the mating surfaces of both the valve cover and the cylinder head.

7. Apply a continuous $3/16''$ wide bead of R.T.V. (room temperature vulcanizing) sealer to the mating surface of the valve cover. Be sure to run the R.T.V. on the INSIDE of the valve cover bolt holes.

CAUTION: *Do not allow sealer to get into the valve cover bolt holes of the cylinder head.*

8. Install the valve cover and tighten the retaining bolts to about 7 ft. lbs.

9. Reattach the spark plug wires, install the P.C.V. valve and hose, then install the air cleaner assembly.

6-173 Engine—Front

1. Disconnect the negative battery cable at the battery.

2. Remove the air cleaner assembly, being sure to tag all disconnected hoses for reassembly purposes.

3. Remove the forward engine support strut, which is bolted to the radiator support and the engine bracket.

4. Disconnect all vacuum hoses and plug wires which would interfere with removal of the cover. Tag these items so that they may be properly reconnected.

5. Remove the engine support strut bracket from the cylinder head.

6. Remove the valve cover retaining bolts then remove the valve cover. If the cover sticks, tap it loose with a rubber mallet. DON'T attempt to pry it off of the head, as the cover may be easily damaged.

7. Refer to steps 6–8 of the previous 4-151 procedure to prepare and seal the valve cover during installation.

8. The remainder of the installation is performed in the reverse of removal. Torque the front engine strut bracket bolts to 35 ft. lbs.

6-173 Engine—Rear

1. Disconnect the negative battery cable at the battery.

2. Remove the air cleaner assembly, being sure to tag all disconnected hoses for reassembly purposes.

3. Remove the spark plug wires from the spark plugs and the locating clips. Be sure to tag the wires so that they may be reattached properly.

4. Disconnect the accelerator linkage and springs from the carburetor.

5. If your vehicle has an automatic transaxle, disconnect the T.V. (throttle valve) linkage at the carburetor.

6. If your vehicle has cruise control, remove the diaphragm actuator mounting bracket.

7. Remove the air management valve and the necessary hoses (see the Emission Control chapter).

8. Remove the valve cover retaining bolts then remove the valve cover. If the cover sticks, tap it loose with a rubber mallet. DON'T attempt to pry it off of the head, as the cover may be easily damaged.

9. Refer to steps 6–8 of the previous 4-151 procedure to prepare and seal the valve cover during installation. The valve cover retaining bolts must be torqued to 11 ft. lbs.

10. The remainder of the installation is performed in the reverse order of removal.

6-183 Engine

Please refer to the previous procedures for the 173 engine.

6-263 Diesel Engine—Front

1. Disconnect the negative battery cable.

2. Remove the fuel injection lines.

3. Remove the forward engine support strut, which is bolted to the radiator support strut and an engine bracket.

4. Unbolt and remove the strut bracket from the engine.

5. If necessary, remove any additional piece(s) which may interfere with removal of the cover.

6. Unbolt and remove the cover. If the cover sticks, tap it loose with a rubber mallet. DON'T attempt to pry it off of the head, as the cover may be easily damaged.

7. Refer to steps 6–8 of the previous 4-151 procedure to prepare and seal the valve cover during installation.

8. The remainder of the installation is performed in the reverse of removal. Torque the engine strut bracket bolts to 35 ft. lbs.

6-263 Diesel Engine—Rear

1. Disconnect the negative battery cable.

2. Remove the fuel injection lines.

3. Disconnect the crankcase ventilation system pipes, grommets, filter and crankcase depression regulator from the valve cover.

4. Unbolt and remove the forward engine support strut.

5. Position a floor jack under the front crossmember of the engine cradle.

6. Raise the jack until it just starts to lift the vehicle.

7. Remove the two front body mount bolts from the cradle, along with the cushions and the retainers. Remove the cushions from the bolts.

8. Thread the body mount bolts (with the retainers) back into place, making sure to turn them at least three full turns each.

9. Carefully and slowly lower the jack until the cradle contacts the retainers. While you are lowering the jack, be sure to watch for any component interference and correct as required.

CAUTION: *DO NOT attempt to lower the cradle without the bolts and retainers in place, as this could cause damage of various underhood components.*

10. Unbolt and remove the cover. If the cover sticks, tap it loose with a rubber mallet. DON'T attempt to pry it off of the head, as the cover may be easily damaged.

11. Refer to steps 6–8 of the previous 4-151 procedure to prepare and seal the valve cover during installation.

12. Installation is the reverse of removal.

Rocker Arm and Pushrod
REMOVAL AND INSTALLATION
4-151 Engine

1. Remove the valve cover.

2. On fuel injected engines, see the fuel pump section to relieve pressure in the fuel system before disconnecting any fuel lines.

3. If only the pushrod is being removed, loosen the rocker arm bolt and swing the rocker arm aside.

4. Remove the rocker arm nut and ball.

NOTE: AT TIME OF INSTALLATION, FLANGES MUST BE FREE OF OIL. A ⅛ BEAD OF SEALANT MUST BE APPLIED TO FLANGES AND SEALANT MUST BE WET TO TOUCH WHEN BOLTS ARE TORQUED.

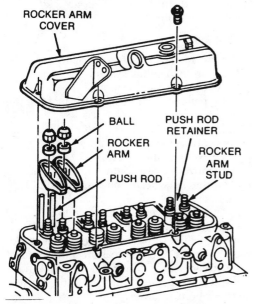

Exploded view of the rocker arm assembly

5. Lift the rocker arm off the stud, keeping rocker arms in order for installation.

6. Installation is the reverse of removal. Tighten the rocker arm bolt to 20 ft. lb.; the rocker cover to 5 ft. lb.

6-173 Engine

Rocker arms are removed by removing the adjusting nut. Be sure to adjust valve lash after replacing rocker arms.

NOTE: *When replacing an exhaust rocker, move an old intake rocker arm to the exhaust rocker arm stud and install the new rocker arm on the intake stud.*

Cylinder heads use threaded rocker arm studs. If the threads in the head are damaged or stripped, the head can be retapped and a helical type insert installed.

NOTE: *If engine is equipped with the A.I.R. exhaust emission control system, the interfering components of the system must be removed. Disconnect the lines at the air injection nozzles in the exhaust manifolds.*

6-183 Engine

1. Remove the rocker arm cover(s).
2. Remove the rocker arm shaft(s).
3. Place the shaft on a clean surface.
4. Remove the nylon rocker arm retainers. A pair of slip joint pliers is good for this.
5. Slide the rocker arms off the shaft and

inspect them for wear or damage. Keep them in order!

6. Installation is the reverse of removal. If new rocker arms are being installed, note that they are stamped R (right) or L (left), meaning that they be used on the right or left of each cylinder, NOT right and left cylinder banks. Each rocker arm must be centered over its oil hole. New nylon retainers must be used.

6-263 Diesel Engine

NOTE: *This procedure requires that the valve lifters be bled!*

1. Remove the valve cover(s). See the Valve Cover procedure.

2. Remove the rocker arm nuts, pivot and rocker arms.

3. If rocker arms are being replaced, they must be replaced in cylinder sets. Never replace just one rocker arm per cylinder! If a stud was replaced, coat the threads with locking compound and torque it to 11 ft. lb.

4. Installation is the reverse of removal. See the section on Valve lifter bleeddown. This is absolutely necessary! If lifters are not bled, engine damage will be unavoidable! Torque the rocker arm nuts to 28 ft. lbs.; the cover to 5 ft. lb.

Intake Manifold
REMOVAL AND INSTALLATION
4-151 Engine

CAUTION: *Bleed pressure from the fuel system, if equipped with fuel injection, before servicing.*

1. Remove the air cleaner and the PCV valve.

2. Drain the cooling system into a clean container.

3. Disconnect the fuel and vacuum lines and the electrical connections at the carburetor and manifold.

4. Disconnect the throttle linkage at the EFI unit and disconnect the transaxle downshift linkage and cruise control linkage.

5. Remove the carburetor and the spacer.

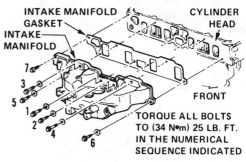

4-151 intake manifold bolt torquing sequence

6. Remove the bell crank and the throttle linkage. Position to the side for clearance.

7. Remove the heater hose at the intake manifold.

8. Remove the pulse air check valve bracket from the manifold.

9. Remove the manifold attaching bolts and remove the manifold.

6-173 Engine

1. Remove the rocker covers.

2. Drain the cooling system.

3. If equipped, remove the AIR pump and bracket.

4. Remove the distributor cap. Mark the position of the ignition rotor in relation to the distributor body, and remove the distributor. Do not crank the engine with the distributor removed.

5. Remove the heater and radiator hoses from the intake manifold.

6. Remove the power brake vacuum hose.

7. Disconnect and label the vacuum hoses. Remove the EFE pipe from the rear of the manifold.

8. Remove the carburetor linkage. Disconnect and plug the fuel line.

9. Remove the manifold retaining bolts and nuts.

10. Remove the intake manifold. Remove and discard the gaskets, and scrape off the old silicone seal from the front and rear ridges.

To install:

1. The gaskets are marked for right and left side installation; do not interchange them. Clean the sealing surface of the engine block, and apply a $3/16$ in. bead of silicone sealer to each ridge.

2. Install the new gaskets onto the heads. The gaskets will have to be cut slightly to fit past the center pushrods. Do not cut any more material than necessary. Hold the gaskets in place by extending the ridge bead of sealer $1/4$ in. onto the gasket ends.

3. Install the intake manifold. The area between the ridges and the manifold should be completely sealed.

4. Install the retaining bolts and nuts, and tighten in sequence to 23 ft. lbs. Do not overtighten; the manifold is made from alumini-

mum, and can be warped or cracked with excessive force.

5. The rest of installation is the reverse of removal. Adjust the ignition timing after installation, and check the coolant level after the engine has warmed up.

6-183 Engine

1. Disconnect the battery ground.

2. Drain the cooling system.

3. Remove the air cleaner.

4. Disconnect all hoses and wiring from the manifold.

5. Disconnect the accelerator linkage and cruise control chain.

6. Disconnect the fuel line.

7. Remove the distributor cap and rotor and remove the Torx head bolt from the left side of the manifold.

8. Unbolt and remove the manifold.

9. Installation is the reverse of removal. When installing the front and rear seals, make sure that the ends of the seals fit snugly against the block and head. Install nos. 1 & 2 bolts first and tighten them until snug, then install the other bolts in order.

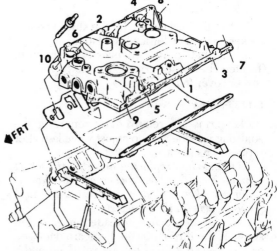

6-183 intake manifold torque sequence

6-263 Diesel Engine

NOTE: *This procedure requires the removal, disassembly draining and reassembly of the valve lifters. Read that procedure, below, before continuing.*

1. Remove the air cleaner assembly.

2. Drain the radiator, then disconnect the upper radiator hose from the water outlet.

3. Disconnect the heater inlet hose from the outlet on intake manifold and disconnect the heater outlet pipe from the intake manifold attachments and move it aside.

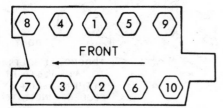

173 V6 intake manifold torque sequence

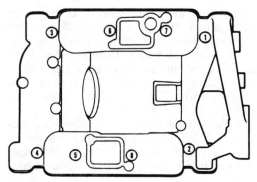

6-263 intake manifold torque sequence

4. Remove air crossover and the fuel injection pump.

5. Disconnect wiring as necessary at the generator (and A/C compressor) and switches, if so equipped).

6. Remove the cruise control servo if so equipped.

7. Remove the A/C compressor bracket and brace bolts and position the compressor (if so equipped) with lines attached out of the way.

8. Remove the generator assembly.

9. Disconnect the engine mounting strut.

10. Remove the fuel lines, filter and brackets. Cap all openings.

11. Disconnect the electrical leads to the glow plug controller and sending units.

12. Disconnect the exhaust crossover pipe heat shield.

13. Remove the left (forward) injection lines and cap all openings. Use a backup wrench on the nozzles.

14. Disconnect the throttle and T.V. cables from the bracket.

15. Remove the drain tube.

16. Remove the intermediate pump adapter.

17. Remove pump adapter and seal.

18. Remove the intake manifold.

19. Clean the machined surfaces of cylinder head and intake manifold with a putty knife. Use care not to gouge or scratch the machined surfaces. Clean all bolts and bolt holes.

20. Coat both sides of gasket sealing surface that seal the intake manifold to the head with 1050026 sealer or equivalent and position intake manifold gasket. Install end seals, making sure that ends are positioned under the cylinder heads. The seals and mating surfaces must be dry. Any liquid, including sealer will act as a lubricant and cause the seal to move during assembly. Use RTV sealer only on each end of the seal.

21. Position intake manifold on engine. Lubricate the entire intake manifold bolt (all) with lubricant 1052080 or equivalent.

22. Torque the bolts in sequence shown to 20 ft. lb. Then retorque to 41 ft. lbs.

23. Install the drain tube.

24. Install the pump adapter.

25. Apply chassis lube to seal area of intake manifold and pump adapter.

26. Apply chassis lube to inside and outside diameter of seal and seal area of tool J-28425.

27. Install seal on tool and install the seal.

28. Install intermediate pump adapter.

29. Reverse the order of removal and install all other removed parts except the air crossover.

30. Fill the cooling system.

31. Install manifold covers, J-29657.

32. Start engine and check for leaks.

33. Check and if necessary, reset the injection pump timing.

34. Remove screen covers from manifold.

35. Install air crossover.

36. Install the air cleaner.

37. Road test car and inspect for leaks.

Diesel Engine Valve Lifter Bleed-Down

If the intake manifold and valve rocker arms have been removed, it will be necessary to remove, disassemble, drain and reassemble the lifters on that side. If the rocker arms have been loosened or removed, but the intake manifold was not removed, skip down to the Bleed-Down procedure.

REMOVAL

Keep lifters and pushrods in order! This is absolutely necessary for installation, since these parts have differences which could result in engine damage if not installed in their original positions!

1. Remove intake manifold. Refer to "Intake Manifold."

2. Remove valve covers, rocker arm assemblies and pushrods.

3. Remove the valve lifter guide retainer bolts.

4. Remove the retainer guides and valve lifters.

DISASSEMBLY

1. Remove the retainer ring with a small screwdriver.

2. Remove pushrod seat and oil metering valve.

3. Remove plunger and plunger spring.

4. Remove check valve retainer from plunger, then remove valve and spring.

CLEANING AND INSPECTION

After lifters are disassembled, all parts should be cleaned in clean solvent. A small particle of foreign material under the check valve will cause malfunctioning of the lifter. Close inspection should be made for nicks, burrs or scoring of parts. If either the roller body or plunger is defective, replace with a new lifter assembly. Whenever lifters are removed, check as follows:

1. Roller should rotate freely, but without excessive play.

2. Check for missing or broken needle bearings.

3. Roller should be free of pits or roughness. If present, check camshaft for similar condition. If pits or roughness are evident replace lifter and camshaft.

ASSEMBLY

1. Coat all lifter parts with a coating of clean kerosene or diesel fuel.

2. Assemble the ball check, spring and retainer into the plunger.

3. Install plunger spring over check retainer.

4. Hold plunger with spring up and insert into lifter body. Hold plunger vertically to prevent cocking spring.

5. Submerge the lifter in clean kerosene or diesel fuel.

6. Install oil metering valve and push rod seat into lifter and install retaining ring.

INSTALLATION

Prime new lifters by working lifter plunger while submerged in clean kerosene or diesel fuel. Lifter could be damaged when starting engine if dry.

1. When a rocker arm is loosened or removed, valve lifter bleed down is required. Lifters must be bled down as possible valve to piston interference due to the close tolerances could exist. Before installing a new or used lifter in the engine, lubricate the roller and bearings of the lifter with No. 1052365 lubricant or equivalent.

2. Install lifters and pushrods into original position in cylinder block. See note under Removal.

3. Install manifold gaskets and manifold.

4. Position rocker arms, pivots and bolts on cylinder head.

5. Install valve covers.

6. Install intake manifold assembly.

BLEED-DOWN

1. Before installing any removed rocker arms, rotate the engine crankshaft to a position of number 1 cylinder being 32° before top dead center. This is a 50 mm (2″) counterclockwise from the 0° pointer. If only the right valve cover was removed, remove No. 1 cylinder's glow plug to determine if the position of the piston is the correct one. The compression pressure will tell you that you are in the right position.

If the left valve cover was removed, rotate the crankshaft until the number 5 cylinder intake valve pushrod ball is 7.0 mm (.28″) above the number 5 cylinder exhaust valve pushrod ball.

NOTE: *Use only hand wrenches to torque the rocker arm pivot nuts to avoid engine damage.*

2. If removed, install the No. 5 cylinder pivot and rocker arms. Torque the nuts alternately between the intake and exhaust valves until the intake valve begins to open, then stop.

3. Install remaining rocker arms except No. 3 exhaust valve. (If this rocker arm was removed.)

4. If removed, install but do not torque No. 3 valve pivots beyond the point that the valve would be fully open. This is indicated by strong resistance while still turning the pivot retaining bolts. Going beyond this would bend the pushrod. Torque the nuts SLOWLY allowing the lifter to bleed down.

5. Finish torquing No. 5 cylinder rocker arm pivot nut SLOWLY. Do not go beyond the point that the valve would be fully open. This is indicated by strong resistance while still turning the pivot retaining bolts. Going beyond this would bend the pushrod.

6. DO NOT turn the engine crankshaft for at least 45 minutes.

7. Finish reassembling the engine as the lifters are being bled.

NOTE: *Do not rotate the engine until the valve lifters have been bled down, or damage to the engine will occur.*

Exhaust Manifold

REMOVAL AND INSTALLATION

4-151 Engine

1. Remove the air cleaner and the EFI preheat tube.

2. Remove the manifold strut bolts from the radiator support panel and the cylinder head.

3. Remove the A/C compressor bracket bolts and position the compressor to one side. Do not disconnect any of the refrigerant lines.

4. If necessary, remove the dipstick tube attaching bolt, and the engine mount bracket from the cylinder head.

5. Raise the car and disconnect the exhaust pipe from the manifold.

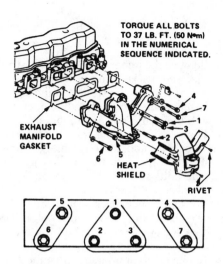

TORQUE ALL BOLTS TO 37 LB. FT. (50 N•m) IN THE NUMERICAL SEQUENCE INDICATED.

EXHAUST MANIFOLD GASKET

HEAT SHIELD

RIVET

BOLT LOCATIONS

4-151 exhaust manifold torque sequence

6. Remove the manifold attaching bolts and remove the manifold.

7. Reverse to install.

6-173 Engine—Left Side

1. Remove the air cleaner. Remove the carburetor heat stove pipe.

2. Remove the air supply plumbing from the exhaust manifold.

3. Raise and support the car. Unbolt and remove the exhaust pipe at the manifold.

4. Unbolt and remove the manifold.

To install:

1. Clean the mating surfaces of the cylinder head and manifold. Install the manifold onto the head, and install the retaining bolts finger tight.

2. Tighten the manifold bolts in a circular pattern, working from the center to the ends, to 25 ft. lbs. in two stages.

3. Connect the exhaust pipe to the manifold.

4. The remainder of installation is the reverse of removal.

6-183 Engine—Left Side

1. Disconnect the battery ground.

2. Unbolt and remove the crossover pipe.

3. Remove the upper engine support strut.

4. Unbolt and remove the manifold.

5. Installation is the reverse of removal.

6-263 Diesel Engine—Left Side

1. Remove the crossover pipe from the manifolds.

2. Raise and support the car on jackstands.

3. Unbolt and remove the manifold.

4. Installation is the reverse of removal.

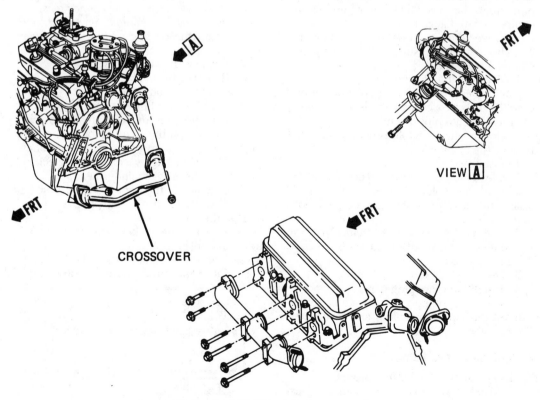

CROSSOVER

VIEW Ⓐ

Exhaust manifold installation—typical

Lubricate the entire length of each manifold bolt with lubricant 1052080 or its equivalent.

6-263 Diesel Engine—Right Side

1. Remove the engine support strut.
2. Place a floor jack under the front crossmember and take up the weight of the car.
3. Remove the two front body mount bolts. Remove the cushions from the bolts.
4. Thread the body mount bolts with their retainers into the cage nuts so that the bolts restrict movement of the engine cradle.
5. Lower the jack until the crossmember contacts the body mount bolt retainers. Check for any hose or wire interference.
6. Remove the crossover pipe.
7. Raise and support the car on jackstands.
8. Disconnect the exhaust pipe from the manifold.
9. Lower the car.
10. Unbolt and remove the manifold.
11. Installation is the reverse of removal. Lubricate the entire length of each manifold bolt with lubricant 1052080 or its equivalent.

6-173 Engine—Right Side

1. Raise and support the car.
2. Tighten the exhaust pipe-to-manifold flange bolts until they break off. Remove the pipe from the manifold. Later models are equipped with flange bolts.
3. Lower the car. Remove the spark plug wires from the plugs. Number them first if they are not already labeled.
4. Remove the air supply pipes from the manifold. Remove the PULSAIR bracket bolt from the rocker cover, on models so equipped, then remove the pipe assembly.
5. Remove the manifold retaining bolts and remove the manifold.
To install:
1. Clean the mating surfaces of the cylinder head and manifold. Position the manifold against the head and install the retaining bolts finger tight.
2. Tighten the bolts in a circular pattern, working from the center to the ends, to 25 ft. lbs. in two stages.
3. Install the air supply system.
4. Install the spark plug wires.
5. Raise and support the car. Connect the exhaust pipe to the manifold and install new flange bolts.

6-183 Engine—Right Side

1. Disconnect the battery ground.
2. Raise and support the car on jackstands.

3. Unbolt the exhaust pipe from the manifold.
4. Lower the car.
5. Remove the upper engine support strut.
6. Place a floor jack under the front crossmember and take up the weight of the car.
7. Remove the two front body mount bolts along with their cushions and retainers.
8. Remove the cushions from the bolts and thread the bolts and their retainers a minimum of three turns into the cradle cage nuts so that the bolts serve to hold the cradle and prevent movement.
9. Lower the floor jack so that the crossmember contacts the body mount bolt retainers. Check for any hose or wire interference problems.
10. Remove the alternator, disconnect the power steering pump and remove its bracket.
11. Disconnect the manifold from the crossover pipe.
12. Unbolt and remove the manifold.
13. Installation is the reverse of removal.

Cylinder Head

REMOVAL AND INSTALLATION

4-151 Engine

CAUTION: *On fuel injected engines, relieve the pressure in the fuel system before disconnecting any fuel line connections.*
NOTE: *The engine should be overnight cold.*

1. Drain the cooling system into a clean container.
2. Remove the air cleaner.
3. Remove the intake and exhaust manifolds as previously outlined.
4. Remove the alternator bracket bolts.
5. Remove the A/C compressor bracket bolts and position the compressor to one side. Do not disconnect any of the refrigerant lines.
6. Disconnect all vacuum and electrical connections from the cylinder head.
7. Disconnect the upper radiator hose.
8. Disconnect the spark plug wires and remove the plugs.
9. Remove the rocker arm cover, rocker arms, and pushrods.
10. Unbolt and remove the cylinder head.
11. Clean the gasket surfaces thoroughly.

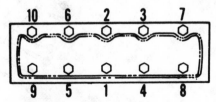

4-151 head bolt torque sequence

12. Install a new gasket over the dowels and position the cylinder head.

13. Coat the head bolt threads with sealer and install finger tight.

14. Tighten the bolts in sequence, in three equal steps to the specified torque.

15. Install all parts in the reverse of removal.

6-173 Engine—Left Side

1. Raise and support the car.

2. Drain the coolant from the block and lower the car.

3. Remove the intake manifold.

4. Remove the crossover.

5. Remove the alternator and AIR pump brackets.

6. Remove the dipstick tube.

7. Loosen the rocker arm bolts and remove the pushrods. Keep the pushrods in the same order as removed.

8. Remove the cylinder head bolts in stages and in the reverse order of the tightening sequence.

9. Remove the cylinder head. Do not pry on the head to loosen it.

10. Installation is the reverse of removal. The words "This side Up" on the new cylinder head gasket should face upward. Coat the cylinder head bolts with sealer and torque to specifications in the sequence shown. Make sure the pushrods seat in the lifter seats and adjust the valves.

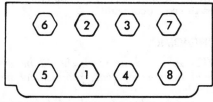

6-173 head bolt torque sequence

6-173 Engine—Right Side

1. Raise the car and drain the coolant from the block.

2. Disconnect the exhaust pipe and lower the car.

3. If equipped, remove the cruise control servo bracket.

4. Remove the air management valve and hose.

5. Remove the intake manifold.

6. Remove the exhaust crossover.

7. Loosen the rocker arm nuts and remove the pushrods. Keep the pushrods in the order in which they were removed.

8. Remove the cylinder head bolts in stages and in the reverse order of the tightening sequence.

9. Remove the cylinder head. Do not pry on the cylinder head to loosen it.

10. Installation is the reverse of removal. The words "This Side Up" on the new cylinder head gasket should face upwards. Coat the cylinder head bolts with sealer and tighten them to specifications in the sequence shown. Make sure the lower ends of the pushrods seat in the lifter seats and adjust the valves.

6-183 Engine

1. Disconnect negative battery cable.

2. Remove intake manifold.

3. Loosen and remove belt(s).

4. When removing LEFT cylinder head;
   a. Remove oil dipstick.
   b. Remove air and vacuum pumps with mounting bracket if present, and move out of the way with hoses attached.

5. When removing RIGHT cylinder head;
   a. Remove alternator.
   b. Disconnect power steering gear pump and brackets attached to cylinder head.

6. Disconnect wires from spark plugs, and remove the spark plug wire clips from the rocker arm cover studs.

7. Remove exhaust manifold bolts from head being removed.

8. With air hose and cloths, clean dirt off cylinder head and adjacent area to avoid getting dirt into engine. *It is extremely important to avoid getting dirt into the hydraulic valve lifters.*

9. Remove rocker arm cover and rocker arm and shaft assembly from cylinder head. Lift out pushrods.

If lifters are to be serviced, remove them at this time and place them in a container with numbered holes or a similar device, to keep them identified as to engine position. If they are not to be removed, protect lifters and cam-

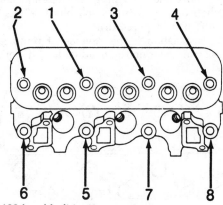

6-183 head bolt torque sequence

shaft from dirt by covering area with a clean cloth.

10. Loosen all cylinder head bolts, then remove bolts and lift off the cylinder head.

11. With cylinder head on bench, remove all spark plugs for cleaning and to avoid damaging them during work on the head.

12. Installation is the reverse of removal. Clean all gasket surfaces thoroughly. Always use a new head gasket. The head gasket is installed with the bead downward. Coat the head bolt threads with heavybodied thread sealer. Torque the head bolts in three equal stages. Recheck head bolt torque after the engine has been warmed to operating temperature.

6-263 Diesel Engine

NOTE: *This procedure requires the complete disassembly of the valve lifters as explained under Diesel Engine Valve Lifter Bleed-Down.*

1. Remove intake manifold.

2. Remove valve cover. Loosen or remove any accessory brackets or pipe clamps which interfere.

3. Disconnect glow plug wiring (and block heater lead if so equipped on rear bank).

4. Remove the ground strap from the rear cylinder head.

5. Remove rocker arm nuts, pivots, rocker arms and pushrods. Scribe pivots and keep rocker arms separated so they can be installed in their original locations.

6. Disconnect the exhaust crossover pipe from the exhaust manifold on the side being worked on and loosen it on the other.

7. Remove engine block drain plug, from side of the block where head is being removed.

8. Remove the pipe plugs covering the upper cylinder head bolts.

9. Remove all the cylinder head bolts and remove the cylinder head.

10. If necessary to remove the prechamber, remove the glow plug and inection nozzle, then tap out with a small blunt ⅛" drift. Do NOT use a tapered drift.

11. Installation is the reverse of removal. Do not use sealer on the head gasket. If a pre-chamber was replaced, measure the chamber height and grind the new one to within 0.001 inch of the old chamber's height, using #80 grit wet sandpaper to polish it. Coat the head bolts with sealer, preventing coolant leakage.

CLEANING AND INSPECTION

Chip carbon away from the valve heads, combustion chambers, and ports, using a chisel made of hardwood. Remove the remaining deposits with a stiff wire brush.

CAUTION: *DO NOT use a steel wire brush to clean an aluminum cylinder head. Special brushes are sold just for use on aluminum.*

NOTE: *Be sure that the deposits are actually removed, rather than burnished.*

Have the cylinder head hot-tanked to remove grease, corrosion, and scale from the water passages. Clean the remaining cylinder head parts in an engine cleaning solvent. Do not remove the protective coating from the springs.

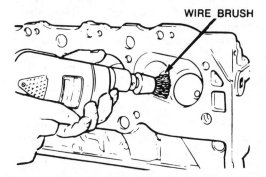

Remove the carbon from the cylinder head with a wire brush and electric drill

RESURFACING

NOTE: *All machine work should be performed by a competent, professional machine shop.*

Place a straight-edge across the gasket surface of the cylinder head. Using feeler gauges, determine the clearance at the center of the straightedge. If warpage exceeds .003" in a 6" span, or .006" over the total length, the cylinder head must be resurfaced.

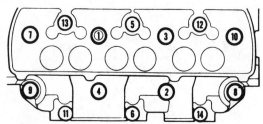

6-263 head bolt torque sequence

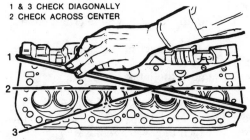

Check the cylinder head for warpage

NOTE: *If warpage exceeds the manufacturer's maximum tolerance for material removal, the cylinder head must be replaced.*

When milling the cylinder heads of V-type engines, the intake manifold mounting position is altered, and must be corrected by milling the manifold flange a proportionate amount.

Valves

REMOVAL AND INSPECTION

1. Remove the cylinder head(s) from the vehicle as previously outlined.

2. Using a suitable valve spring compressor, compress the valve spring and remove the valve keys using a magnetic retrieval tool.

3. Slowly release the compressor and remove the valve spring caps (or rotators) and the valve springs.

4. Fabricate a valve arrangement board to use when you remove the valves, which will indicate the port in which each valve was originally installed (and which cylinder head on V6 models). Also note that the valve keys, rotators, caps, etc. should be arranged in a manner which will allow you to reinstall them on the valve on which they were originally used.

5. Remove and discard the valve seals. On models using the umbrella type seals, note the location of the large and small seals for assembly purposes.

6. Thoroughly clean the valves on the wire wheel of a bench grinder, then clean the cylinder head mating surface with a) a soft wire wheel, b) a soft wire brush, or c) a wooden scraper. Avoid using a metallic scraper, since this can cause damage to the cylinder head mating surface, especially on models with aluminum heads.

7. Using a valve guide cleaner chucked into a drill, clean all of the valve guides.

8. Reinstall each valve into its respective port (guide) of the cylinder head.

9. Mount a dial indicator so that the stem is at 90° to the valve stem, as close to the valve guide as possible.

10. Move the valve off its seat, and measure the valve guide-to-stem clearance by rocking the stem back and forth to actuate the dial indicator.

11. Measure the valve stems using a micrometer, and compare to specifications, to determine whether stem or guide wear is responsible for excessive clearance.

NOTE: *Consult the Specifications tables earlier in this chapter.*

REFACING

Using a valve grinder, resurface the valves according to specifications in this chapter.

NOTE: *All machine work should be performed by a competent, professional machine shop.*

CAUTION: *Valve face angle is not always identical to valve seat angle.*

A minimum margin of $^1/_{32}$″ should remain after grinding the valve. The valve stem top should also be squared and resurfaced, by placing the stem in the V-block of the grinder, and turning it while pressing lightly against the grinding wheel. Be sure to chamfer the edge of the tip so that the squared edges don't dig into the rocker arm.

LAPPING

This procedure should be performed after the valves and seats have been machined, to insure that each valve mates to each seat precisely.

Lapping the valves by hand

HAND DRILL

ROD

SUCTION CUP

Home-made valve lapping tool

1. Invert the cylinder head, lightly lubricate the valve stems, and install the valves in the head as numbered.

2. Coat valve seats with fine grinding compound, and attach the lapping tool suction cup to a valve head.

NOTE: *Moisten the suction cup.*

3. Rotate the tool between the palms, changing position and lifting the tool often to prevent grooving.

4. Lap the valve until a smooth, polished seat is evident.

5. Remove the valve and tool, and rinse away all traces of grinding compound.

Valve Guide Service

The valve guides used in any of the A-Body engines are integral with the cylinder head, that is, they cannot be replaced.

NOTE: *Refer to the previous "Values—Removal and Installation" to check the valve guides for wear.*

Valve guides are most accurately repaired using the bronze wall rebuilding method. In this operation, "threads" are cut into the bore of the valve guide and bronze wire is turned into the threads. The bronze "wall" is then reamed to the proper diameter. This method is well received for a number of reasons: a) it is relatively inexpensive, b) offers better valve lubrication (the wire forms channels which retain oil), c) less valve friction, and d) preserves the original valve guide-to-seat relationship.

Another popular method of repairing valve guides is to have the guides "knurled." The knurling entails cutting into the bore of the valve guide with a special tool. The cutting action "raises" metal off of the guide bore which actually narrows the inner diameter of the bore, thereby reducing the clearance between the valve guide bore and the valve stem. This method offers the same advantages as the bronze wall method, but will generally wear faster.

Either of the above services must be performed by a professional machine shop which has the specialized knowledge and tools necessary to perform the service.

Valve Seat Service

The valve seats are integral with the cylinder head on all engines except the 1982 (only) V6 diesel with aluminum cylinder heads. On all engines except that particular diesel, the seats are machined into the cylinder head casting itself. On the aluminum head diesel, the valve seats are separate inserts, which may be replaced by a competent machine shop if re-

quired. The reason for using inserts on this engine is basically because the aluminum could not withstand the constant pounding of the valves opening and closing as well as the hardened steel insert which is used.

Machining of the valve seats, or replacement of the seats in the case of the diesel, should be referred to a professional machine shop.

Valve Spring Testing

Place the spring on a flat surface next to a square. Measure the height of the spring, and rotate it against the edge of the square to measure distortion. If spring height varies (by comparison) by more than $1/16''$ or if distortion exceeds $1/16''$, replace the spring.

In addition to evaluating the spring as above, test the spring pressure at the installed and compressed (installed height minus valve lift) height using a valve spring tester. Spring pressure should be ∓ 1 lb of all other springs in either position.

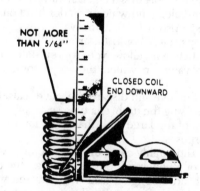

Check the valve spring free length and squareness

Check the valve spring test pressure

Valve and Spring Installation

NOTE: *Be sure that all traces of lapping compound have been cleaned off before the valves are installed.*

1. Lubricate all of the valve stems with a

light coating of engine oil, then install the valves into the proper ports/guides.

2. If umbrella-type valve seals are used, install them at this time. Be sure to use a seal protector to prevent damage to the seals as they are pushed over the valve keeper grooves.

If O-ring seals are used, don't install them yet.

3. Install the valve springs and the spring retainers (or rotators), and using the valve compressing tool, compress the springs.

4. If umbrella-type seals are used, just install the valve keepers (white grease may be used to hold them in place) and release the pressure on the compressing tool. If O-ring type seals are used, carefully work the seals into the second groove of the valve (closest to the head), install the valve keepers and release the pressure on the tool.

NOTE: *If the O-ring seals are installed BEFORE the springs and retainers are compressed, the seal will be destroyed.*

5. After all of the valves are installed and retained, tap each valve spring retainer with a rubber mallet to seat the keepers in the retainer.

Timing Gear Cover
REMOVAL AND INSTALLATION
4-151 Engine

CAUTION: *On fuel injected engines, relieve the pressure in the fuel system before disconnecting the fuel line connections.*

1. Remove the crankshaft hub. It is necessary to remove the inner fender splash shield.

2. Remove the alternator lower bracket.

3. Remove the front engine mounts.

4. Using a floor jack, raise the engine.

5. Remove the engine mount mounting bracket-to-cylinder block bolts. Remove the bracket and mount as an assembly.

6. Remove the oil pan-to-front cover screws.

7. Remove the front cover-to-block screws.

8. Pull the cover slightly forward, just enough to allow cutting of the oil pan front seal flush with the block on both sides.

9. Remove the front cover and attached portion of the pan seal.

10. Clean the gasket surfaces thoroughly.

11. Cut the tabs from the new oil pan front seal.

12. Install the seal on the front cover, pressing the tips into the holes provided.

13. Coat the new gasket with sealer and position it on the front cover.

14. Apply a ⅛ in. bead of silicone sealer to the joint formed at the oil pan and block.

15. Align the front cover seal with a centering tool and install the front cover. Tighten the screws. Install the hub.

6-173 Engine

CAUTION: *The engines use a harmonic balancer. Breakage may occur as the balancer is hammered back onto the crankshaft. A press or special installation tool is necessary.*

1. Remove the water pump.

2. Remove the compressor without disconnecting any A/C lines and lay it aside.

3. Remove harmonic balancer, using a puller.

NOTE: *The outer ring (weight) of the harmonic balancer is bonded to the hub with rubber. The balancer must be removed with a puller which acts on the inner hub only. Pulling on the outer portion of the balancer will break the rubber bond or destroy the tuning of the torsional damper.*

4. Disconnect the lower radiator hose and heater hose.

5. Remove timing gear cover attaching screws, cover and gasket.

6. Clean all the gasket mounting surfaces on the front cover and block. Apply a continuous ³/₃₂ in. bead of sealer (1052357 or equivalent) to front cover sealing surface and around coolant passage ports and central bolt holes.

7. Apply a bead of silicone sealer to the oil pan-to-cylinder block joint.

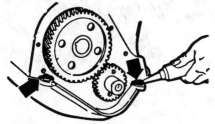

Apply sealant where shown on the 4-151

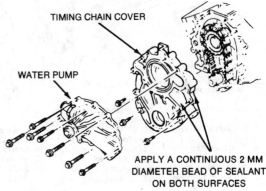

TIMING CHAIN COVER

WATER PUMP

APPLY A CONTINUOUS 2 MM
DIAMETER BEAD OF SEALANT
ON BOTH SURFACES

6-173 timing cover removal

8. Install a centering tool in the crankshaft snout hole in the front cover and install the cover.

9. Install the front cover bolts finger tight, remove the centering tool and tighten and cover bolts. Install the harmonic balancer, pulley, water pump, belts, radiator, and all other parts.

6-183 Engine

1. Drain the cooling system.
2. Disconnect the lower radiator hose and the heater hose at the water pump.
3. Remove the water pump pulley and all drive belts.
4. Remove the alternator and brackets.
5. Remove the distributor.
6. Remove the balancer bolt and washer, and using a puller, remove the balancer.
7. Remove the cover-to-block bolts. Remove the two oil pan-to-cover bolts.
8. Remove the cover and gasket.
9. Installation is the reverse of removal. Always use a new gasket coated with sealer. Remove the oil pump cover and pack the area around the gears with petroleum jelly so that no air space is left within the pump. Apply sealer to the cover bolt threads.

6-263 Diesel Engine

1. Drain the cooling system.
2. Disconnect the lower radiator hose and the heater hose at the water pump. Disconnect the heater outlet pipe at the manifold.
3. Disconnect the power steering pump, vacuum pump, belt tensioner, air conditioning compressor and alternator brackets.

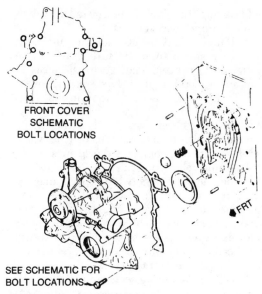

FRONT COVER
SCHEMATIC
BOLT LOCATIONS

SEE SCHEMATIC FOR
BOLT LOCATIONS

6-183 timing cover removal

CAUTION: *Do not disconnect any refrigerant lines.*

4. Remove the crankshaft balancer using a puller.
5. Unbolt and remove the front cover and gasket.
6. Installation is the reverse of removal. Grind a chamfer on the end of each dowel pin to aid in cover installation. Trim 1/8 inch from the ends of the new front pan seal. Apply RTV sealer to the oil pan seal retainer. After the cover gasket is in place, apply sealer to the junction of the pan, gasket and block. When installing the cover, rotate it right and left while

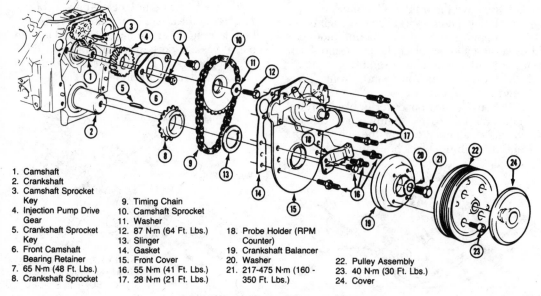

1. Camshaft
2. Crankshaft
3. Camshaft Sprocket Key
4. Injection Pump Drive Gear
5. Crankshaft Sprocket Key
6. Front Camshaft Bearing Retainer
7. 65 N·m (48 Ft. Lbs.)
8. Crankshaft Sprocket
9. Timing Chain
10. Camshaft Sprocket
11. Washer
12. 87 N·m (64 Ft. Lbs.)
13. Slinger
14. Gasket
15. Front Cover
16. 55 N·m (41 Ft. Lbs.)
17. 28 N·m (21 Ft. Lbs.)
18. Probe Holder (RPM Counter)
19. Crankshaft Balancer
20. Washer
21. 217-475 N·m (160 - 350 Ft. Lbs.)
22. Pulley Assembly
23. 40 N·m (30 Ft. Lbs.)
24. Cover

6-263 timing cover and chain removal

guiding the pan seal into place with a small screwdriver.

Timing Gear and/or Chain
REMOVAL AND INSTALLATION

4-151 Engine

See the camshaft removal and installation procedure.

6-173 Engine

To replace the chain, remove the crankcase front cover. This will allow access to the timing chain. Crank the engine until the marks punched on both sprockets are closest to one another and in line between the shaft centers. Take out the three bolts that hold the camshaft sprocket to the camshaft. This sprocket is a light press fit on the camshaft and will come off readily. It is located by a dowel. The chain comes off with the camshaft sprocket. A gear puller will be required to remove the crankshaft sprocket.

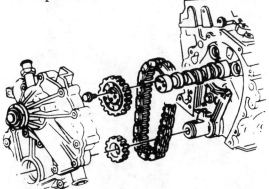

6-173 timing chain and sprockets

Without disturbing the position of the engine, mount the new crank sprocket on the shaft, then mount the chain over the camshaft sprocket. Arrange the camshaft sprocket in such a way that the timing marks will line up between the shaft centers and the camshaft locating dowel will enter the dowel hole in the cam sprocket.

Place the cam sprocket, with its chain mounted over it, in position on the front of the camshaft and pull up with the three bolts that hold it to the camshaft.

After the sprockets are in place, turn the engine two full revolutions to make certain that the timing marks are in correct alignment between the shaft centers.

6-183 Engine

1. Remove the timing chain cover.
2. Turn the crankshaft so that the timing marks are aligned.

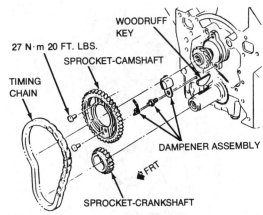

6-183 timing chain and sprockets

3. Remove the crankshaft oil slinger.
4. Remove the camshaft sprocket bolts.
5. Use two prybars to alternately pry the camshaft and crankshaft sprocket free along with the chain.
6. Installation is the reverse of removal. If the engine was turned, make sure that the #1 cylinder is at TDC.

6-263 Diesel Engine

NOTE: *The following procedure requires the bleed-down of the valve lifters. Read that procedure before proceding.*

1. Remove the front cover.
2. Loosen all the rocker arms. See Rocker Arm Removal and Installation.
3. Remove the crankshaft oil slinger.
4. Remove the camshaft sprocket bolt.
5. Using two prybars, work the camshaft and crankshaft sprockets alternately off their shafts along with the chain. It may be necessary to remove the crankshaft sprocket with a puller.
6. Installation is the reverse of removal. If the engine was turned, make sure that the #1 piston is at TDC. Bleed the lifters following

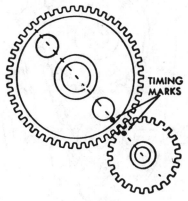

4-151 timing gear alignment

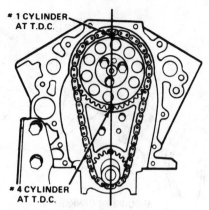

6-173 timing gear alignment

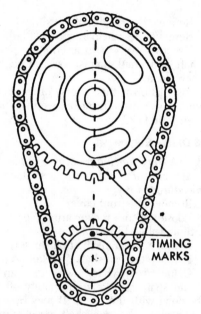

6-183 timing gear alignment

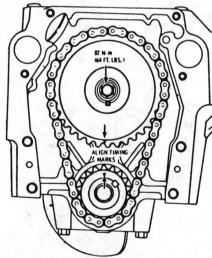

6-263 timing gear alignment

the procedure under Diesel Engine Valve Lifter Bleed-Down.

Oil Seal
REMOVAL AND INSTALLATION

1. After removing the timing cover, pry oil seal out of front of cover.

2. Install new lip seal with lip (open side of seal) inside and drive or press seal carefully into place.

NOTE: *The timing cover oil seal can be replaced without removing the cover. Remove the fan belts, crankshaft pulley and harmonic balancer. Pry the oil seal out the cover working carefully to prevent damage to the seal mating surface. Lubricate the new seal and drive it into place with the open side toward the engine. Use a seal installer to avoid damaging or cocking the seal.*

Installing an oil seal with the front cover removed—typical

Camshaft
REMOVAL AND INSTALLATION

4-151 Engine

CAUTION: *Relieve the pressure in the EFI system on fuel injected engines before disconnecting the fuel line connections.*

1. Remove the engine as previously outlined.

2. Remove the rocker cover, rocker arms, and pushrods.

3. Remove the distributor, spark plugs, and fuel pump.

4. Remove the pushrod cover and gasket. Remove the lifters.

5. Remove the alternator, the alternator

lower bracket and the front engine mount bracket assembly.

6. Remove the oil pump driveshaft and gear assembly.

7. Remove the crankshaft hub and timing gear cover.

8. Remove the two camshaft thrust plate screws by working through the holes in the gear.

9. Remove the camshaft and gear assembly by pulling it through the front of the block. Take care not to damage the bearings.

10. Install in the reverse order. Torque the thrust plate screws to 75 in. lbs.

6-173 Engine

Follow the 6-173 engine removal procedure then remove the camshaft as follows:

1. Remove intake manifold, valve lifters and timing chain cover as described in this section. If the car is equipped with air conditioning, unbolt the condenser and move it aside *without disconnecting any lines*.

2. Remove fuel pump and pump pushrod.

3. Remove camshaft sprocket bolts, sprocket and timing chain. A light blow to the lower edge of a tight sprocket should free it (use a plastic mallet).

4. Install two bolts in cam bolt holes and pull cam from block.

5. To install, reverse removal procedure aligning the sprocket timing marks.

6-183 Engine

1. Remove the engine as described earlier.

2. Remove the intake manifold.

3. Remove the rocker arm covers.

4. Remove the rocker arm assemblies, pushrods and lifters.

5. Remove the timing chain and camshaft sprocket as described earlier.

6. Installation is the reverse of removal.

6-263 Diesel Engine

NOTE: *This procedure requires the removal, disassembly, cleaning, reassembly and bleed-down of all the valve lifters. Read that procedure, described earlier, before proceding.*

1. Remove the engine as described earlier.

2. Remove the intake manifold.

3. Remove the oil pump drive assembly.

4. Remove the timing chain cover.

5. Align the timing marks.

6. Remove the rocker arms, pushrods and lifters, keeping them in order for reassembly.

7. Remove the timing chain and camshaft sprocket as described earlier.

8. Remove the camshaft bearing retainer.

9. Remove the cam sprocket key.

10. Remove the injection pump drive gear.

11. Remove the injection pump driven gear, intermediate pump adapter and pump adapter. Remove the snap ring and selective washer. Remove the driven gear and spring.

12. Carefully slide the camshaft out of the block.

13. If the camshaft bearings are being replaced, you'll have to remove the oil pan.

14. Installation is the reverse of removal. Perform the complete valve lifter bleed-down procedure mentioned earlier.

Camshaft Bearings

REMOVAL AND INSTALLATION

4-151 Engine

1. Remove the engine from the vehicle as previously outlined.

2. Remove the camshaft from the engine as previously outlined.

3. Unbolt and remove the engine flywheel.

4. Drive the rear camshaft expansion plug out of the engine block from the inside.

5. Using a camshaft bearing service tool, drive the front camshaft bearing towards the rear and the rear bearing towards the front.

6. Install the appropriate extension on the service tool and drive the center bearing out towards the rear.

7. Drive all of the new bearings into place in the opposite direction of which they were removed, making sure to align the oil holes of each bearing with each of the feed holes in the engine block bores.

NOTE: *The front camshaft bearing must be driven approximately ⅛" behind the front of the cylinder block to uncover the oil hole to the timing gear oiling nozzle.*

8. Install the camshaft into the engine then reinstall the engine as previously outlined.

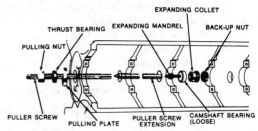

Camshaft bearing removal and installation tool (OHV engines only)

6-173 Engine

Camshaft bearings can be replaced with engine completely or partially disassembled. To replace bearings without complete disassembly remove the camshaft and crankshaft leaving cylinder heads attached and pistons in place. Before removing crankshaft, tape threads of connecting rod bolts to prevent damage to crankshaft. Fasten connecting rods against sides of engine so they will not be in the way while replacing camshaft bearings.

1. Remove the camshaft rear cover.

2. Using Tool J-6098 or its equivalent, with nut and thrust washer installed to end of threads, index pilot in camshaft front bearing and install puller screw through pilot.

3. Install remover and installer tool with shoulder toward bearing, making sure a sufficient amount of threads are engaged.

4. Using two wrenches, hold puller screw while turning nut. When bearing has been pulled from bore, remove remover and installer tool and bearing from puller screw.

5. Remove remaining bearings (except front and rear) in the same manner. It will be necessary to index pilot in camshaft rear bearing to remove the rear intermediate bearing.

6. Assemble remover and installer tool on driver handle and remove camshaft front and rear bearings by driving towards center of cylinder block.

The camshaft front and rear bearings should be installed first. These bearings will act as guides for the pilot and center the remaining bearings being pulled into place.

1. Assemble remover and installer tool on driver handle and install camshaft front and rear bearings by driving towards center of cylinder block.

2. Using Tool Set J-6098, or its equivalent with nut then thrust washer installed to end of threads, index pilot in camshaft front bearing and install puller screw through pilot.

3. Index camshaft bearing in bore (with oil hole aligned as outlined below), then install remover and installer tool on puller screw with shoulder toward bearing.

• The rear and intermediate bearing oil holes must be aligned at 2:30 o'clock.

• The front bearing oil holes must be aligned at 1:00 and 2:30 o'clock (two holes)

4. Using two wrenches, hold puller screw while turning nut. After bearing has been pulled into bore, remove the remover and installer tool from puller screw and check alignment of oil hole in camshaft bearing.

5. Install remaining bearings in the same manner. It will be necessary to index pilot in the camshaft rear bearing to install the rear intermediate bearing.

Clean the rear cover mating surfaces and bolt holes then apply a ⅛″ bead of R.T.V. to the cover. Install the cover.

6-183 Engine

Care must be exercised during bearing removal and installation, not to damage bearings that are not being replaced.

1. Remove camshaft as previously outlined.

2. Assemble puller screw to required length.

3. Select proper size expanding collect and back-up nut.

4. Install expanding collet on expanding mandrel. Install back-up nut.

5. Insert this assembly into camshaft bearing to be removed. Tighten back-up nut to expand collet fo fit I.D. of bearing.

6. Thread end of puller screw assembly into end of expanding mandrel and collet assembly.

7. Install pulling plate, thrust bearing, and pulling nut on threaded end of puller screw.

8. Bearing can then be removed by turning pulling nut.

NOTE: *Make certain to grip the ⅝″ hex end of the puller screw with a wrench to keep it from rotating when the pulling nut is turned. Failure to do this will result in the "locking up" of all threads in the pulling assembly and possible over expansion of the collet.*

9. Repeat the above procedure to remove any other bearings, except the front bearing, which may be pulled from the rear of the engine.

NOTE: *When removing rear cam bearing, it is necessary to remove welch plug at the back of cam bore. However, if only the front bearing is being replaced, it is not necessary to remove the engine or welch plug. The front bearing can be removed by using a spacer between the pulling plate and the cylinder block.*

To install the bearings:

10. Assemble puller screw to required length.

11. Select proper size expanding collet and back-up nut.

12. Install expanding collet on expanding mandrel.

13. Install back-up nut.

14. Place new camshaft bearing on collet and GENTLY hand tighten back-up nut to expand collet to fit bearing. Do not over tighten back-up nut. A loose sliding fit between collet and bearing surface is adequate. This will provide just enough clearance to allow for the "collapse" which will occur when the new bearing is pulled into the engine block.

15. Slide mandrel assembly and bearing into bearing bore as far as it will go without force.

16. Thread end of puller screw onto the end of the mandrel. Make certain to align oil holes in bearing and block properly. One of the collet separation lines may be used as a reference point.

17. Install pulling plate, thrust bearing and pulling nut on threaded end of puller screw.

18. Install bearing in the same manner as described in Steps 8 and 9 under "Bearing Removal."

NOTE: *When installing rear cam bearing, install new welch plug at back of cam bore. Coat O.D. of plug with non-hardening sealer before installation.*

6-263 Diesel Engine

The front camshaft bearing may be replaced separately but numbers 2, 3 and 4 must be replaced as a completed set. This is because it is necessary to remove the forward bearings to gain access to the rearward bearings.

Camshaft Bearing Remover and Installer Set BT-6409 and camshaft bearing pilot spacer BT-7817 are available tools. This set can be used to remove cam bearings. To replace bearings with engine in car, proceed as follows:

NOTE: *The equivalents of special tools mentioned here may be used.*

1. Remove the camshaft as previously outlined.

2. Remove the rear camshaft plug:

   a. Drill a 12 mm or ½" hole in the center of the plug.

   b. Drive the plug inward carefully just enough to loosen it in the block.

   c. Place a punch or screwdriver in the drilled hole and remove the plug.

   d. Remove all the metal particles that entered the block and all traces of the old sealer.

NOTE: *Failure to remove the metal particles will result in engine damage.*

3. Front bearing removal and installation:

   a. To remove the front (No. 1) camshaft bearing, support the retainer in a vise and drive the bearing out using BT-6409-2 with driver BT-6409-7.

   b. To install the bearing use the same tools but make certain that the oil hole in the bearing is in alignment with the oil hole in the retainer.

4. #2, 3, & 4 bearing removal and installation:

   a. Install tool BT-6409-2 on handle BT-6409-7 and drive out No. 2 cam bearing.

   b. Remove the No. 3 bearing in the same manner using BT-6409-3 on handle BT-6409-7.

   c. Remove the No. 4 bearing using puller BT-6409-8.

To aid aligning the bearings with the oil passages, place each bearing in the front of the bore with tapered edge toward the block and align the oil hole in the bearing with the center of the oil slot in the bore. Mark bottom of bearing. When installing the bearings, the mark will act as a guide.

Using pilot BT-6409-1 will aid in installing the No. 4 and 3 bearings by preventing cocking of the bearings.

   d. Install No. 4 bearing using tool BT-6409-4.

NOTE: *Drive the bearing in carefully, stopping to make certain that the oil holes are in alignment otherwise it is possible to drive the bearing in beyond the oil passage opening. Use a piece of $^3/_{32}$" brass rod with a 90° bend at the end to check the oil hole opening as shown in Figure 6A7-76.*

   e. Install the No. 3 bearing using tool BT-6409-3 carefully until the oil holes are in alignment.

   f. Install the No. 2 bearing using tool BT-6409-2 carefully until the oil holes are in alignment.

   g. Use a piece of $^3/_{32}$" brass rod with a 90° bend at the end to check all oil hole openings. Wire must enter hole or the bearing will not receive sufficient lubrication. (See Figure 6A7-76)

5. Install the rear plug:

   a. Coat the block with R.T.V. sealer.

   b. Drive the plug into the block until it is flush or no more than .5 mm (.020") concave.

   c. Install the camshaft and engine assembly. Road test the car and inspect for leaks.

Pistons and Connecting Rod Assemblies

REMOVAL

1. Remove the engine assembly from the car, see "Engine Removal and Installation".

2. Remove the intake manifold, cylinder head or heads.

3. Remove the oil pan.

4. Remove the oil pump assembly.

5. Stamp the cylinder number on the machined surfaces of the bolt bosses of the connecting rod and cap for identification when reinstalling. If the pistons are to be removed from the connecting rod, mark the cylinder number on the piston with a silver pencil or quick drying paint for proper cylinder identification and cap to rod location. The 4-151 engine is numbered 1-4 from front to back; on

the 183 and diesel V6's, the right (rear) bank is numbered 2-4-6, left (front) bank 1-3-5; the V6-173 is numbered 1-3-5 on the right bank, 2-4-6 on the left bank.

6. Examine the cylinder bore above the ring travel. If a ridge exists, remove the ridge with a ridge reamer before attempting to remove the piston and rod assembly.

7. Remove the rod bearing cap and bearing.

8. Install a guide hose over threads of rod bolts. This is to prevent damage to bearing journal and rod bolt threads.

9. Remove the rod and piston assembly through the top of the cylinder bore.

10. Remove any other rod and piston assemblies in the same manner.

CLEANING AND INSPECTION

Connecting Rods

Wash connecting rods in cleaning solvent and dry with compressed air. Check for twisted or bent rods and inspect for nicks or cracks. Replace connecting rods that are damaged.

Pistons

Clean varnish from piston skirts and pins with a cleaning solvent. DO NOT WIRE BRUSH ANY PART OF THE PISTON. Clean the ring grooves with a groove cleaner and make sure oil ring holes and slots are clean.

Inspect the piston for cracked ring lands, skirts or pin bosses, wavy or worn ring lands, scuffed or damaged skirts, eroded areas at top of the piston. Replace pistons that are damaged or show signs of excessive wear.

Inspect the grooves for nicks or burrs that might cause the rings to hang up.

Measure piston skirt (across center line of piston pin) and check piston clearance.

PISTON PIN REMOVAL AND INSTALLATION

Gasoline Engines

Use care at all times when handling and servicing connecting rods and pistons. To prevent possible damage to these units, do not clamp rod or piston in vise since they may become distorted. Do not allow pistons to strike against one another, against hard objects or bench surfaces, since distortion of piston contour or nicks in the soft aluminum material may result.

1. Remove piston rings using suitable piston ring remover.

2. Install guide bushing of piston pin removing and installing tool

3. Install piston and connecting rod assembly on support and place assembly in an arbor press. Press pin out of connecting rod, using the appropriate piston pin tool.

Diesel Engines

The piston pin is a free floating piston pin and the correct piston pin fit in the piston is .0076-.0127 mm (.0003″ to .0005″) and rod is .0076-.033 mm (.0003″ to .0013″) loose. If the pin to piston clearance is to the high limit .0127-.033 mm (.0005″ piston or .0013″ rod), the pin can be inserted in the piston or rod with very little hand pressure and will fall through the piston or rod by its own weight. If the clearance is .0076 mm (.0003″), the pin will not fall through. It is important that the piston and rod pin hole be clean and free of oil when checking pin fit.

The rod may be installed in the piston with either side facing up. Whenever the replacement of a piston pin is necessary, remove the snap ring retaining the pin. Then remove pin.

It is very important that after installing the piston pin retaining snap rings that the rings be rotated to make sure they are fully seated in their grooves. The snap ring must be installed with the flat side out.

MEASURING THE OLD PISTONS

Check used piston to cylinder bore clearance as follows:

1. Measure the cylinder bore diameter with a telescope gage.

2. Measure the piston diameter. When measuring piston for size or taper, measurement must be made with the piston pin removed.

3. Subtract piston diameter from cylinder bore diameter to determine piston-to-bore clearance.

4. Compare piston-to-bore clearance obtained with those clearances recommended. Determine if piston-to-bore clearance is in acceptable range.

5. When measuring taper, the largest reading must be at the bottom of the skirt.

SELECTING NEW PISTONS

1. If the used piston is not acceptable, check service piston sizes and determine if a new piston can be selected. (Service pistons are available in standard, high limit and standard .254 mm (.010″) oversize.)

2. If the cylinder bore must be reconditioned, measure the new piston diameter, then hone cylinder bore to obtain preferable clearance.

3. Select new piston and mark piston to identify the cylinder for which it was fitted. (On some cars oversize pistons may be found. These pistons will be .254 mm (.010″) oversize).

CYLINDER HONING

1. When cylinders are being honed, follow the manufacturer's recommendations for the use of the hone.

2. Occasionally during the honing operation, the cylinder bore should be thoroughly cleaned and the selected piston checked for correct fit.

3. When finish honing a cylinder bore, the hone should be moved up and down at a sufficient speed to obtain very fine uniform surface finish marks in a cross hatch pattern of approximately 45 to 65 degrees included angle. The finish marks should be clean but not sharp, free from imbedded particles and torn or folded metal.

4. Permanently mark the piston for the cylinder to which it has been fitted and proceed to hone the remaining cylinders.

NOTE: *Handle pistons with care. Do not attempt to force pistons through cylinders until the cylinders have been honed to correct size. Pistons can be distorted through careless handling.*

5. Thoroughly clean the bores with hot water and detergent. Scrub well with a stiff bristle brush and rinse thoroughly with hot water. It is extremely essential that a good cleaning operation be performed. If any of the abrasive material is allowed to remain in the cylinder bores, it will rapidly wear the new rings and cylinder bores. The bores should be swabbed several times with light engine oil and a clean cloth and then wiped with a clean dry cloth. *CYLINDERS SHOULD NOT BE CLEANED WITH KEROSENE OR GASOLINE.* Clean the remainder of the cylinder block to remove the excess material spread during the honing operation.

CHECKING CYLINDER BORE

Cylinder bore size can be measured with inside micrometers or a cylinder gage. The most wear will occur at the top of the ring travel.

Reconditioned cylinder bores should be held to not more than .025 mm (.001″) out-of-round and .025 mm (.001″) taper.

If the cylinder bores are smooth, the cylinder walls should not be deglazed. If the cylinder walls are scored, the walls may have to be honed before installing new rings. It is important that reconditioned cylinder bores be thoroughly washed with a soap and water solution to remove all traces of abrasive material to eliminate premature wear.

Piston Rings

The pistons have three rings (two compression rings and one oil ring). The oil ring consists of

two rails and an expander. Pistons do not have oil drain holes behind the rings.

RING TOLERANCES

When installing new rings, ring gap and side clearance should be checked as follows:

PISTON RING AND RAIL GAP

Each ring and rail gap must be measured with the ring or rail positioned squarely and at the bottom of the ring-travel area of the bore.

SIDE CLEARANCE

Each ring must be checked for side clearance in its respective piston groove by inserting a feeler gage between the ring and its upper land. The piston grooves must be cleaned before checking ring for side clearance. See PISTON RING CLEARANCE specifications at the end of this section for ring side clearance specifications. To check oil ring side clearance, the oil rings must be installed on the piston.

RING INSTALLATION

For service ring specifications and detailed installation productions, refer to the instructions furnished with the parts package.

Connecting Rod Bearings

If you have already removed the connecting rod and piston assemblies from the engine, follow only steps 3-7 of the following procedure.

REMOVAL, INSPECTION, INSTALLATION

The connecting rod bearings are designed to have a slight projection above the rod and cap faces to insure a positive contact. The bearings can be replaced without removing the rod and piston assembly from the engine.

1. Remove the oil pan, see "Oil Pan". It may be necessary to remove the oil pump to provide access to rear connecting rod bearings.

2. With the connecting rod journal at the bottom, stamp the cylinder number on the machined surfaces of connecting rod and cap for identification when reinstalling, then remove caps.

3. Inspect journals for roughness and wear. Slight roughness may be removed with a fine grit polishing cloth saturated with engine oil. Burrs may be removed with a fine oil stone by moving the stone on the journal circumference. Do not move the stone back and forth across the journal. If the journals are scored or ridged, the crankshaft must be replaced.

4. The connecting rod journals should be

checked for out-of-round and correct size with a micrometer.

NOTE: *Crankshaft rod journals will normally be standard size. If any undersized crankshafts are used, all will be .254 mm undersize and .254 mm will be stamped on the number 4 counterweight.*

If plastic gaging material is to be used:

5. Clean oil from the journal bearing cap, connecting rod and outer and inner surface of the bearing inserts. Position insert so that tang is properly aligned with notch in rod and cap.

6. Place a piece of plastic gaging material in the center of lower bearing shell.

7. Remove bearing cap and determine bearing clearances by comparing the width of the flattened plastic gaging material at its widest point with the graduation on the container. The number within the graduation on the envelope indicates the clearance in thousandths of an inch or millimeters. If this clearance is excessive, replace the bearing and recheck clearance with plastic gaging material. Lubricate bearing with engine oil before installation. Repeat Steps 2 through 7 on remaining connecting rod bearings. All rods must be connected to their journals when rotating the crankshaft to prevent engine damage.

Piston and Connecting Rod Assembly

INSTALLATION

1. Install connecting rod bolt guide hose over rod bolt threads.

2. Apply engine oil to the rings and piston, then install piston ring compressing tool on the piston.

3. Install the assembly in its respective cylinder bore.

4. Lubricate the crankshaft journal with engine oil and install connecting rod bearing and cap, with bearing index tang in rod and cap on same side.

NOTE: *When more than one rod and piston assembly is being installed, the connecting rod cap attaching nuts should only be tightened enough to keep each rod in position until all have been installed. This will aid installation of remaining piston assemblies.*

5. Torque rod bolt nuts to specification.

6. Install all other removed parts.

7. Install the engine in the car, see "Engine Removal and Installation".

Crankshaft

REMOVAL

1. Remove the engine assembly as previously outlined.

2. Remove the engine front cover.

3. Remove the timing chain and sprockets.

4. Remove the oil pan.

5. Remove the oil pump.

6. Stamp the cylinder number on the machined surfaces of the bolt boses of the connecting rods and caps for identification when reinstalling. If the pistons are to be removed from the connecting rod, mark cylinder number on piston with a silver pencil or quick drying paint for proper cylinder identification and cap to rod location.

7. Remove the connecting rod caps and install thread protectors.

8. Mark the main bearing caps so that they can be reinstalled in their original positions.

9. Remove all the main bearing caps.

10. Note position of keyway in crankshaft so it can be installed in the same position.

11. Lift crankshaft out of block. Rods will pivot to the center of the engine when the crankshaft is removed.

12. Remove both halves of the rear main oil seal.

INSTALLATION

1. Measure the crankshaft journals with a micrometer to determine the correct size rod and main bearings to be used. Whenever a new or reconditioned crankshaft is installed, new connect rod bearings and main bearings should be installed. See "Main Bearings" and "Rod Bearings".

2. Clean all oil passages in the block (and crankshaft if it is being reused).

NOTE: *A new rear main seal should be installed anytime the crankshaft is removed or replaced.*

3. Install sufficient oil pan bolts in the block to align with the connecting rod bolts. Use rubber bands between the bolts to position the connecting rods as required. Connecting rod position can be adjusted by increasing the tension on the rubber bands with additional turns around the pan bolts or thread protectors.

4. Position the upper half of main bearings in the block and lubricate with engine oil.

5. Position crankshaft keyway in the same position as removed and lower into block. The connecting rods will follow the crank pins into the correct position as the crankshaft is lowered.

6. Lubricate the thrust flanges with 1050169 Lubricant or equivalent. Install caps with lower half of bearings lubricated with engine oil. Lubricate cap bolts with engine oil and install, but do not tighten.

7. With a block of wood, bump shaft in

each direction to align thrust flanges of main bearing. After bumping shaft in each direction, wedge the shaft to the front and hold it while torquing the thrust bearing cap bolts.

NOTE: *In order to prevent the possibility of cylinder block and/or main bearing cap damage, the main bearing caps are to be tapped into their cylinder block cavity using a brass or leather mallet before attaching bolts are installed. Do not use attaching bolts to pull main bearing caps into their seats. Failure to observe this information may damage the cylinder block or a bearing cap.*

8. Torque all main bearing caps to specification.

9. Remove the connecting rod bolt thread protectors and lubricate the connecting rod bearings with engine oil.

10. Install the connecting rod bearing caps in their original position. Torque the nuts to specification.

11. Complete the installation by reversing the removal steps.

Main Bearings

CHECKING BEARING CLEARANCE

1. Remove bearing cap and wipe oil from crankshaft journal and outer and inner surfaces of bearing shell.

2. Place a piece of plastic gaging material in the center of bearing.

3. Use a floor jack or other means to hold crankshaft against upper bearing shell. This is necessary to obtain accurate clearance readings when using plastic gaging material.

4. Reinstall bearing cap and bearing. Place engine oil on cap bolts and install Torque bolts to specification.

5. Remove bearing cap and determine bearing clearance by comparing the width of the flattened plastic gaging material at its widest point with graduations on the gaging material container. The number within the graduation on the envelope indicates the clearance in millimeters or thousandths of an inch. If the

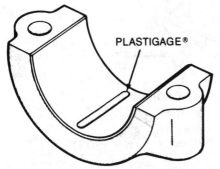

PLASTIGAGE®

Plastigage® installed on the lower bearing shell

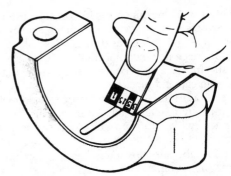

Measure Plastigage® to determine main bearing clearance

clearance is greater than allowed, *REPLACE BOTH BEARING SHELLS AS A SET.* Recheck clearance after replacing shells. (Refer to Main Bearing Replacement.

REPLACEMENT

Main bearing clearances must be corrected by the use of selective upper and lower shells. UNDER NO CIRCUMSTANCES should the use of shims behind the shells to compensate for wear be attempted. To install main bearing shells, proceed as follows:

1. Remove the oil pan as outlined elsewhere in this Chapter. On some models, the oil pump may also have to be removed.

2. Loosen all main bearing caps.

3. Remove bearing cap and remove lower shell.

4. Insert a flattened cotter pin or roll out pin in the oil passage hole in the crankshaft, then rotate the crankshaft in the direction opposite to cranking rotation. The pin will contact the upper shell and roll it out.

5. The main bearing journals should be checked for roughness and wear. Slight roughness may be removed with a fine grit polishing cloth saturated with engine oil. Burrs may be removed with a fine oil stone. If the journals are scored or ridged, the crankshaft must be replaced.

The journals can be measured for out-of-round with the crankshaft installed by using a crankshaft caliper and inside micrometer or a main bearing micrometer. The upper bearing shell must be removed when measuring the crankshaft journals. Maximum out-of-round of the crankshaft journals must not exceed .037 mm (.0015").

6. Clean crankshaft journals and bearing caps thoroughly before installing new main bearings.

7. Apply special lubricant, No. 1050169 or equivalent, to the thrust flanges of bearing shells.

8. Place new upper shell on crankshaft

journal with locating tang in correct position and rotate shaft to turn it into place using cotter pin or roll out pin as during removal.

9. Place new bearing shell in earing cap.

10. Install a new oil seal in the rear main bearing cap and block.

11. Lubricate the removed or replaced main bearings with engine oil. Lubricate the thrust surface with lubricant 1050169 or equivalent.

12. Lubricate the main bearing cap bolts with engine oil.

NOTE: *In order to prevent the possibility of cylinder block and/or main bearing cap damage, the main bearing caps are to be tapped into their cylinder block cavity using a brass or leather mallet before attaching bolts are installed. Do not use attaching bolts to pull main bearing caps into their seats. Failure to observe this information may damage the cylinder block or a bearing cap.*

13. Torque the main bearing cap bolts to 145 N·m (107 ft. lbs.).

Oil Pan

REMOVAL AND INSTALLATION

4-151 Engine

1. Raise and support the car. Drain the oil.

2. Remove the engine cradle-to-front engine mounts.

3. Disconnect the exhaust pipe at both the exhaust manifold and at the rear transaxle mount.

4. Disconnect and remove the starter. Remove the flywheel housing or torque converter cover.

5. Remove the alternator upper bracket.

6. Install an engine lifting chain and raise the engine.

7. Remove the lower alternator bracket. Remove the engine support bracket.

8. Remove the oil pan retaining bolts and remove the pan.

9. Reverse the procedure to install. Clean all gasket surfaces thoroughly. Install the rear oil pan gasket into the rear main bearing cap,

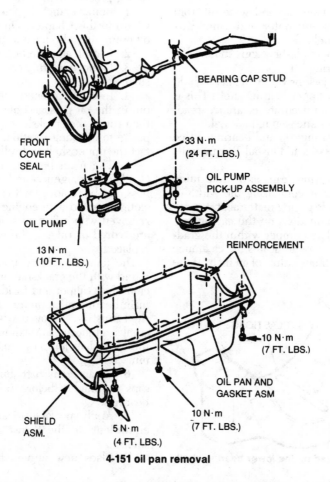

BEARING CAP STUD

FRONT COVER SEAL

33 N·m (24 FT. LBS.)

OIL PUMP PICK-UP ASSEMBLY

OIL PUMP

13 N·m (10 FT. LBS.)

REINFORCEMENT

10 N·m (7 FT. LBS.)

OIL PAN AND GASKET ASM

SHIELD ASM.

5 N·m (4 FT. LBS.)

10 N·m (7 FT. LBS.)

4-151 oil pan removal

then apply a thin bead of silicone sealer to the pan gasket depressions. Install the front pan gasket into the timing cover. Install the side gaskets onto the pan, not the block. They can be retained in place with grease. Apply a thin bead of silicone seal to the mating joints of the gaskets. Install the oil pan; install the timing gear bolts last, after the other bolts have been snugged down.

6-173 Engine

1. Disconnect the battery ground.
2. Raise and support the car on jackstands.
3. Drain the oil.
4. Remove the bellhousing cover.
5. Remove the starter.
6. Support the engine.
7. Unbolt the engine from its mounts.
8. Remove the oil pan bolts.
9. Raise the engine with a jack, just enough to remove the oil pan.
10. Installation is the reverse of removal. The pan is installed using RTV gasket material in place of a gasket. Make sure that the sealing surfaces are free of old RTV material. Use a ⅛ inch bead of RTV material on the pan sealing flange. Torque the pan bolts to 8–10 ft. lb.

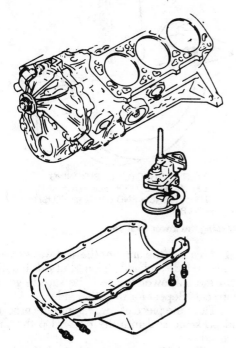

6-173 oil pan removal

6-183 Engine

1. Disconnect the battery ground.
2. Raise and support the car on jackstands.
3. Drain the oil.

4. Remove the bellhousing cover.
5. Unbolt and remove the oil pan.
6. Installation is the reverse of removal. RTV gasket material is used in place of a gasket. Make sure that the sealing surfaces are free of all old RTV material. Use a ⅛ inch bead of RTV material on the oil pan sealing flange. Torque the pan bolts to 10 ft. lb.

6-263 Diesel Engine

CAUTION: *The following procedure will be personally hazardous unless the procedures are followed exactly.*

1. Install the engine support fixture assembly shown in the accompanying illustration. Be certain to arrange washers on the fixture so that the bolt securing the chain to the cylinder head can be torqued to 20 ft. lb. THIS IS ABSOLUTELY NECESSARY!
2. Raise the front and rear of the car and support it on jackstands with the rear slightly lower than the front. The front jackstands should be located at the front lift points shown in your owner's manual.
3. Drain the oil.
4. Remove the left side steering gear cradle bolt and loosen the right side cradle bolt.
5. Remove the front stabilizer bar.
6. Using a ½ inch drill bit, drill through the spot weld located between the rear holes at the left front stabilizer bar mounting.
7. Remove the nuts securing the engine and transaxle to its cradle.
8. Disconnect the left lower ball joint from the knuckle.
9. Place a wood block on a floor jack and raise the transaxle under the pan until the mount studs clear the cradle.
10. Remove the bolts securing the front crossmember to the right side of the cradle.
11. Remove the bolts from the left side front body mounts.
12. Remove the left side and front crossmember assemblies. It will be necessary to lower the rear crossmember below the left side of the body through the careful use of a large prybar.
13. Remove the bellhousing cover.
14. Remove the starter.
15. Remove the engine from mount bracket.
16. Unbolt and remove the oil pan.
17. Installation is the reverse of removal. Apply sealer to both sides of the oil pan gasket and make sure that the tabs on the gaskets are installed in the seal notches. Apply RTV sealer to the front cover oil pan seal retainer, and to each seal where it contacts the block. Wipe the seal area of the pan with clean engine oil

before installing the pan. Torque the pan bolts to 10 ft. lb.

Oil Pump

REMOVAL AND INSTALLATION

4-151 and 6-173 Engines

1. Remove the oil pan as described earlier.
2. Unbolt and remove the oil pump and pickup.
3. Installation is the reverse of removal. Torque the 4-151 pump to 22 ft. lb. and the 6-173 pump bolts to 26–35 ft. lb.

6-183

1. Remove the oil filter.
2. Unbolt the oil pump cover from the timing chain cover.
3. Slide out the oil pump gears. Clean all parts thoroughly in solvent and check for wear. Remove the oil pressure relief valve cap, spring and valve.
4. Installation is the reverse of removal. Torque the pressure relief valve cap to 35 ft. lb. Install the pump gears and check their clearances:
   End clearance: 0.002–0.006 in.
   Side clearance: 0.002–0.005 in.
   Place a straightedge across the face of the pump cover and check that it is flat to within 0.001 in. Pack the oil pump cavity with petroleum jelly so that there is no air space. Install the cover and torque the bolts to 10 ft. lb.

6-263

1. Remove the oil pan.
2. Unbolt and remove the oil pump and drive extension.
3. Installation is the reverse of removal. Torque the pump bolts to 18 ft. lb.

Rear Main Oil Seal

REMOVAL AND INSTALLATION

4-151 Engine

1. Remove the transaxle and flywheel.
2. Being careful not to scratch the crankshaft, pry out the old seal with a screwdriver.
3. Coat the new seal with clean engine oil, and install it by hand onto the crankshaft. The seal backing must be flush with the block opening.
4. Install all other parts in reverse of removal.

6-173 Engine

1. Remove the oil pan and pump.
2. Remove the rear main bearing cap.
3. Gently pack the upper seal into the groove approximately ¼ inch on each side.

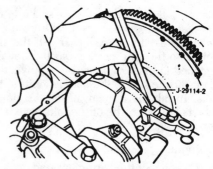

Installing the upper rear main seal on 6-173 engines

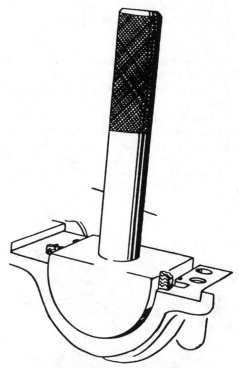

AFTER CORRECTLY POSITIONING SEAL, ROTATE TOOL SLIGHTLY AND CUT OFF EACH END OF SEAL FLUSH WITH BLOCK

Installing the lower seal half

4. Measure the amount the seal was driven in on one side and add $1/16$ in. Cut this length from the old lower cap seal. Be sure to get a sharp cut. Repeat for the other side.
5. Place the piece of cut seal into the groove and pack the seal into the block. Do this for each side.
   NOTE: *G.M. makes a guide tool (J-29114-1) which bolts to the block via an oil pan bolt hole, and a packing tool (J-29114-2) which are machined to provide a built-in stop for the installation of the short cut pieces. Using the packing tool, work the short pieces of seal onto the guide tool, then*

pack them into the block with the packing tool.

6. Install a new lower seal in the rear main cap.

7. Install a piece of Plastigage or the equivalent on the bearing journal. Install the rear cap and tighten to 70 ft. lbs. Remove the cap and check the gauge for bearing clearance. If out of specification, the ends of the seal may be frayed or not flush, preventing the cap from proper sealing. Correct as required.

8. Clean the journal, and apply a thin film of sealer to the mating surfaces of the cap and block. Do not allow any sealer to get onto the journal or bearing. Install the bearing cap and tighten to 70 ft. lbs. Install the pan and pump.

6-183 and 6-263 Engines

Braided fabric seals are pressed into grooves formed in crankcase and rear bearing cap to rear of the oil collecting groove, to seal against leakage of oil around the crankshaft.

A new braided fabric seal can be installed in crankcase only when crankshaft is removed, but it can be repaired while crankshaft is installed, as outlined under Rear Main Bearing Upper Oil Seal Repair. The seal can be replaced in cap whenever the cap is removed. Remove old seal and place new seal in groove with both ends projecting above parting surface of cap. Force seal into groove rubbing down with hammer handle or smooth stick until seal projects above the groove not more than $1/16''$. Cut ends off flush with surface of cap, using sharp knife or razor blade.

The engine must be operated at slow speed when first started after a new braided seal is installed.

Neoprene composition seals are placed in grooves in the sides of bearing cap to seal against leakage in the joints between cap and crankcase. The neoprene composition swells in the presence of oil and heat. The seals are undersize when newly installed and may even leak for a short time until the seals have had time to swell and seal the opening.

The neoprene seals are slightly longer than the grooves in the bearing cap. The seals must not be cut to length. Before installation of seals, soak for 1 to 2 minutes in light oil or kerosene. After installation of bearing cap in crankcase, install seal in bearing cap.

To help eliminate oil leakage at the joint where the cap meets the crankcase, apply silastic sealer, or equivalent, to the rear main bearing cap split line. When applying sealer, use only a thin coat as an over abundance will not allow the cap to seat properly.

After seal is installed, force seals up into the cap with a blunt instrument to be sure of a seal at the upper parting line between the cap and case.

REAR MAIN BEARING UPPER OIL SEAL REPAIR

1. Remove oil pan.

2. Insert packing tool (J-21526-2) against one end of the seal in the cylinder block. Drive the old seal gently into the groove until it is packed tight. This varies from $1/4''$ to $3/4''$ depending on the amount of pack required.

3. Repeat Step 2 on the other end of the seal in the cylinder block.

4. Measure the amount the seal was driven up on one side and add $1/16''$. Using a single edge razor blade, cut that length from the old seal removed from the rear main bearing cap. Repeat the procedure for the other side. Use the rear main bearing cap as a holding fixture when cutting the seal.

5. Install Guide Tool (J-21526-1) onto cylinder block.

6. Using packing tool, work the short pieces cut in Step 4 into the guide tool and then pack into cylinder block. The guide tool and packing tool have been machined to provide a built-in stop. Use this procedure for both sides. It may help to use oil on the short pieces of the rope seal when packing into the cylinder block.

7. Remove the guide tool.

8. Install a new fabric seal in the rear main bearing cap. Install cap and torque to specifications.

9. Install oil pan.

Water Pump

REMOVAL AND INSTALLATION

4-151 Engine

1. Disconnect battery negative cable.

2. Remove accessory drive belts.

3. Remove water pump attaching bolts and remove pump.

4. If installing a new water pump, transfer pulley from old unit. With sealing surfaces cleaned, place a 3mm ($1/8''$) bead of sealant #1052289 or equivalent on the water pump sealing surface. While sealer is still wet, install pump and torque bolts to 6 ft. lb.

5. Install accessory drive belts.

6. Connect battery negative cable.

6-173 Engine

1. Disconnect battery negative cable.

2. Drain cooling system and remove heater hose.

3. Remove water pump attaching bolts and nut and remove pump.

4. With the sealant surfaces cleaned, place

a 2mm ($^3/_{32}$″) bead of sealant #1052357 or equivalent on the water pump sealing surface.

5. Clean old sealant from pump.

6. Coat bolt threads with pipe sealant #1052080 or equivalent.

7. Install pump and torque bolts to 10 ft. lb.

8. Connect battery negative battery cable.

NOTE: *When replacing the water pump on a car equipped with the V-6 engine, the timing cover must be clamped to the cylinder block PRIOR TO removing the water pump bolts. Certain bolts holding the water pump pass through the front cover and when removed, may allow the front cover to pull away from the cylinder block, breaking the seal. This may or may not be readily apparent and if left undetected, could allow coolant to enter the crankcase. To prevent this possible separation during water pump removal, Special Tool #J29176 will have to be installed.*

6-183 Engine

1. Disconnect the negative battery cable.

2. Remove accessory drive belts.

3. Remove water pump attaching bolts.

4. Remove the engine support strut.

5. Place a floor jack under the front crossmember of the cradle and raise the jack until the jack just starts to raise the car.

6. Remove the front two body mount bolts with the lower cushions and retainers.

7. Remove the cushions from the bolts.

8. Thread the body mount bolts with retainers a minimum of three (3) turns into the cage nuts so that the bolts restrain cradle movement.

9. Release the floor jack slowly until the crossmember contacts the body mount bolt retainers. As the jack is being lowered watch and correct any interference with hoses, lines, pipes and cables.

NOTE: *Do not lower the cradle without its being restrained as possible damage can occur to the body and underhood items.*

10. Remove water pump from engine.

11. Reverse removal procedure.

12. Install pump and torque to 25 ft. lb.

13. Connect negative battery cable.

14. Fill with coolant and check for leaks.

6-263 Diesel Engine

1. Drain radiator.

2. Disconnect lower radiator hose at water pump.

3. Disconnect the heater return hose at the water pump, remove the bolt retaining the heater water return pipe to the intake manifold and position the pipe out-of-the-way.

4. If equipped with AC, remove the vacuum pump drivebelt.

5. Remove the serpentine drive belt.

6. Remove the generator, AC compressor or vacuum pump brackets.

7. Remove the water pump attaching bolts and remove the water pump assembly.

8. Remove the water pump pulley.

9. Clean gasket material from engine block.

10. Apply a thin coat of 1050026 sealer or equivalent to the water pump housing to retain the gasket, then position new gasket on the housing. Also apply sealer to water pump mounting bolts. Torque bolts to 12–15 ft. lb.

Radiator

REMOVAL AND INSTALLATION

All Models

1. Disconnect the negative battery cable.

2. Drain the cooling system.

3. Remove the forward strut brace for the engine at the radiator. Loosen the bolt to prevent shearing the rubber bushing, then swing the strut rearward.

4. Disconnect the headlamp wiring harness from the fan frame. Unplug the fan electrical connector.

5. Remove the attaching bolts for the fan.

6. Scribe the hood latch location on the radiator support, then remove the latch.

7. Disconnect the coolant hoses from the radiator. Remove the coolant recovery tank hose from the radiator neck. Disconnect and plug the automatic transmission fluid cooler lines from the radiator, if so equipped.

8. Remove the radiator attaching bolts and remove the radiator. If the car has air conditioning, it first may be necessary to raise the left side of the radiator so that the radiator neck will clear the compressor.

To install:

1. Install the radiator in the car, tightening the mounting bolts to 7 in. lbs. Connect the transmission cooler lines and hoses. Install the coolant recovery hose.

2. Install the hood latch. Tighten to 6 ft. lbs.

3. Install the fan, making sure the bottom leg of the frame fits into the rubber grommet at the lower support. Install the fan wires and the headlamp wiring harness. Swing the strut and brace forward, tightening to 11 ft. lbs. Connect the engine ground strap to the strut brace. Install the negative battery cable, fill the cooling system, and check for leaks.

Thermostat

REMOVAL AND INSTALLATION

All Models

1. Disconnect the negative battery cable.
2. Drain the cooling system.
3. Some models with cruise control have a vacuum modulator attached to the thermostat housing with a bracket. If your vehicle is equipped as such, remove the bracket from the housing.
4. On the four cylinder engine, unbolt the water outlet from the thermostat housing, remove the outlet from the housing and lift the thermostat out of the housing. On all other models, unbolt the water outlet from the intake manifold, remove the outlet and lift the thermostat out of the manifold.

To install the new thermostat:

5. Clean both of the mating surfaces and run

Thermostat installation

a ⅛″ bead of R.T.V. (room temperature vulcanizing) sealer in the groove of the water outlet.

6. Install the thermostat (spring towards engine) and bolt the water outlet into place while the R.T.V. sealer is still wet. Torque the bolts to 21 ft. lbs. The remainder of the installation is the reverse of removal. Check for leaks after the car is started and correct as required.

General Engine Specifications

Year	Engine No. Cyl Displacement (cu. in.)	Carburetor Type	Horsepower @ rpm	Torque @ rpm (ft. lbs.)	Bore x Stroke (in.)	Compression Ratio	Oil Pressure @ rpm
82–83	4-151	T.B.I.①	90 @ 4000	132 @ 2800	4.000 x 3.000	8.2 : 1	36–41
	6-173	2 bbl	112 @ 4800	145 @ 3400	3.500 x 3.000	8.5 : 1	36–41
	6-183	2 bbl	110 @ 4800	145 @ 2600	3.800 x 2.660	8.45 : 1	35–42
	6-263	Diesel	85 @ 3600	165 @ 1600	4.057 x 3.385	21.6 : 1	40–45

① Throttle Body Injection
Note: Some models equipped with the 4-151 engine use a 2 bbl. carburetor rather than T.B.I.

Valve Specifications

Year	Engine No. Cyl Displacement (cu In.)	Seat Angle (deg)	Face Angle (deg)	Spring Test Pressure (lbs. @ In.)	Spring Installed Height (In.)	Stem to Guide Clearance (In.)		Stem Diameter (In.)	
						Intake	Exhaust	Intake	Exhaust
82–83	4-151	46	45	176 @ 1.25	1.66	.0010–.0027	.0010–.0027	.3418–.3425	.3418–.3425
	6-173	46	45	155 @ 1.16	1.61	.0010–.0027	.0010–.0027	.3410–.3416	.3410–.3416
	6-183	45	45	220 @ 1.34	1.727	.0015–.0035	.0015–.0035	.3401–.3412	.3401–.3415
	6-263	①	②	210 @ 1.22	1.67	.0010–.0027	.0015–.0032	.3425–.3432	.3420–.3427

① Intake: 45
Exhaust: 31
② Intake: 44
Exhaust: 30

Crankshaft and Connecting Rod Specifications

All measurements are given in inches

Year	Engine No. Cyl Displacement (cu in.)	Crankshaft				Connecting Rod		
		Main Brg Journal Dia	Main Brg Oil Clearance	Shaft End-Play	Thrust on No.	Journal Diameter	Oil Clearance	Side Clearance
82–83	4-151	2.2995–3.3005	.0005–.0002	.0035–.0085	5	1.9995–2.0005	.0005–.0026	.006–.022
	6-173	2.4937–2.4946	.0017–.0030	.0020–.0067	3	1.9984–1.9994	.0014–.0036	.006–.017
	6-183	2.4990–2.5000	.0003–.0018	.0030–.0090	2	2.2487–2.2495	.0005–.0026	.006–.023
	6-263	2.9993–3.0003	①	.0035–.0135	4	2.2490–2.2510	.0003–.0025	.008–.021

① #1, 2, 3: .0005–.0021
#4: .0020–.0034

Camshaft Specifications

All measurements in inches

Year	Engine	Journal Diameter					Bearing Clearance	Lobe Lift		Camshaft End Play
		1	2	3	4	5		Intake	Exhaust	
82–83	4-151	1.869	1.869	1.869	—	—	.0007–.0027	.398	.398	.0015–.0050
	6-173	1.869	1.869	1.869	1.869	—	.0010–.0040	.231	.263	—
	6-183	1.786	1.786	1.786	1.786	1.786	①	.406	.406	—
	6-263	②	2.205	2.185	2.165	—	.0020–.0059	N/A	N/A	.0008–.0228

① #1: .0005–.0025
#2–5: .0005–.0035
② #1 bearing is not borable, but must be replaced separately
N/A—not available

Piston and Ring Specifications

All measurements are given in inches.

Year	Engine Type/ Disp. cu. in.	Piston-to-Bore Clearance	Ring Gap			Ring Side Clearance		
			Top Compression	Bottom Compression	Oil Control	Top Compression	Bottom Compression	Oil Control
'82–'83	4-151	0.0025–0.0033	0.010–0.022	0.010–0.027	0.015–0.055	0.0015–0.0030	0.0015–0.0030	snug
	6-173	0.0017–0.0027	0.0098–0.0197	0.0098–0.0197	0.020–0.055	0.0012–0.0028	0.0016–0.0037	0.008 max.
	6-183	0.008–0.0020	0.013–0.023	0.013–0.023	0.015–0.035	0.0030–0.0050	0.0030–0.0050	0.0035 max.
	6-263	0.0030–0.0040	0.015–0.025	0.015–0.025	0.015–0.055	0.0050–0.0070	0.0030–0.0070	0.001–0.005

Torque Specifications
(All readings in ft. lbs.)

Year	Engine No. Cyl Displacement (cu. in.)	Cylinder Head Bolts	Rod Bearing Bolts	Main Bearing Bolts	Crankshaft Bolt	Flywheel to Crankshaft Bolts	Manifold	
							Intake	Exhaust
'82–83	4-151	85	32	70	200	44	29	44
	6-173	70	37	68	75	50	23	25
	6-183	80	40	100	225	60	13	25
	6-263	①	42	107	255 ②	76	41	29

① All exc. #5, 6, 11, 12, 13, 14: 142
  #5, 6, 11, 12, 14: 59
② Range: 160–350 ft. lb.

Emission Controls and Fuel Systems

4

EMISSION CONTROLS

There are three sources of automotive pollutants: crankcase fumes, exhaust gases, and gasoline evaporation. The pollutants formed from these substances fall into three categories: unburnt hydrocarbons (HC), carbon monoxide (CO), and oxides of nitrogen (NO_x). The equipment that is used to limit these pollutants is commonly called emission control equipment.

Positive Crankcase Ventilation System

All A Body cars except diesels are equipped with a positive crankcase ventilation (PCV) system to control crankcase blow-by vapors. The system functions as follows:

When the engine is running, a small portion of the gases which are formed in the combustion chamber leak by the piston rings and enter the crankcase. Since these gases are under pressure, they tend to escape from the crankcase and enter the atmosphere. If these gases are allowed to remain in the crankcase for any period of time, they contaminate the engine oil and cause sludge to build up in the crankcase. If the gases are allowed to escape into the atmosphere, they pollute the air with unburned hydrocarbons.

The job of the crankcase emission control equipment is to recycle these gases back into the engine combustion chamber where they are reburned.

The crankcase (blow-by) gases are recycled in the following way: as the engine is running, clean, filtered air is drawn through the air filter and into the crankcase. As the air passes through the crankcase, it picks up the combustion gases and carries them out of the crankcase, through the oil separator, through the PCV valve, and into the induction system.

As they enter the intake manifold, they are drawn into the combustion chamber where they are reburned.

The most critical component in the system is the PCV valve. This valve controls the amount of gases which are recycled into the combustion chamber. At low engine speeds, the valve is partially closed, limiting the flow of gases into the intake manifold. As engine speed increases, the valve opens to admit greater quantities of gases into the intake manifold. If the valve should become blocked or plugged, the gases will be prevented from escaping from the crankcase by the normal route. Since these gases are under pressure, they will find their own way out of the crankcase. This alternate route is usually a weak oil seal or gasket in the engine. As the gas escapes by the gasket, it also creates an oil leak. Besides causing oil leaks, a clogged PCV valve also allows these gases to remain in the crankcase for an extended period of time, promoting the formation of sludge in the engine.

SERVICE

Inspect the PCV system hose and connections at each tune-up and replace any deteriorated hoses. Check the PCV valve at every tune-up and replace it at 30,000 mile intervals.

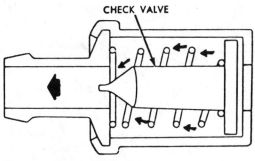

CHECK VALVE

Cross section of a PCV valve

Diesel Crankcase Ventilation

A crankcase depression regulator valve is used to regulate the flow of crankcase gases back into the engine. This valve is designed to limit vacuum in the crankcase. The gases are drawn from the valve cover through the CDRV and into the intake manifold.

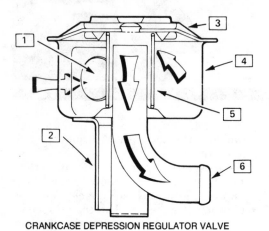

CRANKCASE DEPRESSION REGULATOR VALVE
V-TYPE DIESEL ENGINE

1. Inlet port (2) (Gases from) crankcase
2. Mounting bracket
3. Cover diaphragm
4. Body
5. Spring
6. Outlet tube (Gases to intake manifold)

Crankcase depression regulator valve (C.D.R.V.)

Fresh air enters the engine through the combination filter, check valve, and oil fill cap. This air mixes with blow-by gases and enters the opposite valve cover. These gases pass through a filter on the valve cover and are drawn into the connected tubing.

Intake manifold vacuum acts against a spring loaded diaphragm to control the flow of crank-

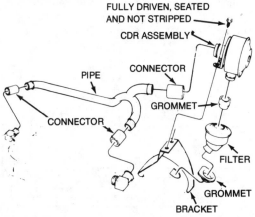

FULLY DRIVEN, SEATED
AND NOT STRIPPED

CDR ASSEMBLY

CONNECTOR

PIPE

GROMMET

CONNECTOR

FILTER

GROMMET

BRACKET

V6 diesel crankcase ventilation

case gases. Higher vacuum levels pull the diaphragm closer to the top of the outlet tube. This reduces the amount of gases being drawn from the crankcase and decreases vacuum in the crankcase. As intake vacuum decreases, the spring pushes the diaphragm away from the top of the outlet tube allowing more gases into the manifold.

CAUTION: *Do not allow solvent to come in contact with the diaphragm of the CDRV, as it will cause diaphragm damage.*

Evaporative Emission Control System

The basic Evaporative Emission Control System (EEC) used on all models is the carbon canister storage method. The system is used to reduce emissions of fuel vapors from the car's fuel system. Evaporated fuel vapors are stored for burning during combustion rather than being vented into the atmosphere when the engine is not running. To accomplish this, the fuel tank and the carburetor float bowl are vented through a vapor canister containing activated charcoal. The system utilizes a sealed fuel tank with a dome that collects fuel vapors and allows them to pass on into a line connected with the vapor canister. In addition, the vapors that form above the float chamber in the carburetor also pass into a line connected with the canister. The canister absorbs these vapors in a bed of activated charcoal and retains them until the canister is purged or cleared by air drawn through the filter at its bottom. The absorbing occurs when the car is not running, while the purging or cleaning occurs when the car is running. The amount of vapor being drawn into the engine at any given time is too small to have an effect on either fuel economy or engine performance.

The Electronic Control Module (ECM) controls the vacuum to the canister purge valve by using an electrically operated solenoid valve. When the system is in the 'Open Loop' mode, the solenoid valve is energized and blocks all vacuum to the canister purge valve. When the system is in the 'Closed Loop' mode, the solenoid valve is de-energized and vacuum is then supplied to operate the purge valve. This releases the fuel vapors, collected in the canister, into the induction system.

It is extremely important that only vapors be transferred to the engine. To avoid the possibility of liquid fuel being drawn into the system, the following features are included as part of the total system:

• A fuel tank overfill protector is provided to assure adequate room for expansion of liquid fuel volume with temperature changes.

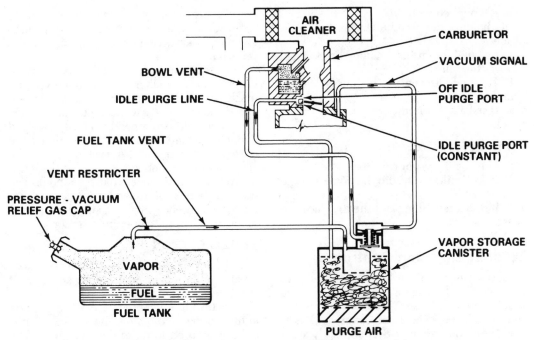

Evaporative emission control system (EECS)—open canister

• A one point fuel tank venting system is provided on all models to assure that the tank will be vented under any normal car attitude. This is accomplished by the use of a domed tank.

• A pressure-vacuum relief valve is located in the fuel cap.

NOTE: *Some canisters are of the "closed"*

design. They draw air from the air cleaner rather than the bottom of the canister.

VAPOR CANISTER REMOVAL AND INSTALLATION

1. Loosen the screw holding the canister retaining bracket.

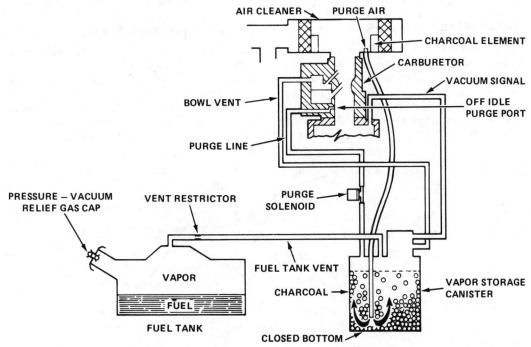

Evaporative emission control system (EECS)—closed canister

2. If equipped with A/C, loosen the attachments holding the accumulator and pipe assembly.

3. Rotate the canister retaining bracket and remove the canister.

4. Tag and disconnect the hoses leading from the canister.

5. Installation is in the reverse order of removal.

FILTER REPLACEMENT

1. Remove the vapor canister.

2. Pull the filter out from the bottom of the canister.

3. Install a new filter and then replace the canister.

Exhaust Emission Controls

Exhaust emission control systems constitute the largest body of emission control devices installed on A body cars. Included in this category are: Thermostatic Air Cleaner (THERMAC); Air Management System; Early Fuel Evaporation System (EFE); Exhaust Gas Recirculation (EGR); Computer Command Control System (CCC); Deceleration Valve; Mixture Control Solenoid (M/C); Throttle Position Sensor (TPS); Idle Speed Control (ISC); Electronic Spark Timing (EST); Transmission Converter Clutch (TCC); Catalytic Converter and the Oxygen Sensor System. A brief description of each system and any applicable service procedures follows.

Thermostatic Air Cleaner (THERMAC)

All engines use the THERMAC system. This system is designed to warm the air entering the carburetor when underhood temperatures are low, and to maintain a controlled air temperature into the carburetor at all times. By allowing preheated air to enter the carbu-retor, the amount of time the choke is on is reduced, resulting in better fuel economy and lower emissions. Engine warm-up time is also reduced.

The THERMAC system is composed of the air cleaner body, a filter, sensor unit, vacuum diaphragm, damper door, and associated hoses and connections. Heat radiating from the exhaust manifold is trapped by a heat stove and is ducted to the air cleaner to supply heated air to the carburetor. A movable door in the air cleaner case snorkel allows air to be drawn in from the heat stove (cold operation). The door position is controlled by the vacuum motor, which receives intake manifold vacuum as modulated by the temperature sensor.

SYSTEM CHECKS

1. Check the vacuum hoses for leaks, kinks, breaks, or improper connections and correct any defects.

2. Wtih the engine off, check the position of the damper door within the snorkel. A mirror can be used to make this job easier. The damper door should be open to admit outside air.

3. Apply at least 7 in. Hg of vacuum to the damper diaphragm unit. The door should close. If it doesn't, check the diaphragm linkage for binding and correct hookup.

4. With the vacuum still applied and the door closed, clamp the tube to trap the vacuum. If the door doesn't remain closed, there is a leak in the diaphragm assembly.

Air Management System

The AIR management system, is used to provide additional oxygen to continue the combustion process after the exhaust gases leave the combustion chamber. Air is injected into either the exhaust port(s), the exhaust manifold(s) or the catalytic converter by an engine driven air pump. The system is in operation at

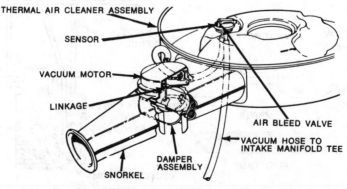

Thermostatic air cleaner

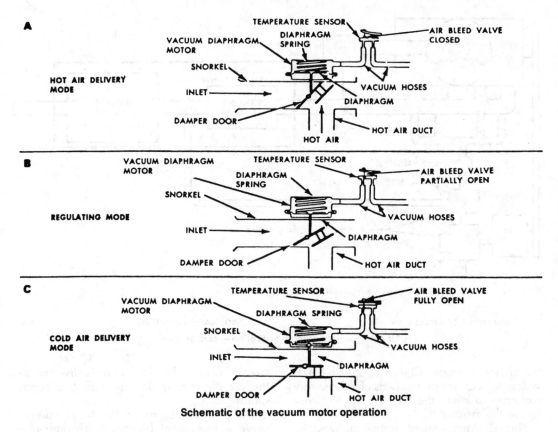

Schematic of the vacuum motor operation

all times and will bypass air only momentarily during deceleration and at high speeds. The bypass function is performed by the AIR Management Valve, while the check valve protects the air pump by preventing any backflow of exhaust gases.

The AIR management system helps reduce HC and CO content in the exhaust gases by injecting air into the exhaust ports during cold engine operation. This air injection also helps the catalytic converter to reach the proper temperature quicker during warmup. When

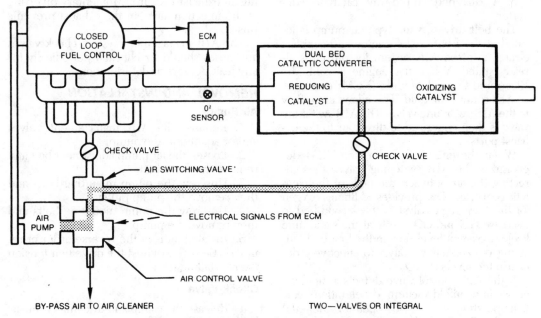

Air management system operation—warm engine

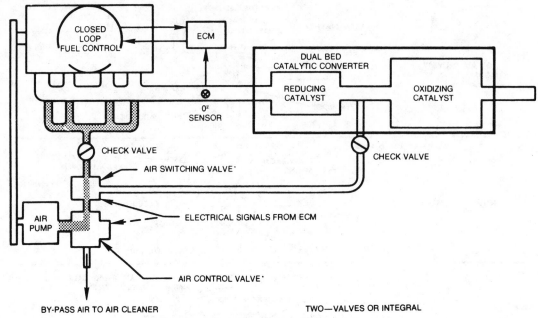

Air management system operation—cold engine

the engine is warm (Closed Loop), the AIR system injects air into the beds of a three-way converter to lower the HC and the CO content in the exhaust.

The Air Management system utilizes the following components:

1. An engine driven AIR pump
2. AIR management valves (Air Control, Air Switching)
3. Air flow and control hoses
4. Check valves
5. A dual-bed, three-way catalytic converter.

The belt driven, vane-type air pump is located at the front of the engine and supplies clean air to the AIR system for purposes already stated. When the engine is cold, the Electronic Control Module (ECM) energizes an AIR control solenoid. This allows air to flow to the AIR switching valve. The AIR switching valve is then energized to direct air to the exhaust ports.

When the engine is warm, the ECM de-energizes the AIR switching valve, thus directing the air between the beds of the catalytic converter. This provides additional oxygen for the oxidizing catalyst in the second bed to decrease HC and CO, while at the same time keeping oxygen levels low in the first bed, enabling the reducing catalyst to effectively decrease the levels of NO_x.

If the AIR control valve detects a rapid increase in manifold vacuum (deceleration), certain operating modes (wide open throttle, etc.) or if the ECM self-diagnostic system detects

any problem in the system, air is diverted to the air cleaner or directly into the atmosphere.

The primary purpose of the ECM's divert mode is to prevent backfiring. Throttle closure at the beginning of deceleration will temporarily create air/fuel mixtures which are too rich to burn completely. These mixtures become burnable when they reach the exhaust if combined with the injection air. The next firing of the engine will ignite this mixture causing an exhaust backfire. Momentary diverting of the injection air from the exhaust prevents this.

The AIR management system check valves and hoses should be checked periodically for any leaks, cracks or deterioration.

REMOVAL AND INSTALLATION

Air Pump

1. Remove the AIR management valves and/or adapter at the pump.
2. Loosen the air pump adjustment bolt and remove the drive belt.
3. Unscrew the pump mounting bolts and then remove the pump pulley.
4. Unscrew the pump mounting bolts and then remove the pump.
5. Installation is in the reverse order of removal. Be sure to adjust the drive belt tension after installing it.

Check Valve

1. Release the clamp and disconnect the air hoses from the valve.

2. Unscrew the check valve from the air injection pipe.

3. Installation is in the reverse order of removal.

Air Management Valve

1. Disconnect the negative battery cable.
2. Remove the air cleaner.
3. Tag and disconnect the vacuum hose from the valve.
4. Tag and disconnect the air outlet hoses from the valve.
5. Bend back the lock tabs and then remove the bolts holding the elbow to the valve.
6. Tag and disconnect any electrical connections at the valve and then remove the valve from the elbow.
7. Installation is in the reverse order of removal.

Computer Command Control System (CCC)

The Computer Command Control System (CCC) is an electronically controlled exhaust emission system that can monitor and control a large number of interrelated emission control systems. It can monitor up to 15 various engine/vehicle operating conditions and then use this information to control as many as 9 engine related systems. The "System" is thereby making constant adjustments to maintain good vehicle performance under all normal driving conditions while at the same time allowing the catalytic converter to effectively control the emissions of HC, CO and NO_x.

In addition, the "System" has a built in diagnostic system that recognizes and identifies possible operational problems and alerts the

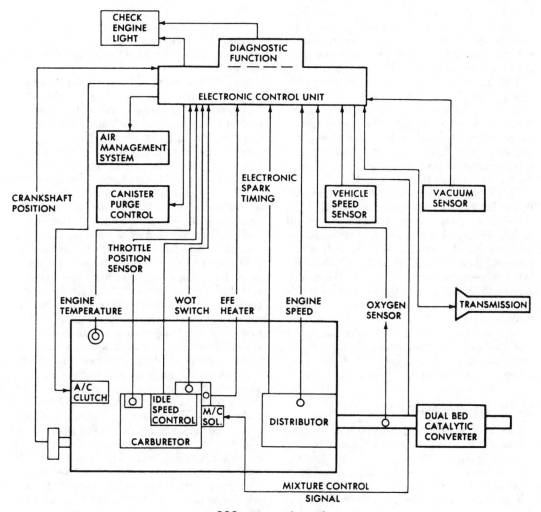

CCC system schematic

driver through a "Check Engine" light in the instrument panel. The light will remain "On" until the problem is corrected. The "System" also has built in back-up systems that in most cases of an operational problem will allow for the continued operation of the vehicle in a near normal manner until the repairs can be made.

The CCC system has some components in common with the old G.M. C-4 system, although they are not interchangeable. These components include the Electronic Control Module (ECM), which controls many more functions than does its predecessor, an oxygen sensor system, an electronically controlled variable-mixture carburetor, a three-way catalytic converter, throttle position and coolant sensors, a Barometric Pressure Sensor (BARO), a Manifold Absolute Pressure Sensor (MAP) and a "Check Engine" light in the instrument panel.

Components unique to the CCC system include the Air Injection Reaction (AIR) management system, a charcoal canister purge solenoid, EGR valve controls, a vehicle speed sensor (in the instrument panel), a transmission converter clutch solenoid (only on models with automatic transmission), idle speed control and Electronic Spark Timing (EST).

The ECM, in addition to monitoring sensors and sending out a control signal to the carburetors, also controls the following components or sub-systems: charcoal canister purge control, the AIR system, idle speed, automatic transmission converter lockup, distributor ignition timing, the EGR valve, and the air conditioner converter clutch.

The EGR valve control solenoid is activated by the ECM in a fashion similar to that of the charcoal canister purge solenoid described earlier in this chapter. When the engine is cold, the ECM energizes the solenoid, which blocks the vacuum signal to the EGR valve. When the engine is warm, the ECM de-energizes the solenoid and the vacuum signal is allowed to reach and then activate the EGR valve.

The idle speed control adjusts the idle speed to all particular engine load conditions and will lower the idle under no-load or low-load conditions in order to conserve fuel.

BASIC TROUBLESHOOTING

NOTE: *The following explains how to activate the Trouble Code signal light in the instrument cluster. This is not a full fledged CCC system troubleshooting and isolation procedure.*

Before suspecting the CCC system, or any of its components as being faulty, check the ignition system (distributor, timing, spark plugs

and wires). Check the engine compression, the air cleaner and any of the emission control components that are not controlled by the ECM. Also check the intake manifold, the vacuum hoses and hose connectors for any leaks. Check the carburetor mounting bolts for tightness.

The following symptoms could indicate a possible problem area with the CCC system:
1. Detonation;
2. Stalling or rough idling when the engine is cold;
3. Stalling or rough idling when the engine is hot;
4. Missing;
5. Hesitation;
6. Surging;
7. Poor gasoline mileage;
8. Sluggish or spongy performance;
9. Hard starting when engine is cold;
10. Hard starting when the engine is hot;
11. Objectionable exhaust odors;
12. Engine cuts out;
13. Improper idle speed.

As a bulb and system check, the "Check Engine" light will come on when the ignition switch is turned to the 'ON' position but the engine is not started.

The "Check Engine" light will also produce the trouble code/codes by a series of flashes which translate as follows: When the diagnostic test terminal under the instrument panel is grounded, with the ignition in the 'ON' position and the engine not running, the "Check Engine" light will flash once, pause, and then flash twice in rapid succession. This is a Code 12, which indicates that the diagnostic system is working. After a long pause, the Code 12 will repeat itself two more times. This whole cycle will then repeat itself until the engine is started or the ignition switch is turned 'OFF'.

When the engine is started, the "Check Engine" light will remain on for a few seconds and then turn off. If the "Check Engine" light remains on, the self-diagnostic system has detected a problem. If the test terminal is then grounded, the trouble code will flash (3) three times. If more than one problem is found to be in existence, each trouble code will flash (3) three times and then change to the next one. Trouble codes will flash in numerical order (lowest code number to highest). The trouble code series will repeat themselves for as long as the test terminal remains grounded.

A trouble code indicates a problem with a given circuit. For example, trouble code 14 indicates a problem in the coolant sensor circuit. This includes the coolant sensor, its electrical harness and the Electronic Control Module (ECM).

Since the self-diagnostic system cannot diagnose every possible fault in the system, the absence of a trouble code does not necessarily mean that the system is trouble-free. To determine whether or not a prblem with the system exists that does not activate a trouble code, a system performance check must be made. This job should be left to a qualified service technician.

In the case of an intermittent fault in the system, the "Check Engine" light will go out when the fault goes away, but the trouble code will remain in the memory of the ECM. Therefore, if a trouble code can be obtained even though the "Check Engine" light is not on, it must still be evaluated. It must be determined if the fault is intermittent or if the engine must be operating under certain conditions (acceleration, deceleration, etc.) before the "Check Engine" light will come on. In some cases, certain trouble codes will not be recorded in the ECM until the engine has been operated at part throttle for at least 5 to 18 minutes.

On the CCC system, a trouble code will be stored until the terminal 'R' at the ECM has been disconnected from the battery for at least 10 seconds.

ACTIVATING THE TROUBLE CODE

On the CCC system, locate the test terminal under the instrument panel (see illustration). Use a jumper wire and ground only the lead.

NOTE: *Ground the test terminal according to the instructions given previously in the "Basic Troubleshooting" section.*

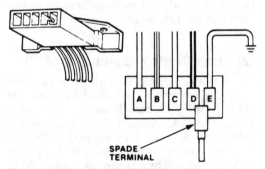

Test terminal and ground location

Pulse Air Injection (PULSAIR)

All engines use the Pulsair air injection system, which uses exhaust system air pulses to siphon fresh air into the exhaust manifold. The injected air supports continued combustion of the hot exhaust gases in the exhaust manifold, reducing exhaust emissions. A secondary purpose of the Pulsair system is to introduce more oxygen into the exhaust system upstream of the catalytic converter, to supply the con-

Trouble Code Identification Chart

NOTE: *Always ground the test terminal AFTER the engine is running.*

Trouble Code	Refers To:
12	No reference pulses to the ECM. This is not stored in the memory and will only flash when the fault is present (not to be confused with the Code 12 discussed earlier).
13	Oxygen sensor circuit. The engine must run for at least 5 min. before this code will set.
14	Shorted coolant circuit. The engine must run at least 2 min. before this code will set.
15	Open coolant sensor circuit. The engine must run at least 5 min. before this code will set.
21	Throttle position sensor circuit. The engine must run up to 25 sec., below 800 rpm, before this code will set.
23	Open or grounded carburetor solenoid circuit.
24	Vehicle Speed Sensor (VSS) circuit. The engine must run for at least 5 min. at road speed for this code to set.
32	Altitude Compensator circuit.
34	Vacuum sensor circuit. The engine must run up to 5 min., below 800 rpm, before this code will set.
35	Idle speed control switch circuit shorted. Over ½ throttle for at least 2 sec.
41	No distributor reference pulses to the ECM at specified engine vacuum. This code will store in memory.
42	Electronic Spark Timing (EST) bypass circuit grounded.
44	Lean oxygen sensor indication. The engine must run at least 5 min., in closed loop, at part throttle and road load for this code to set.
45	Rich system indication. The engine must run at least 5 min., in closed loop, at part throttle and road load for this code to set.
44&45	(at same time) Faulty oxygen sensor circuit.
51	Faulty calibration unit (PROM) or installation. It takes 30 sec. for this code to set.
54	Shorted M/C solenoid circuit and/or faulty ECM.
55	Gounded Vref (terminal 21), faulty oxygen sensor or ECM.

verter with the oxygen required for the oxidation reaction.

Air is drawn into the Pulsair valve through a hose connected to the air cleaner. The air

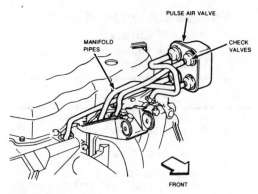

Pulsair installed on the four cylinder engine; V6 similar

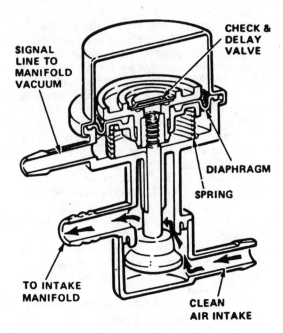

OPEN POSITION

Cross section of the deceleration valve

passes through a check valve (there is one check valve for each cylinder; all check valves are installed in the Pulsair valve), then through a manifold pipe to the exhaust manifold. All manifold pipes are the same length, to prevent uneven pulsation. The check valves open during pulses of negative exhaust back pressure, admitting air into the manifold pipe and the exhaust manifold. During pulses of positive exhaust back pressure, the check valves close, preventing backfiring into the Pulsair valve and air cleaner.

The Pulsair check valves, hoses and pipes should be checked occasionally for leaks, cracks, or breaks.

REMOVAL AND INSTALLATION

1. Remove the air cleaner case. Disconnect the rubber hose(s) from the Pulsair valve(s).

2. Disconnect the support bracket, if present. Some V6 engines have a Pulsair solenoid and bracket, which must be removed.

3. Unscrew the attaching nuts and remove the Pulsair tubes from the exhaust manifold(s).

4. To install, first apply a light coat of clean oil to the ends of the Pulsair tubes.

5. Install the tubes to the exhaust manifold(s), tightening the nuts to 10–13 ft. lbs. (10 Nm.). Connect the support bracket and solenoid and bracket, if used. Connect the rubber hose(s) and install the air cleaner.

Deceleration Valve

The purpose of the deceleration valve is to prevent backfiring in the exhaust system during deceleration. The normal position of the valve is closed. When deceleration causes a sudden vacuum increase in the vacuum signal lines, the pressure differential on the diaphragm will overcome the closing force of the spring, opening the valve and bleeding air into the intake manifold.

Air trapped in the chamber above the vacuum diaphragm will bleed at a calibrated rate through the delay valve portion of the integral 'check and delay valve', reducing the vacuum acting on the diaphragm. When the vacuum load on the diaphragm and the spring load equalize, the valve assembly will close, shutting off the air flow into the intake manifold.

The check valve portion of the 'check and delay valve' provides quick balancing of chamber pressure when a sudden decrease in vacuum is caused by acceleration rather than deceleration.

Mixture Control Solenoid (M/C)

The fuel flow through the carburetor idle main metering circuits is controlled by a mixture control (M/C) solenoid located in the carburetor. The M/C solenoid changes the air/fuel mixture to the engine by controlling the fuel flow through the carburetor. The ECM controls the solenoid by providing a ground. When the solenoid is energized, the fuel flow through the carburetor is reduced, providing a leaner mixture. When the ECM removes the ground, the solenoid is de-energized, increasing the fuel flow and providing a richer mixture. The M/C solenoid is energized and de-energized at a rate of 10 times per second.

Throttle Position Sensor (TPS)

The throttle position sensor is mounted in the carburetor body and is used to supply throttle

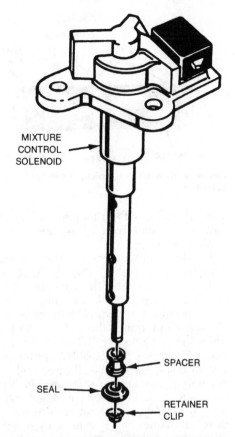

MIXTURE
CONTROL
SOLENOID

SPACER

SEAL

RETAINER
CLIP

The mixture control (M/C) solenoid is located in the carburetor

position information to the ECM. The ECM memory stores an average of operating conditions with the ideal air/fuel ratios for each of those conditions. When the ECM receives a signal that indicates throttle position change, it immediately shifts to the last remembered set of operating conditions that resulted in an ideal air/fuel ratio control. The memory is continually being updated during normal operations.

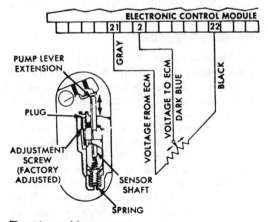

ELECTRONIC CONTROL MODULE

21   2   22

PUMP LEVER
EXTENSION

GRAY

VOLTAGE FROM ECM

VOLTAGE TO ECM
DARK BLUE

BLACK

PLUG

ADJUSTMENT
SCREW
(FACTORY
ADJUSTED)

SENSOR
SHAFT

SPRING

Throttle position sensor

Idle Speed Control (ISC)

The idle speed control does just what its name implies—it controls the idle. The ISC is used to maintain low engine speeds while at the same time preventing stalling due to engine load changes. The system consists of a motor assembly mounted on the carburetor which moves the throttle lever so as to open or close the throttle blades.

The whole operation is controlled by the ECM. The ECM moniters engine load to determine the proper idle speed. To prevent stalling, it moniters the air conditioning compressor switch, the transmission, the park/neutral switch and the ISC throttle switch. The ECM processes all this information and then uses it to control the ISC motor which in turn will vary the idle speed as necessary.

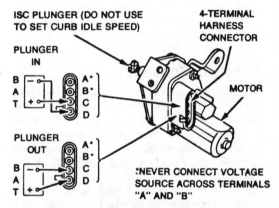

ISC PLUNGER (DO NOT USE
TO SET CURB IDLE SPEED)

4-TERMINAL
HARNESS
CONNECTOR

PLUNGER
IN

B
A
T

A·
B·
C
D

MOTOR

PLUNGER
OUT

B
A
T

A·
B·
C
D

·NEVER CONNECT VOLTAGE
SOURCE ACROSS TERMINALS
"A" AND "B"

The idle speed control motor (ISC) is mounted on the carburetor

Electronic Spark Timing (EST)

All models use EST. The EST distributor, as described in an earlier chapter, contains no vacuum or centrifugal advance mechanism and uses a seven terminal HEI module. It has four wires going to a four terminal connector in addition to the connectors normally found on HEI distributors. A reference pulse, indicating engine rpm is sent to the ECM. The ECM determines the proper spark advance for the engine operating conditions and then sends an 'EST' pulse back to the distributor.

Under most normal operating conditions, the ECM will control the spark advance. However, under certain operating conditions such as cranking or when setting base timing, the distributor is capable of operating without ECM control. This condition is called BYPASS and is determined by the BYPASS lead which runs from the ECM to the distributor. When the BYPASS lead is at the proper voltage (5), the ECM will control the spark. If the lead is grounded or open circuited, the HEI module itself will control the spark. Disconnecting the 4-terminal EST connector will also cause the engine to operate in the BYPASS mode.

Transmission Converter Clutch (TCC)

All models with an automatic transmission use TCC. The ECM controls the converter by means of a solenoid mounted in the transmission. When the vehicle speed reaches a certain level, the ECM energizes the solenoid and allows the torque converter to mechanically couple the transmission to the engine. When the operating conditions indicate that the transmission should operate as a normal fluid coupled transmission, the ECM will de-energize the solenoid. Depressing the brake will also return the transmission to normal automatic operation.

Catalytic Converter

The catalytic converter is a muffler-like container built into the exhaust system to aid in the reduction of exhaust emissions. The catalyst element consists of individual pellets or a honeycomb monolithic substrate coated with a noble metal such as platinum, palladium, rhodium or a combination. When the exhaust gases come into contact with the catalyst, a chemical reaction occurs which will reduce the pollutants into harmless substances like water and carbon dioxide.

There are essentially two types of catalytic converters: an oxidizing type and a three-way type. The oxidizing type requires the addition of oxygen to spur the catalyst into reducing the engine's HC and CO emissions into H_2O and CO_2. The oxidizing catalytic converter, while effectively reducing HC and CO emis-

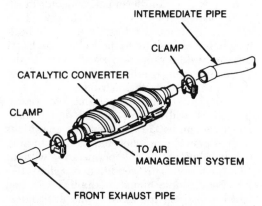

The catalytic converter is upstream of the muffler

INTERMEDIATE PIPE
CLAMP
CATALYTIC CONVERTER
CLAMP
TO AIR MANAGEMENT SYSTEM
FRONT EXHAUST PIPE

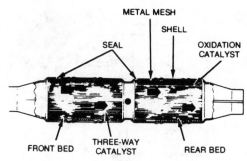

Cutaway view of the typical three-way catalytic converter

METAL MESH
SHELL
SEAL
OXIDATION CATALYST
FRONT BED
THREE-WAY CATALYST
REAR BED

sions, does little, if anything in the way of reducing NO_x emissions. Thus, the three-way catalytic converter.

The three-way converter, unlike the oxidizing type, is capable of reducing HC, CO and NO_x emmissions; all at the same time. In theory, it seems impossible to reduce all three pollutants in one system since the reduction of HC and CO requires the addition of oxygen, while the reduction of NO_x calls for the removal of oxygen. In actuality, the three-way system really can reduce all three pollutants, but only if the amount of oxygen in the exhaust system is precisely controlled. Due to this precise oxygen control requirement, the three-way converter system is used only in conjunction with an oxygen sensor system.

There are no service procedures required for the catalytic converter, although the converter body should be inspected occasionally for damage.

PRECAUTIONS

1. Use only unleaded fuel.
2. Avoid prolonged idling; the engine should run no longer than 20 min. at curb idle and no longer than 10 min. at fast idle.
3. Do not disconnect any of the spark plug leads while the engine is running.
4. Make engine compression checks as quickly as possible.

CATALYST TESTING

At the present time there is no known way to reliably test catalytic converter operation in the field. The only reliable test is a 12 hour and 40 min. "soak" test (CVS) which must be done in a laboratory.

An infrared HC/CO tester is not sensitive enough to measure the higher tailpipe emissions from a failing converter. Thus, a bad converter may allow enough emissions to escape so that the car is no longer in compliance with Federal or state standards, but will still not cause the needle on a tester to move off zero.

The chemical reactions which occur inside a catalytic converter generate a great deal of heat. Most converter problems can be traced to fuel or ignition system problems which cause unusually high emissions. As a result of the increased intensity of the chemical reactions, the converter literally burns itself up.

A completely failed converter might cause a tester to show a slight reading. As a result, it is occasionally possible to detect one of these.

As long as you avoid severe overheating and the use of leaded fuels it is reasonably safe to assume that the converter is working properly. If you are in doubt, take the car to a diagnostic center that has a tester.

Oxygen Sensor

An oxygen sensor is used on all models. The sensor protrudes into the exhaust stream and monitors the oxygen content of the exhaust gases. The difference between the oxygen content of the exhaust gases and that of the outside air generates a voltage signal to the ECM. The ECM monitors this voltage and, depending upon the value of the signal received, issues a command to adjust for a rich or a lean condition.

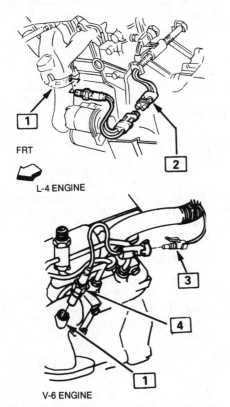

1. Exhaust manifold   3. Terminal (Wiring harness)
2. Engine harness   4. Oxygen sensor

Oxygen sensor mounting

No attempt should ever be made to measure the voltage output of the sensor. The current drain of any conventional voltmeter would be such that it would permanently damage the sensor. No jumpers, test leads or any other electrical connections should ever be made to the sensor. Use these tools ONLY on the ECM side of the wiring harness connector AFTER disconnecting it from the sensor.

REMOVAL AND INSTALLATION

The oxygen sensor must be replaced every 30,000 miles (48,000 km.). The sensor may be difficult to remove when the engine temperature is below 120°F (48°C). Excessive removal force may damage the threads in the exhaust manifold or pipe; follow the removal procedure carefully.

1. Locate the oxygen sensor. It protrudes from the center of the exhaust manifold at the front of the engine compartment (it looks somewhat like a spark plug).

2. Disconnect the electrical connector from the oxygen sensor.

3. Spray a commercial heat riser solvent onto the sensor threads and allow it to soak in for at least five minutes.

4. Carefully unscrew and remove the sensor.

5. To install, first coat the new sensor's threads with G.M. anti-seize compound No. 5613695 or the equivalent. This is *not* a conventional anti-seize paste. The use of a regular compound may electrically insulate the sensor, rendering it inoperative. You must coat the threads with an electrically conductive anti-seize compound.

6. Installation torque is 30 ft. lbs. (42 Nm.). Do not overtighten.

7. Reconnect the electrical connector. Be careful not to damage the electrical pigtail. Check the sensor boot for proper fit and installation.

Early Fuel Evaporation (EFE)

All models are equipped with this system to reduce engine warm-up time, improve driveability and reduce emissions. The system is electric and uses a ceramic heater grid located underneath the primary bore of the carburetor as part of the carburetor insulator/gasket. When the ignition switch is turned on and the engine coolant temperature is low, voltage is applied to the EFE relay by the ECM. The EFE relay in turn energizes the heater grid. When the coolant temperature increases, the ECM de-energizes the relay which will then "shut off" the EFE heater.

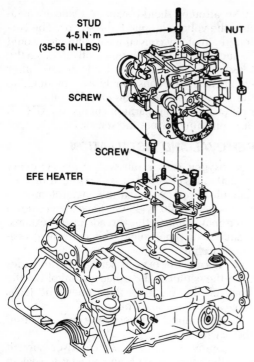

EFE heater grid

REMOVAL AND INSTALLATION

1. Remove the air cleaner and disconnect the negative battery cable.
2. Disconnect all electrical, vacuum and fuel connections from the carburetor.
3. Disconnect the EFE heater electrical lead.
4. Remove the carburetor as detailed later in this chapter.
5. Life off the EFE heater grid.
6. Installation is in the reverse order of removal.

EFE HEATER RELAY REPLACEMENT

1. Disconnect the negative battery cable.
2. Remove the retaining bracket.
3. Tag and disconnect all electrical connections.

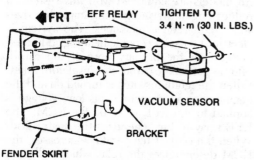

Heater relay installation details

4. Unscrew the retaining bolts and remove the relay.
5. Installation is in the reverse order of removal.

Exhaust Gas Recirculation (EGR)

All gasoline models are equipped with this system, which consists of a metering valve, a vacuum line to the carburetor or intake manifold, and cast-in exhaust passages in the intake manifold. The EGR valve is controlled by vacuum, and opens and closes in response to the vacuum signals to admit exhaust gases into the air/fuel mixture. The exhaust gases lower peak combustion temperatures, reducing the formation of NO_x. The valve is closed at idle and wide open throttle, but is open between the two extreme positions.

There are actually two types of EGR systems: Vacuum Modulated and Exhaust Back Pressure Modulated. The principle of both systems is the same; the only difference is in the method used to control how far the EGR valve opens.

In the Vacuum Modulated system, the amount of exhaust gas admitted into the intake manifold depends on a ported vacuum signal. A ported vacuum signal is one taken from the carburetor above the throttle plates; thus, the vacuum signal (amount of vacuum) is dependent on how far the throttle plates are opened. When the throttle is closed (idle or deceleration) there is no vacuum signal. Thus, the EGR valve is closed, and no exhaust gas enters the intake manifold. As the throttle is opened, a vacuum is produced, which opens the EGR valve, admitting exhaust gas into the intake manifold.

In the Exhaust Back Pressure Modulated system, a transducer is installed in the EGR valve body. The vacuum is still ported vacuum, but the transducer uses exhaust gas pressure to control an air bleed within the valve to modify this vacuum signal.

SYSTEM CHECKS

1. Check to see if the EGR valve diaphragm moves freely. Use your finger to reach up under the valve and push on the diaphragm. If it doesn't move freely, the valve should be replaced. The use of a mirror will aid the inspection process.

CAUTION: *If the engine is hot, wear a glove to protect your hand.*

2. Install a vacuum gauge into the vacuum line between the EGR valve and the carburetor. Start the engine and allow it to reach operating temperature.

3. With the car in either Park or Neutral,

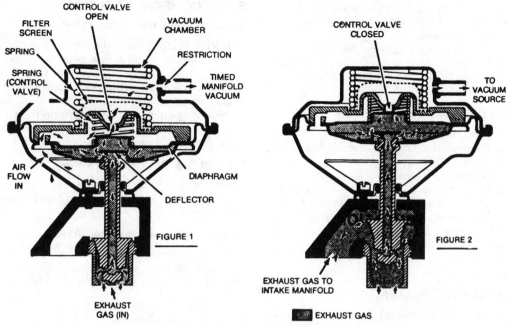

Exhaust gas modulated EGR valve

increase the engine speed until at least 5 in. Hg. is showing on the gauge.

4. Remove the vacuum hose from the EGR valve. The diaphragm should move downward (valve closed). The engine speed should increase.

5. Install the vacuum hose and watch for the EGR valve to open (diaphragm moving upward). The engine speed should decrease to its former level, indcating exhaust recirculation.

If the diaphragm doesn't move:

1. Check engine vacuum; it should be at least 5 in. Hg. with the throttle open and engine running.

2. Check to see that the engine is at normal operating temperature.

3. Check for vacuum at the EGR hose. If

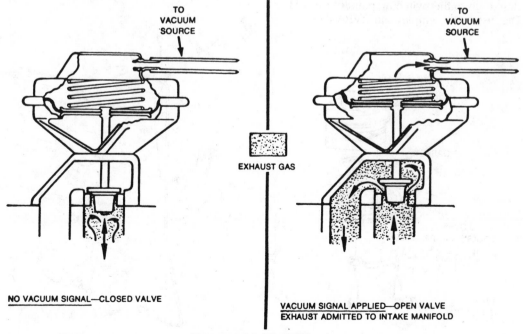

Vacuum modulated EGR valve

no vacuum is present, check the hose for leaks, breaks, kinks, improper connections, etc., and replace as necessary.

If the diaphragm moves, but the engine speed doesn't change, check the EGR passages in the intake manifold for blockage.

REMOVAL AND INSTALLATION

1. Disconnect the vacuum hose.
2. Remove the bolts or nuts holding the EGR valve to the engine.
3. Remove the valve.
4. Clean the mounting surfaces before replacing the valve. Install the valve onto the manifold, using a new gasket. Be sure to install the spacer, if used. Connect the vacuum hose and check the valve operation.

Diesel EGR System

The diesel EGR systems work in the same basic manner as gasoline engine EGR systems: exhaust gases are introduced into the combustion chambers to reduce combustion temperatures, and thus lower the formation of nitrogen oxides (NO_x).

Vacuum from the vacuum pump is modulated by the Vacuum Regulator Valve (VRV) mounted on the injection pump.

The amount of EGR valve opening is further modulated by a Vacuum Modulator Valve (VMV). The VMV allows for an increase in vacuum to the EGR valve as the throttle is closed, up to the switching point of the VMV. The system also employs an RVR valve.

BASIC COMPONENT TESTING

Vacuum Regulator Valve (VRV)

The VRV is attached to the side of the injection pump and regulates vacuum in proportion to throttle angle. Vacuum from the vacuum pump is supplied to port A and vacuum at port B (see illustration) is reduced as the throttle is opened. At closed throttle the vacuum is 15 in. Hg; at half throttle, 6 in.; at wide open throttle there should be zero vacuum.

Exhaust Gas Recirculation Valve

Apply vacuum to the vacuum port. The valve should be fully open at 12 in. Hg and closed below 6 in.

Response Vacuum Reducer (RVR)

Connect a vacuum gauge to the port marked "To EGR valve or TCC solenoid." Connect a hand operated vacuum pump to the VRV port.

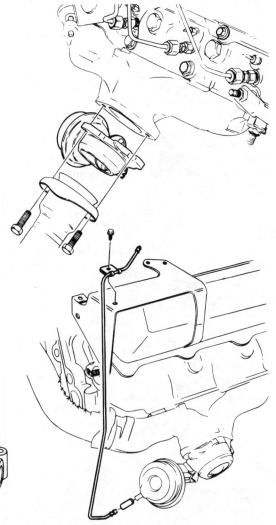

EGR VALVE

GASKET

LOCK-BEND OVER
AFTER BOLTS ARE TORQUED

24 N·m
(17 FT. LBS.)

EGR valve—V6 diesel

Exhaust pressure regulator valve (EPR)

Draw 15 in. of vacuum on the pump and the reading on the vacuum gauge should be lower than the vacuum pump reading by .75 in.

Exhaust Pressure Regulator Valve

Apply vacuum to the vacuum port of the valve. The valve should be fully closed at 12 in. Hg and open below 6 in.

Vacuum Modulator Valve (VMV)

To test the VMV, block the drive wheels, and apply the parking brake. With the shift lever in Park, start the engine and run at a slow idle. Connect a vacuum gauge to the hose that connects to the port marked "MAN." There should be at least 14 in. Hg of vacuum. If not, check the vacuum pump, VRV, RVR, solenoid, and all connecting hoses. Reconnect the hose to the "MAN" port. Connect a vacuum gauge to the "DIST" port on the VMV. The vacuum reading should be 12 in. Hg except on High Altitude cars, which should be 9 in. Hg.

GASOLINE FUEL SYSTEM

Fuel Pump

Mechanical fuel pumps are used on both the four cylinder and V6 engines. The V6 engine pump has a vapor return line for both emission control purposes and to reduce the likelihood of vapor lock.

TESTING THE FUEL PUMP

To determine if the pump is in good condition, tests for both volume and pressure should be performed. The tests are made with the pump installed, and the engine at normal operating temperature and idle speed. Never replace a fuel pump without first performing these simple tests.

Be sure that the fuel filter has been changed

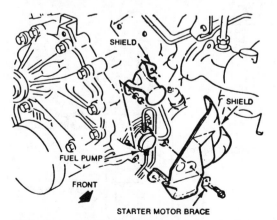

V6 fuel pump installation; four cylinder similar

at the specified interval. If in doubt, install a new filter first.

Pressure Test

1. Disconnect the fuel line at the carburetor and connect a fuel pump pressure gauge. Fill the carburetor float bowl with gasoline.
2. Start the engine and check the pressure with the engine at idle. If the pump has a vapor return hose, squeeze it off so that an accurate reading can be obtained. Pressure for the four cylinder engine should be 6.5–8.0 psi; for the V6, it should measure 6.0–7.5 psi.
3. If the pressure is incorrect, replace the pump. If it is ok, go on to the volume test.

Volume Test

4. Disconnect the pressure gauge. Run the fuel line into a graduated container.
5. Run the engine at idle until one pint of gasoline has been pumped. One pint should be delivered in 30 seconds or less. There is normally enough fuel in the carburetor float bowl to perform this test, but refill it if necessary.
6. If the delivery rate is below the minimum, check the lines for restrictions or leaks, then replace the pump.

REMOVAL AND INSTALLATION

All Models

The fuel pump is located at the center rear of the four cylinder engine, and at the right front of the V6.

1. Disconnect the negative cable at the battery. Raise and support the car.
2. On models with the V6 engine, remove the pump shields and the oil filter, if so equipped.
3. Disconnect the inlet hose from the pump. Disconnect the vapor return hose, if equipped.
4. Loosen the fuel line at the carburetor, then disconnect the outlet pipe from the pump.
5. Remove the two mounting bolts and remove the pump from the engine.
6. To install, place a new gasket on the pump and install the pump on the engine. Tighten the two mounting bolts alternately and evenly.
7. Install the pump outlet pipe. This is easier if the pipe is disconnected from the carburetor. Tighten the fitting while backing up the pump nut with another wrench. Install the pipe at the carburetor.
8. Install the inlet and vapor hoses. Install the shields (if so equipped) and oil filter on the V6 engine. Lower the car, connect the negative battery cable, start the engine, and check for leaks.

Carburetor

The Rochester E2SE is used on all 1982 and later A-body cars. It is a two barrel, two stage carburetor of downdraft design used in conjunction with the Computer Command Control system of fuel control. The carburetor has special design features for optimum air/fuel mixture control during all ranges of engine operation.

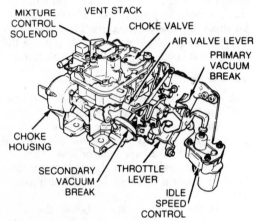

MIXTURE CONTROL SOLENOID
VENT STACK
CHOKE VALVE
AIR VALVE LEVER
PRIMARY VACUUM BREAK
CHOKE HOUSING
SECONDARY VACUUM BREAK
THROTTLE LEVER
IDLE SPEED CONTROL

Rochester E2SE carburetor

MODEL IDENTIFICATION

General Motors Rochester carburetors are identified by their model code. The first number indicates the number of barrels, while one of the last letters indicates the type of choke used. These are V for the manifold mounted choke coil, C for the choke coil mounted in the carburetor body, and E for electric choke, also mounted on the carburetor. Model codes ending in A indicate an altitude-compensating carburetor.

REMOVAL AND INSTALLATION

1. Remove the air cleaner and gasket.
2. Disconnect the fuel pipe and all vacuum lines.
3. Tag and disconnect all electrical connections.
4. Disconnect the downshift cable.
5. If equipped with cruise control, disconnect the linkage.
6. Unscrew the carburetor mounting bolts and remove the carburetor.
7. Inspect the EFE heater for damage. Be sure that the throttle body and EFE mating surfaces are clean.
8. Install the carburetor and tighten the nuts alternately to the proper specifications.
9. Installation of the remaining components is in the reverse order of removal.

OVERHAUL

Efficient carburetion depends greatly on careful cleaning and inspection during overhaul, since dirt, gum, water, or varnish in or on the carburetor parts are often responsible for poor performance.

Overhaul your carburetor in a clean, dust-free area. Carefully disassemble the carburetor, referring often to the exploded views and directions packaged with the rebuilding kit. Keep all similar and look-alike parts segregated during disassembly and cleaning to avoid accidental interchange during assembly. Make a note of all jet sizes.

When the carburetor is disassembled, wash all parts (except diaphragms, electric choke units, pump plunger, and any other plastic, leather, fiber, or rubber parts) in clean carburetor solvent. Do not leave parts in the solvent any longer than is necessary to sufficiently loosen the deposits. Excessive cleaning may

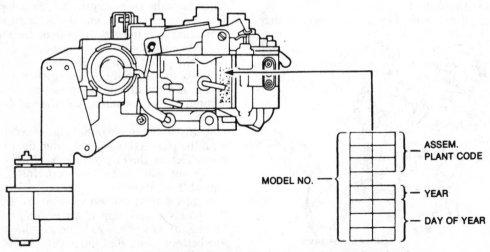

MODEL NO. —
ASSEM. PLANT CODE
YEAR
DAY OF YEAR

The carburetor identification number is stamped on the float bowl

CHILTON'S
FUEL ECONOMY
& TUNE-UP TIPS

Tune-Up • Spark Plug Diagnosis • Emission Controls

Fuel System • Cooling System • Tires and Wheels

General Maintenance

CHILTON'S FUEL ECONOMY & TUNE-UP TIPS

Fuel economy is important to everyone, no matter what kind of vehicle you drive. The maintenance-minded motorist can save both money and fuel using these tips and the periodic maintenance and tune-up procedures in this Repair and Tune-Up Guide.

There are more than 130,000,000 cars and trucks registered for private use in the United States. Each travels an average of 10-12,000 miles per year, and, in total they consume close to 70 billion gallons of fuel each year. This represents nearly ⅔ of the oil imported by the United States each year. The Federal government's goal is to reduce consumption 10% by 1985. A variety of methods are either already in use or under serious consideration, and they all affect your driving and the cars you will drive. In addition to "down-sizing", the auto industry is using or investigating the use of electronic fuel delivery, electronic engine controls and alternative engines for use in smaller and lighter vehicles, among other alternatives to meet the federally mandated Corporate Average Fuel Economy (CAFE) of 27.5 mpg by 1985. The government, for its part, is considering rationing, mandatory driving curtailments and tax increases on motor vehicle fuel in an effort to reduce consumption. The government's goal of a 10% reduction could be realized — and further government regulation avoided — if every private vehicle could use just 1 less gallon of fuel per week.

How Much Can You Save?

Tests have proven that almost anyone can make at least a 10% reduction in fuel consumption through regular maintenance and tune-ups. When a major manufacturer of spark plugs sur-

TUNE-UP

1. Check the cylinder compression to be sure the engine will really benefit from a tune-up and that it is capable of producing good fuel economy. A tune-up will be wasted on an engine in poor mechanical condition.

2. Replace spark plugs regularly. New spark plugs alone can increase fuel economy 3%.

3. Be sure the spark plugs are the correct type (heat range) for your vehicle. See the Tune-Up Specifications.

Heat range refers to the spark plug's ability to conduct heat away from the firing end. It must conduct the heat away in an even pattern to avoid becoming a source of pre-ignition, yet it must also operate hot enough to burn off conductive deposits that could cause misfiring.

The heat range is usually indicated by a number on the spark plug, part of the manufacturer's designation for each individual spark plug. The numbers in bold-face indicate the heat range in each manufacturer's identification system.

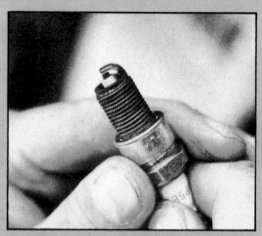

Periodically, check the spark plugs to be sure they are firing efficiently. They are excellent indicators of the internal condition of your engine.

Manufacturer	Typical Designation
AC	R **45** TS
Bosch (old)	WA **145** T30
Bosch (new)	HR **8** Y
Champion	RBL **15** Y
Fram/Autolite	**4**15
Mopar	P-**62** PR
Motorcraft	BRF-**42**
NGK	BP **5** ES-15
Nippondenso	W **16** EP
Prestolite	14GR **5** 2A

On AC, Bosch (new), Champion, Fram/Autolite, Mopar, Motorcraft and Prestolite, a higher number indicates a hotter plug. On Bosch (old), NGK and Nippondenso, a higher number indicates a colder plug.

4. Make sure the spark plugs are properly gapped. See the Tune-Up Specifications in this book.

5. Be sure the spark plugs are firing efficiently. The illustrations on the next 2 pages show you how to "read" the firing end of the spark plug.

6. Check the ignition timing and set it to specifications. Tests show that almost all cars

veyed over 6,000 cars nationwide, they found that a tune-up, on cars that needed one, increased fuel economy over 11%. Replacing worn plugs alone, accounted for a 3% increase. The same test also revealed that 8 out of every 10 vehicles will have some maintenance deficiency that will directly affect fuel economy, emissions or performance. Most of this mileage-robbing neglect could be prevented with regular maintenance.

Modern engines require that all of the functioning systems operate properly for maximum efficiency. A malfunction anywhere wastes fuel. You can keep your vehicle running as efficiently and economically as possible, by being aware of your vehicles operating and performance characteristics. If your vehicle suddenly develops performance or fuel economy problems it could be due to one or more of the following:

PROBLEM	POSSIBLE CAUSE
Engine Idles Rough	Ignition timing, idle mixture, vacuum leak or something amiss in the emission control system.
Hesitates on Acceleration	Dirty carburetor or fuel filter, improper accelerator pump setting, ignition timing or fouled spark plugs.
Starts Hard or Fails to Start	Worn spark plugs, improperly set automatic choke, ice (or water) in fuel system.
Stalls Frequently	Automatic choke improperly adjusted and possible dirty air filter or fuel filter.
Performs Sluggishly	Worn spark plugs, dirty fuel or air filter, ignition timing or automatic choke out of adjustment.

Check spark plug wires on conventional point type ignition for cracks by bending them in a loop around your finger.

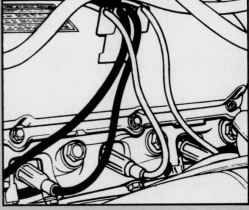

Be sure that spark plug wires leading to adjacent cylinders do not run too close together. (Photo courtesy Champion Spark Plug Co.)

have incorrect ignition timing by more than 2°.

7. If your vehicle does not have electronic ignition, check the points, rotor and cap as specified.

8. Check the spark plug wires (used with conventional point-type ignitions) for cracks and burned or broken insulation by bending them in a loop around your finger. Cracked wires decrease fuel efficiency by failing to deliver full voltage to the spark plugs. One misfiring spark plug can cost you as much as 2 mpg.

9. Check the routing of the plug wires. Misfiring can be the result of spark plug leads to adjacent cylinders running parallel to each other and too close together. One wire tends to pick up voltage from the other causing it to fire "out of time".

10. Check all electrical and ignition circuits for voltage drop and resistance.

11. Check the distributor mechanical and/or vacuum advance mechanisms for proper functioning. The vacuum advance can be checked by twisting the distributor plate in the opposite direction of rotation. It should spring back when released.

12. Check and adjust the valve clearance on engines with mechanical lifters. The clearance should be slightly loose rather than too tight.

SPARK PLUG DIAGNOSIS

Normal

APPEARANCE: This plug is typical of one operating normally. The insulator nose varies from a light tan to grayish color with slight electrode wear. The presence of slight deposits is normal on used plugs and will have no adverse effect on engine performance. The spark plug heat range is correct for the engine and the engine is running normally.

CAUSE: Properly running engine.

RECOMMENDATION: Before reinstalling this plug, the electrodes should be cleaned and filed square. Set the gap to specifications. If the plug has been in service for more than 10-12,000 miles, the entire set should probably be replaced with a fresh set of the same heat range.

Oil Deposits

APPEARANCE: The firing end of the plug is covered with a wet, oily coating.

CAUSE: The problem is poor oil control. On high mileage engines, oil is leaking past the rings or valve guides into the combustion chamber. A common cause is also a plugged PCV valve, and a ruptured fuel pump diaphragm can also cause this condition. Oil fouled plugs such as these are often found in new or recently overhauled engines, before normal oil control is achieved, and can be cleaned and reinstalled.

RECOMMENDATION: A hotter spark plug may temporarily relieve the problem, but the engine is probably in need of work.

Incorrect Heat Range

APPEARANCE: The effects of high temperature on a spark plug are indicated by clean white, often blistered insulator. This can also be accompanied by excessive wear of the electrode, and the absence of deposits.

CAUSE: Check for the correct spark plug heat range. A plug which is too hot for the engine can result in overheating. A car operated mostly at high speeds can require a colder plug. Also check ignition timing, cooling system level, fuel mixture and leaking intake manifold.

RECOMMENDATION: If all ignition and engine adjustments are known to be correct, and no other malfunction exists, install spark plugs one heat range colder.

Photos Courtesy Champion Spark Plug Co.

Carbon Deposits

APPEARANCE: Carbon fouling is easily identified by the presence of dry, soft, black, sooty deposits.

CAUSE: Changing the heat range can often lead to carbon fouling, as can prolonged slow, stop-and-start driving. If the heat range is correct, carbon fouling can be attributed to a rich fuel mixture, sticking choke, clogged air cleaner, worn breaker points, retarded timing or low compression. If only one or two plugs are carbon fouled, check for corroded or cracked wires on the affected plugs. Also look for cracks in the distributor cap between the towers of affected cylinders.

RECOMMENDATION: After the problem is corrected, these plugs can be cleaned and reinstalled if not worn severely.

MMT Fouled

APPEARANCE: Spark plugs fouled by MMT (Methycyclopentadienyl Maganese Tricarbonyl) have reddish, rusty appearance on the insulator and side electrode.

CAUSE: MMT is an anti-knock additive in gasoline used to replace lead. During the combustion process, the MMT leaves a reddish deposit on the insulator and side electrode.

RECOMMENDATION: No engine malfunction is indicated and the deposits will not affect plug performance any more than lead deposits (see Ash Deposits). MMT fouled plugs can be cleaned, regapped and reinstalled.

High Speed Glazing

APPEARANCE: Glazing appears as shiny coating on the plug, either yellow or tan in color.

CAUSE: During hard, fast acceleration, plug temperatures rise suddenly. Deposits from normal combustion have no chance to fluff-off; instead, they melt on the insulator forming an electrically conductive coating which causes misfiring.

RECOMMENDATION: Glazed plugs are not easily cleaned. They should be replaced with a fresh set of plugs of the correct heat range. If the condition recurs, using plugs with a heat range one step colder may cure the problem.

Ash (Lead) Deposits

APPEARANCE: Ash deposits are characterized by light brown or white colored deposits crusted on the side or center electrodes. In some cases it may give the plug a rusty appearance.

CAUSE: Ash deposits are normally derived from oil or fuel additives burned during normal combustion. Normally they are harmless, though excessive amounts can cause misfiring. If deposits are excessive in short mileage, the valve guides may be worn.

RECOMMENDATION: Ash-fouled plugs can be cleaned, gapped and reinstalled.

Detonation

APPEARANCE: Detonation is usually characterized by a broken plug insulator.

CAUSE: A portion of the fuel charge will begin to burn spontaneously, from the increased heat following ignition. The explosion that results applies extreme pressure to engine components, frequently damaging spark plugs and pistons.

Detonation can result by over-advanced ignition timing, inferior gasoline (low octane) lean air/fuel mixture, poor carburetion, engine lugging or an increase in compression ratio due to combustion chamber deposits or engine modification.

RECOMMENDATION: Replace the plugs after correcting the problem.

EMISSION CONTROLS

13. Be aware of the general condition of the emission control system. It contributes to reduced pollution and should be serviced regularly to maintain efficient engine operation.

14. Check all vacuum lines for dried, cracked or brittle conditions. Something as simple as a leaking vacuum hose can cause poor performance and loss of economy.

15. Avoid tampering with the emission control system. Attempting to improve fuel econ-

FUEL SYSTEM

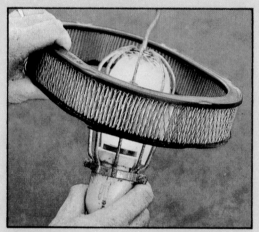

Check the air filter with a light behind it. If you can see light through the filter it can be reused.

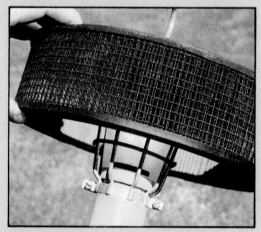

Extremely clogged filters should be discarded and replaced with a new one.

18. Replace the air filter regularly. A dirty air filter richens the air/fuel mixture and can increase fuel consumption as much as 10%. Tests show that ⅓ of all vehicles have air filters in need of replacement.

19. Replace the fuel filter at least as often as recommended.

20. Set the idle speed and carburetor mixture to specifications.

21. Check the automatic choke. A sticking or malfunctioning choke wastes gas.

22. During the summer months, adjust the automatic choke for a leaner mixture which will produce faster engine warm-ups.

COOLING SYSTEM

29. Be sure all accessory drive belts are in good condition. Check for cracks or wear.

30. Adjust all accessory drive belts to proper tension.

31. Check all hoses for swollen areas, worn spots, or loose clamps.

32. Check coolant level in the radiator or expansion tank.

33. Be sure the thermostat is operating properly. A stuck thermostat delays engine warm-up and a cold engine uses nearly twice as much fuel as a warm engine.

34. Drain and replace the engine coolant at least as often as recommended. Rust and scale

TIRES & WHEELS

38. Check the tire pressure often with a pencil type gauge. Tests by a major tire manufacturer show that 90% of all vehicles have at least 1 tire improperly inflated. Better mileage can be achieved by over-inflating tires, but never exceed the maximum inflation pressure on the side of the tire.

39. If possible, install radial tires. Radial tires deliver as much as ½ mpg more than bias belted tires.

40. Avoid installing super-wide tires. They only create extra rolling resistance and decrease fuel mileage. Stick to the manufacturer's recommendations.

41. Have the wheels properly balanced.

omy by tampering with emission controls is more likely to worsen fuel economy than improve it. Emission control changes on modern engines are not readily reversible.

16. Clean (or replace) the EGR valve and lines as recommended.

17. Be sure that all vacuum lines and hoses are reconnected properly after working under the hood. An unconnected or misrouted vacuum line can wreak havoc with engine performance.

---

23. Check for fuel leaks at the carburetor, fuel pump, fuel lines and fuel tank. Be sure all lines and connections are tight.

24. Periodically check the tightness of the carburetor and intake manifold attaching nuts and bolts. These are a common place for vacuum leaks to occur.

25. Clean the carburetor periodically and lubricate the linkage.

26. The condition of the tailpipe can be an excellent indicator of proper engine combustion. After a long drive at highway speeds, the inside of the tailpipe should be a light grey in color. Black or soot on the insides indicates an overly rich mixture.

27. Check the fuel pump pressure. The fuel pump may be supplying more fuel than the engine needs.

28. Use the proper grade of gasoline for your engine. Don't try to compensate for knocking or "pinging" by advancing the ignition timing. This practice will only increase plug temperature and the chances of detonation or pre-ignition with relatively little performance gain.

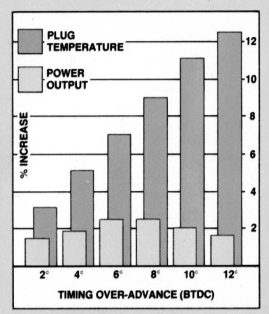

Increasing ignition timing past the specified setting results in a drastic increase in spark plug temperature with increased chance of detonation or preignition. Performance increase is considerably less. (Photo courtesy Champion Spark Plug Co.)

---

that form in the engine should be flushed out to allow the engine to operate at peak efficiency.

35. Clean the radiator of debris that can decrease cooling efficiency.

36. Install a flex-type or electric cooling fan, if you don't have a clutch type fan. Flex fans use curved plastic blades to push more air at low speeds when more cooling is needed; at high speeds the blades flatten out for less resistance. Electric fans only run when the engine temperature reaches a predetermined level.

37. Check the radiator cap for a worn or cracked gasket. If the cap does not seal properly, the cooling system will not function properly.

---

42. Be sure the front end is correctly aligned. A misaligned front end actually has wheels going in different directions. The increased drag can reduce fuel economy by .3 mpg.

43. Correctly adjust the wheel bearings. Wheel bearings that are adjusted too tight increase rolling resistance.

Check tire pressures regularly with a reliable pocket type gauge. Be sure to check the pressure on a cold tire.

GENERAL MAINTENANCE

Check the fluid levels (particularly engine oil) on a regular basis. Be sure to check the oil for grit, water or other contamination.

A vacuum gauge is another excellent indicator of internal engine condition and can also be installed in the dash as a mileage indicator.

44. Periodically check the fluid levels in the engine, power steering pump, master cylinder, automatic transmission and drive axle.

45. Change the oil at the recommended interval and change the filter at every oil change. Dirty oil is thick and causes extra friction between moving parts, cutting efficiency and increasing wear. A worn engine requires more frequent tune-ups and gets progressively worse fuel economy. In general, use the lightest viscosity oil for the driving conditions you will encounter.

46. Use the recommended viscosity fluids in the transmission and axle.

47. Be sure the battery is fully charged for fast starts. A slow starting engine wastes fuel.

48. Be sure battery terminals are clean and tight.

49. Check the battery electrolyte level and add distilled water if necessary.

50. Check the exhaust system for crushed pipes, blockages and leaks.

51. Adjust the brakes. Dragging brakes or brakes that are not releasing create increased drag on the engine.

52. Install a vacuum gauge or miles-per-gallon gauge. These gauges visually indicate engine vacuum in the intake manifold. High vacuum = good mileage and low vacuum = poorer mileage. The gauge can also be an excellent indicator of internal engine conditions.

53. Be sure the clutch is properly adjusted. A slipping clutch wastes fuel.

54. Check and periodically lubricate the heat control valve in the exhaust manifold. A sticking or inoperative valve prevents engine warm-up and wastes gas.

55. Keep accurate records to check fuel economy over a period of time. A sudden drop in fuel economy may signal a need for tune-up or other maintenance.

remove the special finish from the float bowl and choke valve bodies, leaving these parts unfit for service. Rinse all parts in clean solvent and blow them dry with compressed air or allow them to air dry. Wipe clean all cork, plastic, leather, and fiber parts with a clean, lint-free cloth.

Blow out all passages and jets with compressed air and be sure that there are no restrictions or blockages. Never use wire or similar tools to clean jets, fuel passages, or air bleeds. Clean all jets and valves separately to avoid accidental interchange.

Check all parts for wear or damage. If wear or damage is found, replace the defective parts. Especially check the following:

1. Check the float needle and seat for wear. If wear is found, replace the complete assembly.

2. Check the float hinge pin for wear and the float(s) for dents or distortion. Replace the float if fuel has leaked into it.

3. Check the throttle and choke shaft bores for wear or an out-of-round condition. Damage or wear to the throttle arm, shaft, or shaft bore will often require replacement of the throttle body. These parts require a close tolerance of fit; wear may allow air leakage, which could affect starting and idling.

NOTE: *Throttle shafts and bushings are not included in overhaul kits. They can be purchased separately.*

4. Inspect the idle mixture adjusting needles for burrs or grooves. Any such condition requires replacement of the needle, since you will not be able to obtain a satisfactory idle.

5. Test the accelerator pump check valves. They should pass air one way but not the other. Test for proper seating by blowing and sucking on the valve. Replace the valve check ball and spring as necessary. If the valve is satisfactory, wash the valve parts again to remove breath moisture.

6. Check the bowl cover for warped surfaces with a straightedge.

7. Closely inspect the accelerator pump plunger for wear and damage, replacing as necessary.

8. After the carburetor is assembled, check the choke valve for freedom of operation.

Carburetor overhaul kits are recommended for each overhaul. These kits contain all gaskets and new parts to replace those which deteriorate most rapidly. Failure to replace all parts supplied with the kit (especially gaskets) can result in poor performance later.

Some carburetor manufacturers supply overhaul kits for three basic types: minor repair; major repair; and gasket kits. Basically, they contain the following:

Minor Repair Kits:
• All gaskets
• Float needle valve
• All diagrams
• Spring for the pump diaphragm

Major Repair Kits:
• All jets and gaskets
• All diaphragms
• Float needle valve
• Pump ball valve
• Float
• Complete intermediate rod
• Intermediate pump lever
• Some cover hold-down screws and washers

Gasket Kits:
All gaskets

After cleaning and checking all components, reassemble the carburetor, using new parts and referring to the exploded view. When reassembling, make sure that all screws and jets are tight in their seats, but do not overtighten as the tips will be distorted. Tighten all screws gradually, in rotation. Do not tighten needle valves into their seats; uneven jetting will result. Always use new gaskets. Be sure to adjust the float level when reassembling.

PRELIMINARY CHECKS

The following should be observed before attempting any adjustments.

1. Thoroughly warm the engine. If the engine is cold, be sure that it reaches operating temperature.

2. Check the torque of all carburetor mounting nuts and assembly screws. Also check the intake manifold-to-cylinder head bolts. If air is leaking at any of these points, any attempts at adjustment will inevitably lead to frustration.

3. Check the manifold heat control valve (if used) to be sure that it is free.

4. Check and adjust the choke as necessary.

5. Adjust the idle speed and mixture. If the mixture screws are capped, don't adjust them unless all other causes of rough idle have been eliminated. If any adjustments are performed that might possibly change the idle speed or mixture, adjust the idle and mixture again when you are finished.

Before you make any carburetor adjustments make sure that the engine is in tune. Many problems which are thought to be carburetor-related can be traced to an engine which is simply out-of-tune. Any trouble in these areas will have symptoms like those of carburetor problems.

FLOAT ADJUSTMENT

1. Remove the air horn from the throttle body.

2. Use your fingers to hold the retainer in place, and to push the float down into light contact with the needle.

3. Measure the distance from the toe of the float (furthest from the hinge) to the top of the carburetor (gasket removed).

4. To adjust, remove the float and gently bend the arm to specification. After adjustment, check the float alignment in the chamber.

PUMP ADJUSTMENT

E2SE carburetors have a non-adjustable pump lever. No adjustments are either necessary or possible.

FAST IDLE ADJUSTMENT

1. Set the ignition timing and curb idle speed, and disconnect and plug hoses as directed on the emission control decal.

2. Place the fast idle screw on the highest step of the cam.

3. Start the engine and adjust the engine speed to specification with the fast idle screw.

CHOKE COIL LEVER ADJUSTMENT

1. Remove the three retaining screws and remove the choke cover and coil. On models with a riveted choke cover, drill out the three rivets and remove the cover and choke coil.

NOTE: *A choke stat cover retainer kit is required for reassembly.*

2. Place the fast idle screw on the high step of the cam.

3. Close the choke by pushing in on the intermediate choke lever.

4. Insert a drill or gauge of the specified size into the hole in the choke housing. The choke lever in the housing should be up against the side of the gauge.

5. If the lever does not just touch the gauge, bend the intermediate choke rod to adjust.

FAST IDLE CAM (CHOKE ROD) ADJUSTMENT

NOTE: *A special angle gauge should be used. If it is not available, an inch measurement can be made.*

1. Adjust the choke coil lever and fast idle first.

2. Rotate the degree scale until it is zeroed.

3. Close the choke and install the degree scale onto the choke plate. Center the leveling bubble.

4. Rotate the scale so that the specified degree is opposite the scale pointer.

5. Place the fast idle screw on the second step of the cam (against the high step). Close

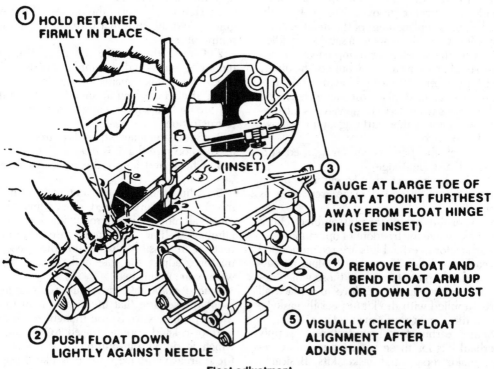

① HOLD RETAINER FIRMLY IN PLACE

(INSET)

③ GAUGE AT LARGE TOE OF FLOAT AT POINT FURTHEST AWAY FROM FLOAT HINGE PIN (SEE INSET)

④ REMOVE FLOAT AND BEND FLOAT ARM UP OR DOWN TO ADJUST

⑤ VISUALLY CHECK FLOAT ALIGNMENT AFTER ADJUSTING

② PUSH FLOAT DOWN LIGHTLY AGAINST NEEDLE

Float adjustment

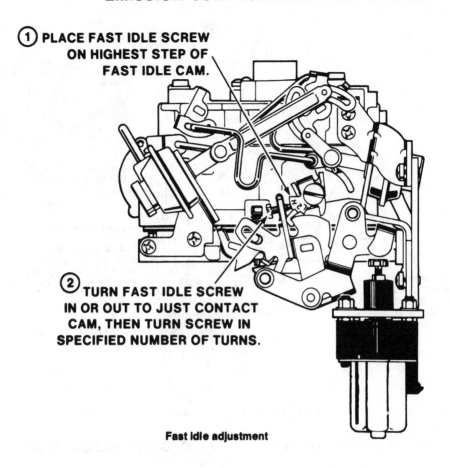

① PLACE FAST IDLE SCREW ON HIGHEST STEP OF FAST IDLE CAM.

② TURN FAST IDLE SCREW IN OR OUT TO JUST CONTACT CAM, THEN TURN SCREW IN SPECIFIED NUMBER OF TURNS.

Fast idle adjustment

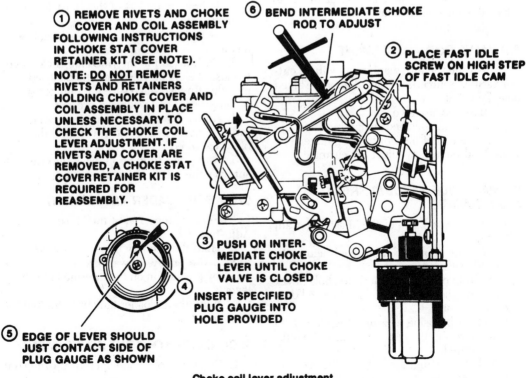

① REMOVE RIVETS AND CHOKE COVER AND COIL ASSEMBLY FOLLOWING INSTRUCTIONS IN CHOKE STAT COVER RETAINER KIT (SEE NOTE).

NOTE: <u>DO NOT</u> REMOVE RIVETS AND RETAINERS HOLDING CHOKE COVER AND COIL ASSEMBLY IN PLACE UNLESS NECESSARY TO CHECK THE CHOKE COIL LEVER ADJUSTMENT. IF RIVETS AND COVER ARE REMOVED, A CHOKE STAT COVER RETAINER KIT IS REQUIRED FOR REASSEMBLY.

⑥ BEND INTERMEDIATE CHOKE ROD TO ADJUST

② PLACE FAST IDLE SCREW ON HIGH STEP OF FAST IDLE CAM

③ PUSH ON INTERMEDIATE CHOKE LEVER UNTIL CHOKE VALVE IS CLOSED

④ INSERT SPECIFIED PLUG GAUGE INTO HOLE PROVIDED

⑤ EDGE OF LEVER SHOULD JUST CONTACT SIDE OF PLUG GAUGE AS SHOWN

Choke coil lever adjustment

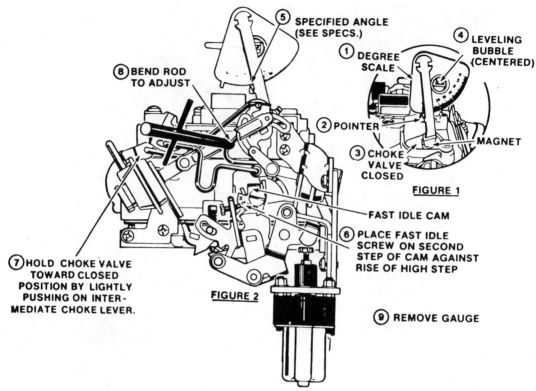

Fast Idle cam (choke rod) adjustment

the choke by pushing in the intermediate lever.

6. Bend the fast idle cam rod at the U to adjust the angle to specifications.

AIR VALVE ROD ADJUSTMENT

1. Seat the vacuum diaphragm with an outside vacuum source. Tape over the purge bleed hole if present.
2. Close the air valve.
3. Insert the specified gauge between the rod and the end of the slot in the plunger.
4. Bend the rod to adjust the clearance.

PRIMARY SIDE VACUUM BREAK ADJUSTMENT

1. Follow Steps 1–4 of the "Fast Idle Cam Adjustment."
2. Seat the choke vacuum diaphragm with an outside vacuum source.
3. Push in on the intermediate choke lever to close the choke valve, and hold closed during adjustment.
4. Adjust by using a ⅛ in. Hex wrench to turn the screw in the rear cover until the bubble is centered.
5. After adjusting, apply RTV silicone sealant over the screw to seal the setting.

SECONDARY VACUUM BREAK ADJUSTMENT

1. Follow Steps 1–4 of the "Fast Idle Cam Adjustment."
2. Seat the choke vacuum diaphragm with an outside vacuum source.
3. Push in on the intermediate choke lever to close the choke valve, and hold closed during adjustment. Make sure the plunger spring is compressed and seated, if present.
4. Adjust by using a ⅛ in. Hex wrench to turn the screw in the rear cover until the bubble is centered.
5. After adjusting, apply RVT silicone sealant over the screw to seal the setting.

CHOKE UNLOADER ADJUSTMENT

1. Follow Steps 1–4 of the "Fast Idle Cam Adjustment."
2. Hold the primary throttle wide open.
3. If the engine is warm, close the choke valve by pushing in on the intermediate choke lever.
4. Bend the unloader tang until the bubble is centered.

SECONDARY LOCKOUT ADJUSTMENT

1. Pull the choke wide open by pushing out on the intermediate choke lever.

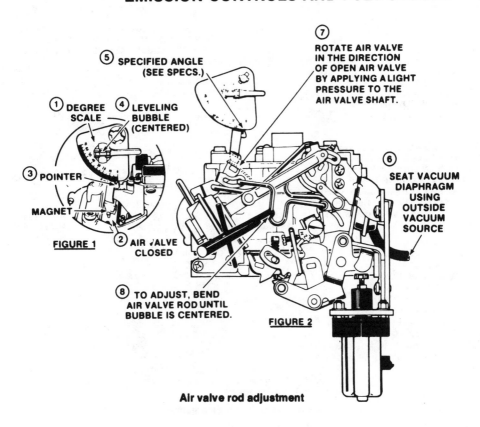

Air valve rod adjustment

NOTE: PRIOR TO ADJUSTMENT, REMOVE VACUUM BREAK FROM CARBURETOR. PLACE BRACKET IN VICE AND, USING SAFETY PRECAUTIONS, GRIND OFF ADJUSTMENT SCREW CAP. REINSTALL VACUUM BREAK.

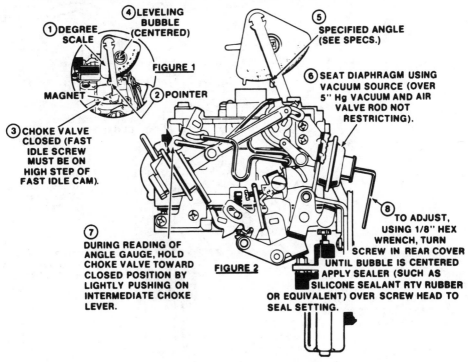

Primary side vacuum break adjustment

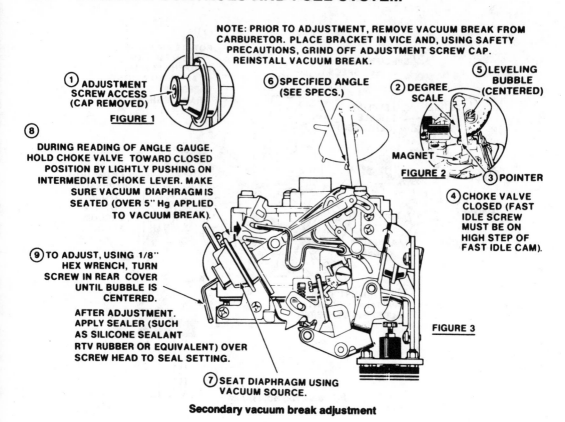

NOTE: PRIOR TO ADJUSTMENT, REMOVE VACUUM BREAK FROM CARBURETOR. PLACE BRACKET IN VICE AND, USING SAFETY PRECAUTIONS, GRIND OFF ADJUSTMENT SCREW CAP. REINSTALL VACUUM BREAK.

① ADJUSTMENT SCREW ACCESS (CAP REMOVED)

FIGURE 1

⑥ SPECIFIED ANGLE (SEE SPECS.)

⑤ LEVELING BUBBLE (CENTERED)

② DEGREE SCALE

MAGNET

FIGURE 2

③ POINTER

⑧ DURING READING OF ANGLE GAUGE, HOLD CHOKE VALVE TOWARD CLOSED POSITION BY LIGHTLY PUSHING ON INTERMEDIATE CHOKE LEVER. MAKE SURE VACUUM DIAPHRAGM IS SEATED (OVER 5" Hg APPLIED TO VACUUM BREAK).

④ CHOKE VALVE CLOSED (FAST IDLE SCREW MUST BE ON HIGH STEP OF FAST IDLE CAM).

⑨ TO ADJUST, USING 1/8" HEX WRENCH, TURN SCREW IN REAR COVER UNTIL BUBBLE IS CENTERED.

AFTER ADJUSTMENT. APPLY SEALER (SUCH AS SILICONE SEALANT RTV RUBBER OR EQUIVALENT) OVER SCREW HEAD TO SEAL SETTING.

FIGURE 3

⑦ SEAT DIAPHRAGM USING VACUUM SOURCE.

Secondary vacuum break adjustment

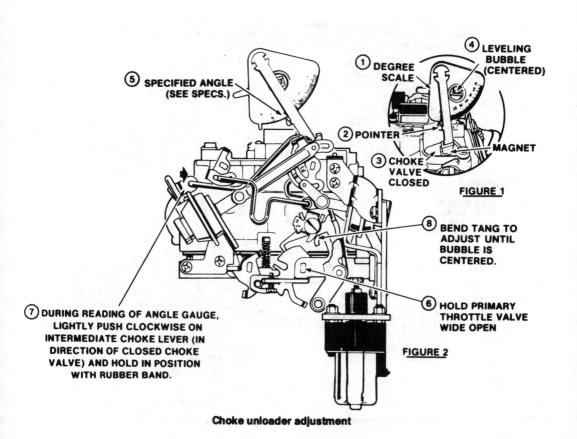

⑤ SPECIFIED ANGLE (SEE SPECS.)

① DEGREE SCALE

④ LEVELING BUBBLE (CENTERED)

② POINTER

③ CHOKE VALVE CLOSED

MAGNET

FIGURE 1

⑧ BEND TANG TO ADJUST UNTIL BUBBLE IS CENTERED.

⑥ HOLD PRIMARY THROTTLE VALVE WIDE OPEN

FIGURE 2

⑦ DURING READING OF ANGLE GAUGE, LIGHTLY PUSH CLOCKWISE ON INTERMEDIATE CHOKE LEVER (IN DIRECTION OF CLOSED CHOKE VALVE) AND HOLD IN POSITION WITH RUBBER BAND.

Choke unloader adjustment

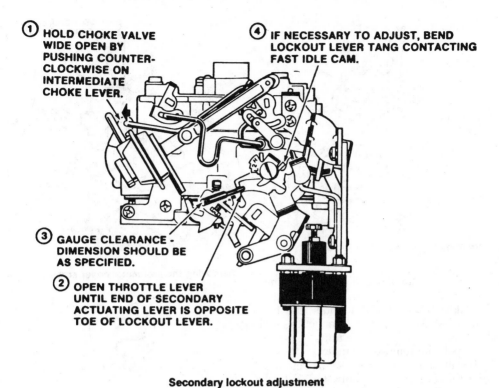

① HOLD CHOKE VALVE WIDE OPEN BY PUSHING COUNTER-CLOCKWISE ON INTERMEDIATE CHOKE LEVER.

④ IF NECESSARY TO ADJUST, BEND LOCKOUT LEVER TANG CONTACTING FAST IDLE CAM.

③ GAUGE CLEARANCE - DIMENSION SHOULD BE AS SPECIFIED.

② OPEN THROTTLE LEVER UNTIL END OF SECONDARY ACTUATING LEVER IS OPPOSITE TOE OF LOCKOUT LEVER.

Secondary lockout adjustment

E2SE Carburetor Specifications

Year	Carburetor Identification	Float Level (in.)	Fast Idle (rpm)	Choke Coil Lever (in.)	Air Valve Rod (deg.)	Primary Vacuum Break (deg./in.)	Secondary Vacuum Break (deg./in.)	Choke Unloader (deg./in.)
82	17082196	5/16	①	.096	—	21°/.117	19°/.103	27°/.157
	17082316	¼	①	.090	10	26°/.149	34°/.211	35°/.203
	17082317	¼	①	.090	10	29°/.171	35°/.220	35°/.220
	17082320	¼	①	.142	10	30°/.179	35°/.220	33°/.203
	17082321	¼	①	.142	10	29°/.171	35°/.220	35°/.220
	17082640	¼	①	.090	10	26°/.149	34°/.211	35°/.220
	17082641	¼	①	.090	10	29°/.171	35°/.220	35°/.220
	17082642	¼	①	.142	10	30°/.179	35°/.220	33°/.203

① See underhood sticker

2. Open the throttle until the end of the secondary actuating lever is opposite the toe of the lockout lever.

3. Gauge clearance between the lockout lever and secondary lever should be as specified.

4. To adjust, bend the lockout lever where it contacts the fast idle cam.

Throttle Body Injection (TBI)

Some models equipped with the 151 cu. in. engine are also equipped with electronic fuel injection. The computer (ECM) is in complete control of fuel metering under all driving conditions. The proper amount of fuel is injected directly into the intake manifold. An electric fuel pump located in the fuel tank maintains a constant fuel pressure between 9 and 13 psi. This electrical fuel pump is controlled by an electric fuel pump relay.

REMOVAL AND INSTALLATION

1. Remove the air cleaner.
2. Disconnect all wiring from the unit.
3. Disconnect the linkage from the unit.

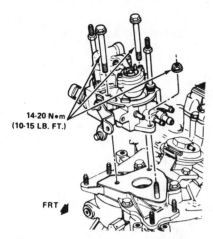

**14-20 N•m
(10-15 LB. FT.)**

FRT

Throttle Body Injection (TBI) unit mounting

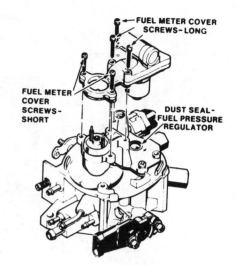

FUEL METER COVER
SCREWS-LONG

FUEL METER
COVER
SCREWS-
SHORT

DUST SEAL-
FUEL PRESSURE
REGULATOR

Removing the fuel meter cover screws

4. Mark and disconnect the vacuum lines from the unit.

5. Follow the CAUTION under the fuel Pressure Test above, then disconnect the fuel feed and return lines from the unit.

6. Unbolt and remove the unit.

7. Installation is the reverse of removal. Torque the TBI attaching bolts to 10–15 ft. lb.; the fuel lines to 19 ft. lb.

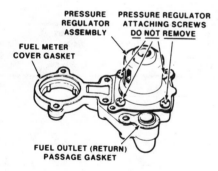

PRESSURE
REGULATOR
ASSEMBLY

PRESSURE REGULATOR
ATTACHING SCREWS
DO NOT REMOVE

FUEL METER
COVER GASKET

FUEL OUTLET (RETURN)
PASSAGE GASKET

Bottom view of the fuel meter cover

FUEL INJECTORS REMOVAL AND INSTALLATION

1. Remove the air cleaner.

2. Disconnect the injector by squeezing the two tabs together and pulling straight up.

3. Remove the fuel meter cover by removing the five attaching bolts; note the positions of the two short bolts.

CAUTION: *Do not remove the four screws securing the pressure regulator to the meter cover. The pressure regulator includes a large spring under heavy tension.*

4. Using a small pliers, grasp the center collar of the injector, between the terminals and remove it with a gentle, upward, twisting motion.

5. Installation is the reverse of removal. Al-

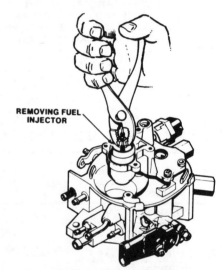

REMOVING FUEL
INJECTOR

Removing a fuel injector from the TBI

ways use new O-ring coated with clean automatic transmission fluid. Make sure all O-rings and steel washers are properly located. Make sure that the injector is fully seated with its locating lug mated with its notch and the electrical terminals parallel with the throttle shaft in the throttle body. Apply thread compound to the first three threads of the fuel meter cover bolts.

IDLE SPEED ADJUSTMENT—FUEL INJECTION

This procedure should be performed only when the throttle body parts have been replaced.

NOTE: *The following procedure requires the use of a special tool.*

1. Remove the air clearner and gasket.

2. Plug the vacuum port on the TBI marked THERMAC.

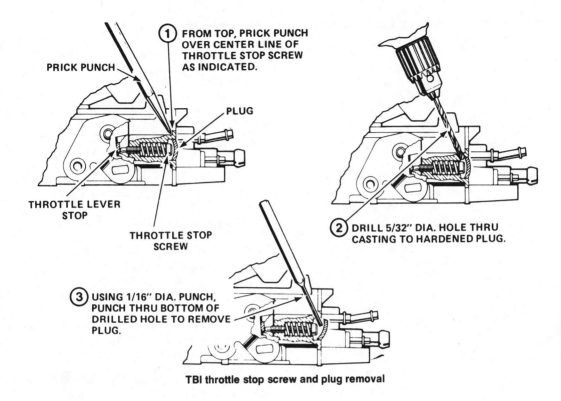

TBI throttle stop screw and plug removal

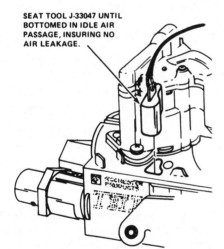

Installing tool J-33047 in the TBI for idle adjustment

sage of the throttle body. Be sure that the tool is fully seated and that no air leaks exist.

8. Using a #20 Torx bit, turn the minimum air screw until the engine rpm is 675–725 with auto. trans. or 725–825 with manual trans. The AT should be in Park; the MT in neutral.

9. Stop the engine and remove the special tool.

10. Install the cable on the throttle body.

11. Use RTV sealant to cover the throttle stop screw.

FUEL PUMP REMOVAL (TBI)

1. Jack up your vehicle and support it with jackstands.

2. Drain the tank.

3. Disconnect the negative battery terminal.

4. Disconnect the tank unit wire from the connector in the rear compartment.

5. Remove the ground wire retainer screw from the underbody.

6. Disconnect all hoses.

7. Support the tank and remove the retaining straps.

8. Remove the tank.

9. Remove the fuel gauge retaining cam using special tool J-24187 or its equal.

10. Remove the sending unit and pump from the tank.

11. Installation is the reverse of removal.

3. If the car is equipped with a tamper resistant plug cover the throttle stop screw, the TBI unit must be removed as instructed above, to remove the plug.

4. Remove the throttle valve cable from the throttle control bracket to allow access to the throttle stop screw.

5. Connect a tachometer to the engine.

6. Start the engine and run it to normal operating temperature.

7. Install tool J-33047 into the idle air pas-

FUEL PUMP PRESSURE RELIEF (TBI)

1. Remove the fuel pump fuse from the fuse block.
2. Start the engine. Allow it to run out of fuel.
3. Engage the starter for 3 seconds to assure that all pressure has been relieved from the system.
4. With the ignition off, replace the fuse.

DIESEL FUEL SYSTEM

The injection system used on the V6 diesel is similar to the V8 diesel system.

The diesel injection pump is mounted on top of the engine. It is gear driven by the camshaft and turns at camshaft speed. A high pressure rotary pump injects a metered amount of fuel into each cylinder at the precise time. Fuel delivery lines are the same length to prevent any difference in timing, from cylinder to cylinder. The timing advance is also controlled by the fuel pump. Engine rpm is controlled by the rotary fuel metering valve.

The fuel filter is located between the fuel pump and the injection pump at the left rear of the engine.

An electric fuel pump is used which is located at the front of the engine next to the fuel heater. Excess fuel returns to the tank via the fuel return line.

NOTE: *Because of the exacting nature of the diesel injection system all major repairs should be referred to your local GM dealer.*

Diesel Electric Fuel Pump
REMOVAL AND INSTALLATION

1. Disconnect the negative battery terminal.
2. Remove the air cleaner.

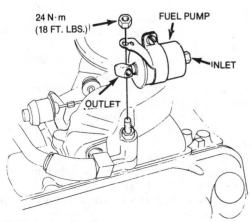

Fuel pump—diesel

3. Unplug the electrical connection.
4. Using a ¾ in. wrench to support the inlet fitting, use a ⅝ in. wrench to unscrew the inlet tube.
5. Remove the outlet tube.
6. Installation is the reverse of removal. After the pump has been replaced disconnect the fuel line at the filter. Turn the ignition on and bleed the lines. If the pump runs with a clicking sound, or air bubbles show up in the fuel, check the line for leaks. Check all connections to be sure they are dry. When the clicking noise disappears, tighten the line.

Injection Pump
REMOVAL AND INSTALLATION

1. Remove the air cleaner.
2. Remove the crankcase ventilation filter and pipes from the valve cover and air crossover.
3. Remove the air crossover and install special cover J-29657 or its equal. Remove the fuel lines, filter and fuel pump as an assembly. Cap all line openings.
4. Disconnect the throttle cable. Remove the return spring.
5. Remove the throttle and TV detent cables from the intake manifold brackets.
6. Disconnect the fuel return line from the injection pump.
7. Disconnect the injection line clamps, closest to the pump.
8. Disconnect the injection lines from the pump. Cap all openings. Carefully reposition the fuel lines.
9. Remove the two bolts retaining the injection pump.
10. Remove the pump. Discard the pump to adapter O-ring.
11. Installation is the reverse of removal, with the following recommendations.

Position the number one cylinder to the firing position. Install a new O-ring, then install the pump fully, seating it by hand. If a new or intermediate adapter plate is used, set the pump at the center slots on the mounting flange. If the original adapter is used align the pump timing mark and the adapter mark. Torque the pump bolts to 35 ft. lbs.

Injector
REMOVAL AND INSTALLATION

NOTE: *When the lines are disconnected use a back-up wrench on the upper injection nozzle hex. It may also be necessary to jack up the engine to gain access to the back bank of injectors.*

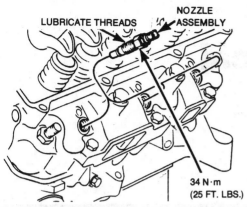

V6 nozzle installation

1. Remove the fuel injection lines as previously outlined.

2. Remove the injector nozzles.

3. Installation is the reverse of removal. When reinstalling the injectors special lubricant (GM part 9985462 or its equal) must be applied to the nozzle threads. Torque the injectors to 25 ft. lbs. Make sure the copper gasket is installed on the nozzle.

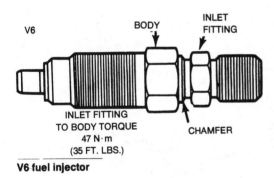

V6 fuel injector

Fuel Pump Lines

REMOVAL AND INSTALLATION

All lines may be removed without moving the injection pump. It not necessary to use a back-up wrench.

1. Remove the air cleaner.

2. Remove the filters and pipes from the valve covers and air crossover.

3. Remove the air crossover. Cap the intake manifold with special cover J-29657 or its equal.

4. Remove the injection pump line clamps. Remove the injection pump lines. Cap open lines, nozzles and pump fittings. Use a back-up wrench on the nozzle hex to prevent a fuel leak.

5. Installation is the reverse of removal.

DIESEL IDLE SPEED ADJUSTMENT

1. Apply the parking brake. Place the transmission in park. Block the drive wheels.

2. Start the engine. Allow it to reach operating temperature.

3. Turn off the engine, and remove the air cleaner.

4. Clean the front cover, rpm counter (probe holder) and the crankshaft balancer.

5. Install tool J-26925 or its equal in the rpm counter. Connect the special tool to the battery.

6. Disconnect the two lead connector at the alternator.

7. Turn off all electrical accessories.

8. Start the engine and set the transmission in drive.

9. Check the idle speed against the emission control sticker. Adjust if required.

10. Unplug the connector from the fast idle cold advance switch (engine temperature). Install a jumper between the connector terminals. Do not allow the jumper to touch ground.

11. Check the fast idle solenoid speed against the emission control label. Adjust if required.

Fuel Tank

REMOVAL AND INSTALLATION

1. Disconnect the negative cable at the battery. Raise and support the car.

2. Drain the tank. There is no drain plug; remaining fuel in the tank must be siphoned through the fuel feed line (the line to the fuel pump), because of the restrictor in the filler neck.

3. Disconnect the hose and the vapor return hose from the level sending unit fittings.

4. Remove the ground wire screw.

5. Unplug the level sending unit electrical connector.

6. Disconnect the vent hose.

7. Unbolt the support straps, and lower and remove the tank. Installation is the reverse.

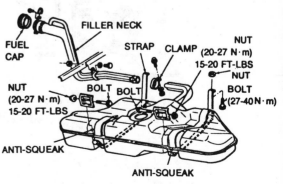

Fuel tank removal and installation details

Chassis Electrical

HEATER

Blower Motor
REMOVAL AND INSTALLATION

NOTE: *This procedure is for all cars, with or without air conditioning.*

1. Disconnect the negative cable at the battery.
2. Working inside the engine compartment, disconnect the blower motor electrical leads.
3. Remove the motor retaining screws, and remove the blower motor.
4. Reverse to install.

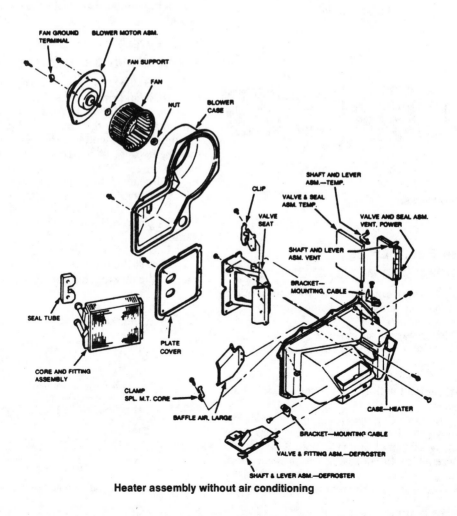

Heater assembly without air conditioning

Heater Core

REMOVAL AND INSTALLATION

Cars Without Air Conditioning

1. Drain the cooling system.
2. Remove the heater inlet and outlet hoses at the firewall, inside the engine compartment.
3. Remove the radio noise suppression strap.
4. Remove the heater core cover retaining screws. Remove the cover.
5. Remove the core. Reverse to install.

Cars With Air Conditioning

1. Drain the cooling system.
2. On the diesel, raise and support the car on jackstands.
3. Disconnect the hoses at the core.
4. On the diesel, remove the instrument panel lower sound absorber.
5. Remove the heater duct and lower side covers.
6. Remove the lower heater outlet.
7. Remove the two housing cover-to-air valve housing clips.

8. Remove the housing cover.
9. Remove the core restraining straps.
10. Remove the core tubing retainers and lift out the core.
11. Installation is the reverse of removal.

RADIO

REMOVAL AND INSTALLATION

1. Disconnect the battery ground.
2. Remove the three screws at the radio bracket if so equipped.
3. Remove any necessary trim plates.
4. Disconnect the electrical connections.
5. Remove the radio.
6. Installation is the reverse of removal.

WINDSHIELD WIPERS

Blade and Arm

REPLACEMENT

Wiper blade replacement procedures are detailed in Chapter 1.

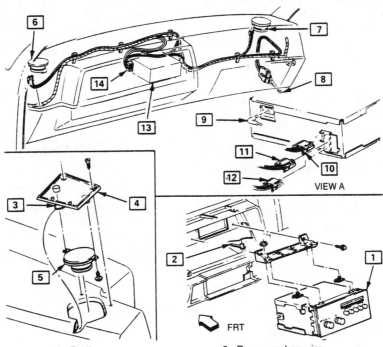

1. Radio
2. Screw on side of radio fits here
3. Retainer
4. Grille
5. Speaker
6. Front speaker assembly
7. Front speaker assembly

8. Rear speaker wire
9. Antenna
10. Rear speakers
11. Front speakers
12. I.P. harness
13. Receiver assembly
14. I.P. harness

Typical radio removal and installation

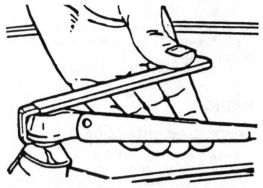

Remove the wiper arm with the special tool

Removal of the wiper arms requires the use of a special tool, G.M. J8966 or its equivalent. Versions of this tool are generally available in auto parts stores.

1. Insert the tool under the wiper arm and lever the arm off the shaft.
2. Disconnect the washer hose from the arm (if so equipped). Remove the arm.
3. Installation is in the reverse order of removal.

The proper park position is at the top of the blackout line on the glass. If the wiper arms and blades were in the proper position prior to removal, adjustment should not be required.

ADJUSTMENT

The only adjustment for the wiper arms is to remove an arm from the transmission shaft, rotate the arm the required distance and direction and then install the arm back in position so it is in line with the blackout line on the glass. The wiper motor must be in the park position.

The correct blade-out wipe position on the driver's side is $1^3/_{32}$ in. (28mm) from the tip of the blade to the left windshield pillar moulding. The correct blade-down wipe position on the passenger side of the car is in line with the blackout line at the bottom of the glass.

Linkage
REMOVAL AND INSTALLATION

1. Remove the wiper arms.
2. Remove the shroud top vent grille.
3. Loosen (but do not remove) the drive link-to-crank arm attaching nuts.
4. Unscrew the linkage-to-cowl panel retaining screws and remove the linkage.
5. Installation is in the reverse order of removal.

Wiper Motor
REMOVAL AND INSTALLATION

1. Loosen (but do not remove) the drive link-to-crank arm attaching nuts and detach the drive link from the motor crank arm.
2. Tag and disconnect all electrical leads from the wiper motor.
3. Unscrew the mounting bolts, rotate the motor up and outward and remove it.
4. Guide the crank arm through the opening in the body and then tighten the mounting bolts to 4–6 ft. lbs.
5. Install the drive link to the crank arm with the motor in the park position.
6. Installation of the remaining components is in the reverse order of removal.

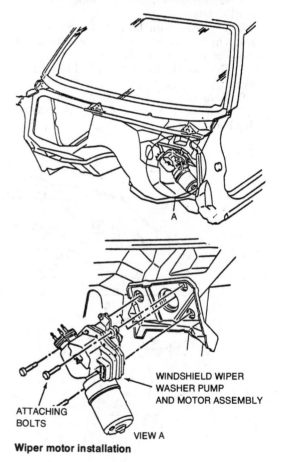

Wiper motor installation

INSTRUMENT CLUSTER

REMOVAL AND INSTALLATION
Century

1. Disconnect the battery ground.
2. Disconnect the speedometer cable and pull it through the firewall.

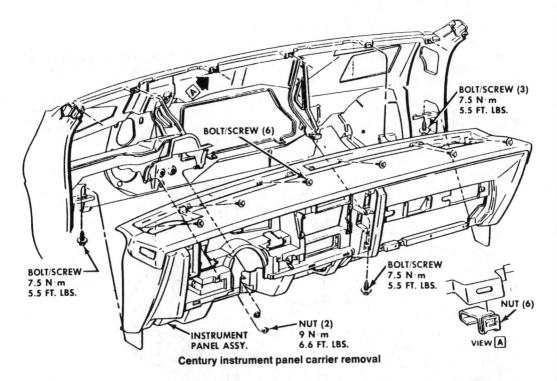

Century instrument panel carrier removal

3. Remove the left side hush panel by removing the three 7mm screws and one 11mm nut.

4. Remove the right side hush panel by removing the five 7mm screws and two 11mm nuts.

5. Remove the shift indicator cable clip.

6. Remove the steering column trim plate.

7. Put the gear selector in LOW, remove the nine retaining screws and gently pull out the instrument panel trim plate.

8. Disconnect the parking brake cable at the lever by pushing it forward and sliding it out of its slot.

9. Unbolt and lower the steering column (3 bolts and 1 nut).

10. Remove the gauge cluster by removing the four screws and pulling the cluster out far enough to disconnect any wires, then pull the cluster out.

11. Installation is the reverse of removal.

Celebrity

1. Disconnect battery ground cable.

2. Remove instrument panel hush panel.

3. Remove vent control housing (heater only vehicles).

4. On non A/C cars remove steering column trim cover screws and lower cover with vent cables attached. On A/C equipped vehicles, remove trim cover attaching screws (6) and remove cover.

5. Remove instrument cluster trim pad.

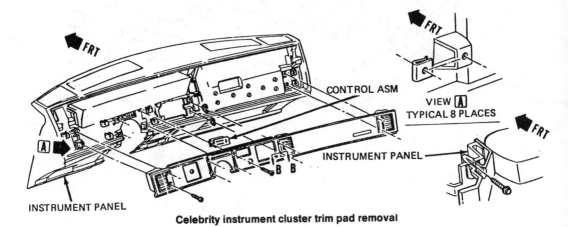

Celebrity instrument cluster trim pad removal

6. Remove ash tray, retainer and fuse block, disconnect wires as necessary.

7. Remove headlamp switch knob and instrument panel trim plate and disconnect electrical connectors of any accessory switches in trim plate.

8. Remove cluster assembly and disconnect speedometer cable. PRNDL and cluster electrical connectors.

9. Installation is the reverse of removal.

Ciera

1. Remove left instrument panel trim pad.
2. Remove instrument panel cluster trim cover.
3. Disconnect speedometer cable at transmission or cruise control tranducer if equipped.
4. Remove steering column trim cover.
5. Disconnect shift indicator clip from steering column shift bowl.

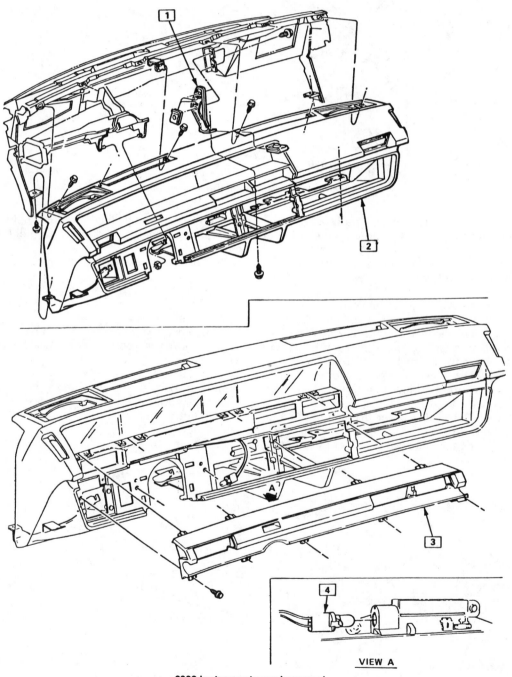

VIEW A

6000 instrument panel removal

6. Remove 4 screws attaching cluster assembly to instrument panel.

7. Pull assembly out far enough to reach behind cluster and disconnect speedometer cable.

8. Remove cluster assembly.

9. Installation is the reverse of removal.

6000

1. Remove center and left-hand lower instrument panel trim plate.

2. Remove six (6) screws holding instrument cluster to instrument panel carrier.

3. Remove instrument cluster lens to gain access to speedometer head and instruments/gages.

4. Disconnect negative battery cable(s).

5. Remove right-hand and left-hand hush panels, steering column trim cover and disconnect parking brake cable and vent cables, if so equipped.

6. Remove steering column retaining bolts and drop steering column.

7. Disconnect temperature control cable, inner to outer A/C wire harness and inner to outer A/C vacuum harness, if so equipped.

8. Disconnect chassis harness behind left lower instrument panel and ECM connectors behind glove box. Disconnect instrument panel harness at cowl.

9. Remove center instrument panel trim plate and remove radio if so equipped.

10. Disconnect neutral switch and brake light switch.

11. Remove six (6) upper instrument panel retaining screws.

12. Remove lower instrument panel retaining screws, nuts and bolts.

13. Pull instrument panel assembly out far enough to disconnect ignition switch, headlight dimmer switch and turn signal switch. Disconnect all other accessory wiring, and vacuum lines necessary to remove instrument panel assembly.

14. Remove instrument panel assembly with wiring harness.

15. Installation is the reverse of removal.

LIGHTING

Headlights

REMOVAL AND INSTALLATION

1. Remove the headlamp trim panel attaching screws.

2. Remove the headlamp bulb retaining screws. Do not touch the two headlamp aiming screws, at the top and side of the retaining

ring, or the headlamp aim will have to be readjusted.

3. Pull the bulb and ring forward and separate them. Unplug the electrical connector from the rear of the bulb.

4. Plug the new bulb into the electrical connector. Install the bulb into the retaining ring and install the ring and bulb. Install the trim panel.

Headlight Switch

REMOVAL AND INSTALLATION

Celebrity

1. Disconnect the battery ground.

2. Remove the headlamp switch knob.

3. Remove the instrument panel trim pad.

4. Unbolt the switch mounting plate from the instrument panel carrier.

5. Disconnect the wiring from the switch.

6. Remove the switch.

7. Installation is the reverse of removal.

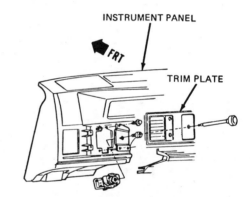

Celebrity headlight switch

Ciera

1. Remove the left side instrument panel trim pad.

2. Unbolt the switch from the instrument panel.

3. Pull the switch rearward and remove it.

4. Installation is the reverse of removal.

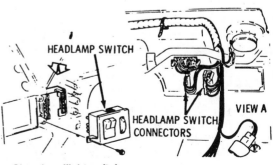

Ciera headlight switch

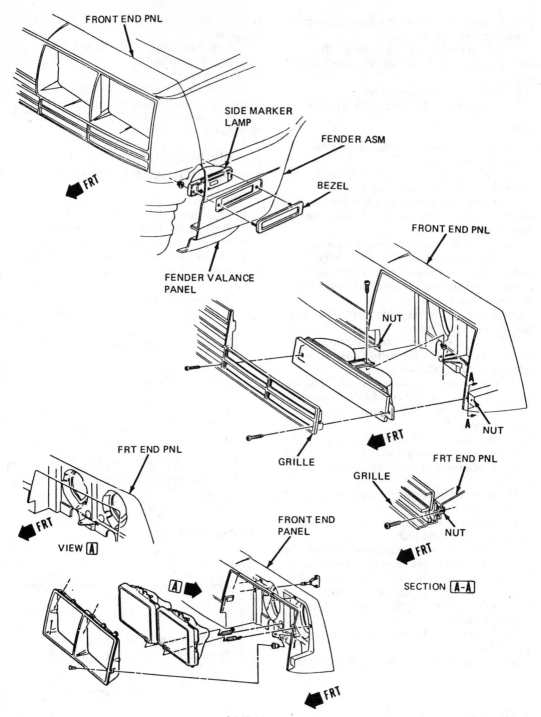

FRONT END PNL

SIDE MARKER LAMP

FENDER ASM

BEZEL

FRT

FENDER VALANCE PANEL

FRONT END PNL

NUT

A

A

NUT

FRT

FRT END PNL

GRILLE

FRT END PNL

GRILLE

NUT

FRT END PNL

FRT

VIEW A

FRONT END PANEL

NUT

FRT

SECTION A-A

FRONT END PANEL

A

FRT

Headlamp assembly

6000

1. Disconnect the battery ground.
2. Remove the steering column trim cover and headlight rod and knob by reaching behind the instrument panel and depressing the lock tab with a screwdriver.
3. Remove the left instrument panel trim plate.
4. Unbolt and remove the switch and bracket assembly from the instrument panel.
5. Loosen the bezel and remove the switch from the bracket.
6. Installation is the reverse of removal.

Century

1. Disconnect the battery ground.
2. Remove the instrument panel trim plate.
3. Remove the left side instrument panel switch trim panel by removing the three screws and gently rocking the panel out.
4. Remove the three screws and pull the switch straight out.
5. Installation is the reverse of removal.

SPEEDOMETER CABLE

1. Remove the instrument cluster.
2. Slide the cable out from the casing. If the cable is broken, the casing will have to be unscrewed from the transaxle and the broken piece removed from that end.
3. Before installing a new cable, slip a piece of cable into the speedometer and spin it between your fingers in the direction of normal rotation. If the mechanism sticks or binds, the speedometer should be repaired or replaced.
4. Inspect the casing; if it is cracked, kinked, or broken, the casing should be replaced.
5. Slide a new cable into the casing, engaging the transaxle end securely. Sometimes it is easier to unscrew the casing at the transaxle end, install the cable into the transaxle fitting, and screw the casing back into place. Install the instrument cluster.

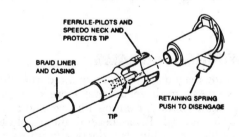

Speedometer cable removal

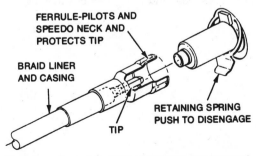

Speedometer cable disengagement at the speedometer

CIRCUIT PROTECTION

Fusible Links

A fusible link is a protective device used in an electrical circuit. When the current increases beyond a certain amperage, the fusible metal of the wire link melts, thus breaking the electrical circuit and preventing further damage to other components and wiring. Whenever a fusible link is melted because of a short circuit, correct the cause before installing a new one.

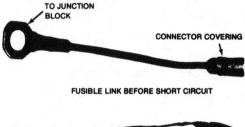

Fusible links before and after a short circuit

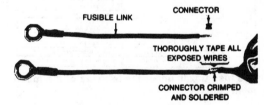

New fusible links are spliced to the wire

To replace a fusible link, cut off the burned link beyond the original splice. Replace the link with a new one of the same rating. If the splice has two wires, two repair links are required, one for each wire. Connect the new fusible link to the wires, then crimp securely.

CAUTION: *Use only replacements of the same electrical capacity as the original, available from your dealer. Replacements of a different electrical value will not provide adequate system protection.*

Fuses

Fuses protect all the major electrical systems in the car. In case of an electrical overload, the fuse melts, breaking the circuit and stopping the flow of electricity.

If a fuse blows, the cause should be investigated and corrected before the installation of a new fuse. This, however, is easier to say than to do. Because each fuse protects a limited

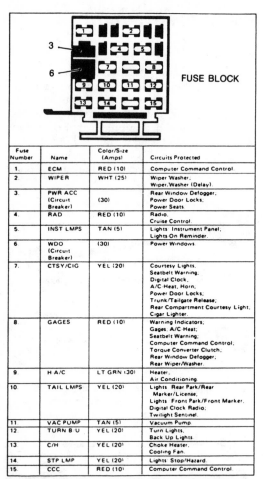

FUSE BLOCK

Fuse Number	Name	Color/Size (Amps)	Circuits Protected
1.	ECM	RED (10)	Computer Command Control.
2.	WIPER	WHT (25)	Wiper Washer; Wiper.Washer (Delay).
3.	PWR ACC (Circuit Breaker)	(30)	Rear Window Defogger; Power Door Locks; Power Seats.
4.	RAD	RED (10)	Radio. Cruise Control.
5.	INST LMPS	TAN (5)	Lights: Instrument Panel; Lights On Reminder.
6.	WDO (Circuit Breaker)	(30)	Power Windows.
7.	CTSY/CIG	YEL (20)	Courtesy Lights. Seatbelt Warning; Digital Clock. A/C-Heat, Horn; Power Door Locks; Trunk/Tailgate Release; Rear Compartment Courtesy Light. Cigar Lighter.
8.	GAGES	RED (10)	Warning Indicators; Gages; A/C-Heat; Seatbelt Warning; Computer Command Control. Torque Converter Clutch; Rear Window Defogger; Rear Wiper/Washer.
9.	H A/C	LT GRN (30)	Heater. Air Conditioning.
10.	TAIL LMPS	YEL (20)	Lights: Rear Park/Rear Marker/License; Lights: Front Park/Front Marker; Digital Clock Radio; Twilight Sentinel.
11.	VAC PUMP	TAN (5)	Vacuum Pump.
12.	TURN B U	YEL (20)	Turn Lights; Back Up Lights.
13.	C/H	YEL (20)	Choke Heater. Cooling Fan.
14.	STP LMP	YEL (20)	Lights: Stop/Hazard.
15.	CCC	RED (10)	Computer Command Control.

The fuse box is under the left side of the instrument panel

number of components, your job is narrowed down somewhat. Begin your investigation by looking for obvious fraying, loose connections, breaks in insulation, etc. Use the techniques outlined at the beginning of this chapter. Electrical problems are almost always a real headache to solve, but if you are patient and persistent, and approach the problem logically (that is, don't start replacing electrical components randomly), you will eventually find the solution.

The amperage of each fuse and the circuit it protects are marked on the fusebox, which is located under the left side (driver's side) of the instrument panel and pulls down for easy access.

Circuit Breakers

The headlights are protected by a circuit breaker in the headlamp switch. If the circuit breaker trips, the headlights will either flash on and off, or stay off altogether. The circuit breaker rests automatically after the overload is removed.

The windshield wipers are also protected by a circuit breaker. If the motor overheats, the circuit breaker will trip, remaining off until the motor cools or the overload is removed. One common cause of overheating is operation of the wipers in heavy snow.

The circuit breakers for the power door locks and power windows are located in the fuse box.

Flashers

The hazard flasher is located in the convenience center', under the dash, on the left side kick panel. The horn relay and the buzzer assembly may be found here also. The turn signal flasher is installed in a clamp attached to the base of the steering column support inside the car. In all cases, replacement is made by unplugging the old unit and plugging in a new one.

WIRING DIAGRAMS

Wiring diagrams have been omitted from this book. As cars have become more complex, wiring diagrams have grown in size and complexity as well. It has become impossible to provide a readable reproduction in a reasonable number of pages. Information on ordering wiring diagrams from the vehicle manufacturer can be found in the owner's manual.

MANUAL TRANSAXLE

"Transaxle" is the term used to identify a unit which combines the transmission and drive axle into one component. All use a model MT-125 manual transaxle as standard equipment. All forward gears in this design are in constant mesh. Final drive from the transmission is taken from the output gear, which is an integral part of the output shaft; the output gear transfers power to the differential ring gear and differential assembly. The differential is of conventional design.

Because of the complexity of the transaxle, no overhaul procedures are given in this book. However, removal and installation, adjustment, and halfshaft removal, installation and overhaul are covered.

REMOVAL AND INSTALLATION

1. Disconnect the negative battery cable from the transaxle case.
2. Remove the two transaxle strut bracket bolts on the left side of the engine compartment, if equipped.
3. Remove the top four engine-to-transaxle bolts, and the one at the rear near the firewall. The one at the rear is installed from the engine side.
4. Loosen the engine-to-transaxle bolt near the starter, but do not remove.
5. Disconnect the speedometer cable at the transaxle, or at the speed control transducer on cars so equipped.
6. Remove the retaining clip and washer from the shift linkage at the transaxle. Remove the clips holding the cables to the mounting bosses on the case.

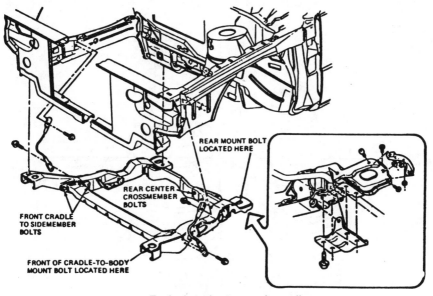

REAR MOUNT BOLT LOCATED HERE

REAR CENTER CROSSMEMBER BOLTS

FRONT CRADLE TO SIDEMEMBER BOLTS

FRONT OF CRADLE-TO-BODY MOUNT BOLT LOCATED HERE

Typical engine/transaxle cradle

7. Support the engine with a lifting chain.

8. Unlock the steering column and raise and support the car. Drain the transaxle. Remove the two nuts attaching the stabilizer bar to the left lower control arm. Remove the four bolts which attach the left retaining plate to the engine cradle. The retaining plate covers and holds the stabilizer bar.

9. Loosen the four bolts holding the right stabilizer bracket.

10. Disconnect and remove the exhaust pipe and crossover if necessary.

11. Pull the stabilizer bar down on the left side.

12. Remove the four nuts and disconnect the front and rear transaxle mounts from the engine cradle. Remove the two rear center crossmember bolts.

13. Remove the three right side front cradle attaching bolts. They are accessible under the splash shield.

14. Remove the top bolt from the lower front transaxle shock absorber if equipped.

15. Remove the left front wheel. Remove the front cradle-to-body bolts on the left side, and the rear cradle-to-body bolts.

16. Pull the left side drive shaft from the transaxle using G.M. special tool J-28468 or the equivalent. The right side axle shaft will simply disconnect from the cage. When the transaxle is removed, the right shaft can be swung out of the way. A boot protector should be used when disconnecting the driveshafts.

17. Swing the cradle to the left side. Secure out of the way, outboard of the fender well.

18. Remove the flywheel and starter shield bolts, and remove the shields.

19. Remove the two transaxle extension bolts from the engine-to-transaxle bracket, if equipped.

20. Place a jack under the transaxle case. Remove the last engine-to-transaxle bolt. Pull the transaxle to the left, away from the engine, then down and out from under the car.

Installation is the reverse.

1. Position the right axle shaft into its bore as the transaxle is bolted to the engine, swing the cradle into position and install the cradle-to-body bolts immediately. Be sure to guide the left axle shaft into place as the cradle is moved back into position.

OVERHAUL

Outer Joint

1. Remove the axle shaft.

2. Cut off the seal retaining clamp. Using a brass drift and a hammer, lightly tap the seal retainer from the outside toward the inside of the shaft to remove from the joint.

3. Use a pair of snap ring pliers to spread the retaining ring apart. Pull the axle shaft from the joint.

4. Using a brass drift and a hammer, lightly tap on the inner race cage until it has tilted sufficiently to remove one of the balls. Remove the other balls in the same manner.

5. Pivot the cage 90° and, with the cage ball windows aligned with the outer joint windows, lift out the cage and the inner race.

6. The inner race can be removed from the cage by pivoting it 90° and lifting out. Clean all parts thoroughly and inspect for wear.

7. To install, put a light coat of the grease provided in the rebuilding kit onto the ball grooves of the inner race and outer joint. In-

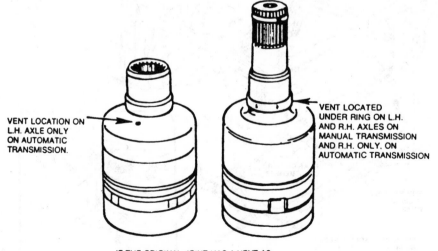

VENT LOCATION ON L.H. AXLE ONLY ON AUTOMATIC TRANSMISSION.

VENT LOCATED UNDER RING ON L.H. AND R.H. AXLES ON MANUAL TRANSMISSION AND R.H. ONLY, ON AUTOMATIC TRANSMISSION

IF THE ORIGINAL JOINT HAS A VENT AS SHOWN ABOVE A NEW SEAL IS REQUIRED.

Comparison of old and new CV joints

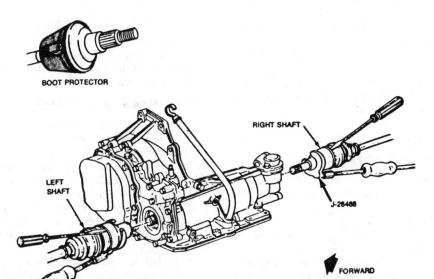

Halfshaft removal using special tools attached to slidehammers

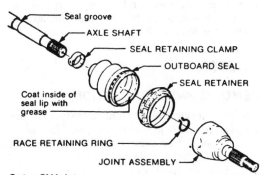

Outer CV joint

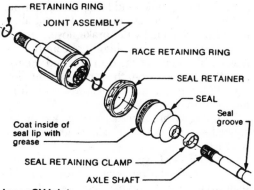

Inner CV joint

stall the parts in the reverse order of removal. To install the seal retainer, install the axle shaft assembly into an arbor press. Support the seal retainer on blocks, and press the axle shaft down until the seal retainer seats on the outer joint. When assembling, apply half the grease provided in the rebuilding kit to the joint; fill the seal (boot) with the rest of the grease.

Inner Joint

1. The joint seal is removed in the same manner as the outer joint seal. Follow Steps 1–3 of the outer joint procedure.

2. To disassemble the inner joint, remove the ball retaining ring from the joint. Pull the cage and inner race from the joint. The balls will come out with the race.

3. Center the inner race lobes in the cage windows, pivot the race 90°, and lift the race from the cage.

4. Assembly of the joint is the reverse. The inner joint seal retainer must be pressed onto

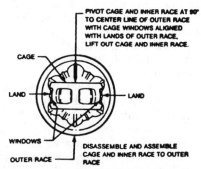

The inner race and cage can be removed from the outer race when pivoted 90°

the joint. See Step 7 of the outer joint procedure.

1. Loosen the wheel nuts, raise the car, and remove the wheel and tire.

2. Remove the brake hose clip-to-strut bolt (if equipped). Do not disconnect the hose from

the caliper. Install a drive axle cover to protect the axle boot.

3. Mark the camber cam eccentric adjuster for assembly.

4. Remove the two lower strut-to-steering knuckle bolts and the three upper strut-to-body nuts. Remove the strut.

Halfshafts

REMOVAL AND INSTALLATION

CAUTION: *Use care when removing the drive axle. Tri-pots can be damaged if the drive axle is over extended.*

1. Remove the hub nut.

2. Raise the front of the car. Remove the wheel and tire.

3. Install an axle shaft boot seal protector, G.M. special tool no. J-28712 or the equivalent, onto the seal.

4. Disconnect the brake hose clip from the MacPherson strut, but do not disconnect the hose from the caliper. Remove the brake caliper from the spindle, and hang the caliper out of the way by a length of wire. Do not allow the caliper to hang by the brake hose.

5. Mark the camber alignment cam bolt for reassembly. Remove the cam bolt and the upper attaching bolt from the strut and spindle.

6. Pull the steering knuckle assembly from the strut bracket.

7. Using G.M. special tool J-28468 or the equivalent, remove the axle shaft from the transaxle.

8. Using G.M. special tool J-28733 or the equivalent spindle remover, remove the axle shaft from the hub and bearing assembly.

To install:

1. If a new drive axle is to be installed, a new knuckle seal should be installed first.

2. Loosely install the drive axle into the transaxle and steering knuckle.

3. Loosely attach the steering knuckle to the suspension strut.

4. The drive axle is an interference fit in the steering knuckle. Press the axle into place, then install the hub nut. When the shaft begins to turn with the hub, insert a drift through the caliper into one of the cooling slots in the rotor to keep it from turning. Insert a long bolt in the hub flange to prevent the shaft from turning. Tighten the hub nut to 70 ft. lbs. to completely seat the shaft.

5. Install the brake caliper. Tighten the bolts to 30 ft. lbs.

6. Load the hub assembly by lowering it onto a jackstand. Align the camber cam bolt marks made during removal, install the bolt and tighten to 140 ft. lbs. Tighten the upper nut to the same value.

7. Install the axle shaft all the way into the transaxle using a screwdriver inserted into the groove provided on the inner retainer. Tap the screwdriver until the shaft seats in the transaxle. Remove the boot seal protector.

SHIFT LINKAGE ADJUSTMENT

1. Remove the shifter boot and retainer inside the car. Shift into first gear.

2. Install two No. 22 drill bits, or two $5/32$ in. rods, into the two alignment holes in the shifter assembly to hold it in first gear.

3. Place the transaxle into first gear by pushing the rail selector shaft down just to the point of feeling the resistance of the inhibitor spring. Then rotate the shift lever all the way counterclockwise.

4. Install the stud, with the cable attached, into the slotted area of the select lever, while gently pulling on the lever to remove all lash.

5. Remove the two drill bits or pins from the shifter.

6. Check the shifter for proper operation. It may be necessary to fine tune the adjustment after road testing.

CLUTCH

REMOVAL AND INSTALLATION

The only service adjustment necessary on the clutch is to maintain the correct pedal free play. Clutch pedal free play, or throwout bearing lash, decreases with driven disc wear.

1. Remove the transaxle.

2. Mark the pressure plate assembly and the flywheel so that they can be assembled in the same position. They were balanced as an assembly at the factory.

3. Loosen the attaching bolts one turn at a time until spring tension is relieved.

4. Support the pressure plate and remove the bolts. Remove the pressure plate and clutch disc. Do not disassemble the pressure plate assembly; replace it if defective.

5. Inspect the flywheel, clutch disc, pressure plate, throwout bearing and the clutch fork and pivot shaft assembly for wear. Replace the parts as required. If the flywheel shows any signs of overheating, or if it is badly grooved or scored, it should be replaced.

6. Clean the pressure plate and flywheel mating surfaces thoroughly. Position the clutch disc and pressure plate into the installed position, and support with a dummy shaft or clutch aligning tool. The clutch plate is assembled with the damper springs offset toward the transaxle. One side of the factory-supplied clutch disc is stamped "Flywheel side."

7. Install the pressure plate-to-flywheel

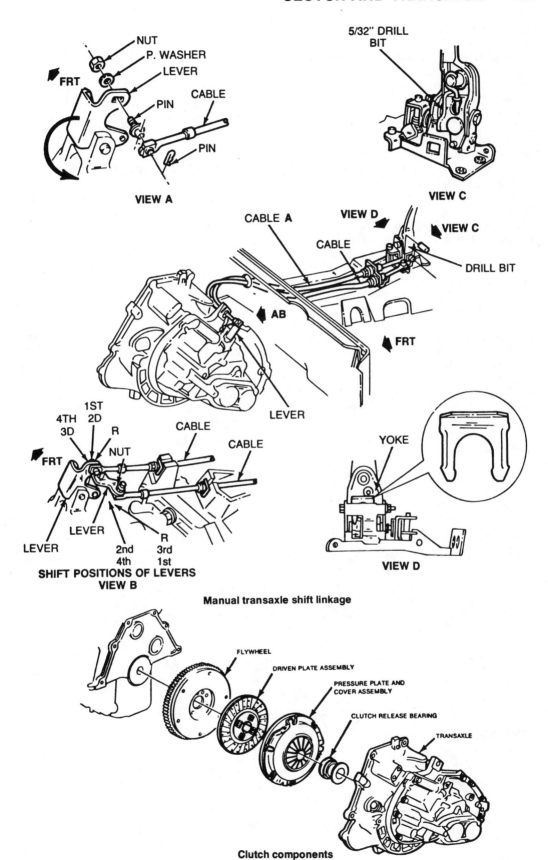

VIEW A

VIEW C

Manual transaxle shift linkage

SHIFT POSITIONS OF LEVERS
VIEW B

VIEW D

Clutch components

bolts. Tighten them gradually in a criss-cross pattern.

8. Lubricate the outside groove and the inside recess of the release bearing with high temperature grease. Wipe off any excess. Install the release bearing.

9. Install the transaxle.

CLUTCH LINKAGE ADJUSTMENT

All cars use a self-adjusting clutch mechanism which may be checked as follows:

As the clutch friction material wears, the cable must be lengthened. This is accomplished by simply pulling the clutch pedal up to its rubber bumper. This action forces the pawl against its stop and rotates it out of mesh with the quadrant teeth, allowing the cable to play out until the quadrant spring load is balanced against the load applied by the release bearing. This adjustment procedure is required every 5,000 miles or less.

1. With engine running and brake on, hold the clutch pedal approximately ½" from floor mat and move shift lever between first and reverse several times. If this can be done smoothly without clashing into reverse, the clutch is fully releasing. If shift is not smooth, clutch is not fully releasing and linkage should be inspected and corrected as necessary.

2. Check clutch pedal bushings for sticking or excessive wear.

3. Have an assistant sit in the driver's seat and fully apply the clutch pedal to the floor.

Observe the clutch fork lever travel at the transaxle. The end of the clutch fork lever should have a total travel of approximately 1.5 to 1.7 inches.

4. If fork lever is not correct, check the adjusting mechanism by depressing the clutch pedal and looking for pawl to firmly engage with the teeth in the quadrant.

AUTOMATIC TRANSAXLE

All models use a Turbo Hydro-Matic 125 or 125C automatic transmission. The 125C is equipped with a torque converter clutch (TCC) which under certain conditions mechanically couples the engine to the transaxle for greater power transfer efficiency and increased fuel mileage. A cable operated throttle valve linkage is used. Automatic transaxle operation is provided through a conventional three element torque converter, a compound planetary gear set, and a dual sprocket and drive link assembly.

No overhaul procedures are given in this book because of the complexity of the transaxle. Transaxle removal and installation, adjustment, and halfshaft removal, installation, and overhaul procedures are covered.

ADJUSTMENTS

The only adjustment required on the TH-M 125C transaxle is the shift linkage (cable) ad-

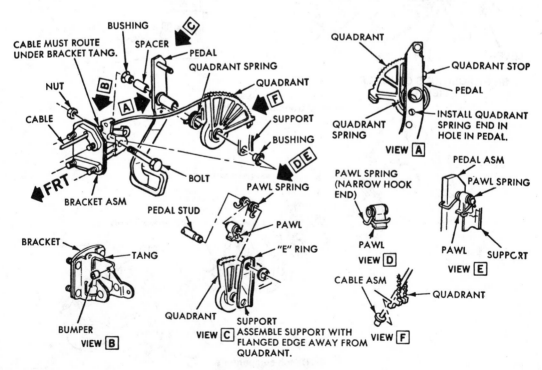

Clutch cable and pedal

justment. The neutral start switch and throttle valve are self-adjusting. The transaxle has only one band, with no provision for periodic adjustment. Pan removal, fluid and filter changes are covered in Chapter One.

SHIFT LINKAGE ADJUSTMENT

1. Place the shift lever inside the car into Neutral.
2. Disconnect the shift cable from the transaxle lever. Place the transaxle lever in Neutral, by moving the lever clockwise to the Low (L) detent, then counterclockwise through the Second (S) and Drive (D) detents to the Neutral detent.
3. Attach the shift cable to the pin on the transaxle lever. Check the shift operation.

CAUTION: *Any inaccuracies in shift linkage adjustments may result in premature failure of the transmission due to operation without the controls in full detent. Such operation results in reduced fluid pressure and in turn, partial engagement of the affected clutches. Partial engagement of the clutches, with sufficient pressure to permit apparently normal vehicle operation will result in failure of the clutches and/or other internal parts after only a few miles of operation.*

REMOVAL AND INSTALLATION

1. Disconnect the negative battery cable from the transaxle. Tape the wire to the upper radiator hose to keep it out of the way.
2. Remove the air cleaner and disconnect the detent cable. Slide the detent cable in the opposite direction of the cable to remove it from the carburetor.
3. Unbolt the detent cable attaching bracket at the transaxle.
4. Pull up on the detent cable cover at the transaxle until the cable is exposed. Disconnect the cable from the rod.
5. Remove the two transaxle strut bracket bolts at the transaxle, if equipped.
6. Remove all the engine-to-transaxle bolts except the one near the starter. The one nearest the firewall is installed from the engine side; you will need a short handled box wrench or ratchet to reach it.
7. Loosen, but do not remove the engine-to-transaxle bolt near the starter.
8. Disconnect the speedometer cable at the upper and lower coupling. On cars with cruise control, remove the speedometer cable at the transducer.
9. Remove the retaining clip and washer from the shift linkage at the transaxle. Remove the two shift linkage at the transaxle. Remove the two shift linkage bracket bolts.

10. Disconnect and plug the two fluid cooler lines at the transaxle. These are inch-size fittings ($\frac{1}{2}$ and $\frac{11}{16}$); use a back-up wrench to avoid twisting the lines.
11. Install an engine holding chain or hoist. Raise the engine enough to take its weight off the mounts.
12. Unlock the steering column and raise the car.
13. Remove the two nuts holding the anti-sway (stabilizer) bar to the left lower control arm (driver's side).
14. Remove the four bolts attaching the covering plate over the stabilizer bar to the engine cradle on the left side (driver's side).
15. Loosen but do not remove the four bolts holding the stabilizer bar bracket to the right side (passenger's side) of the engine cradle. Pull the bar down on the driver's side.
16. Disconnect the front and rear transaxle mounts at the engine cradle.
17. Remove the two rear center cross-member bolts.
18. Remove the three right (passenger) side front engine cradle attaching bolts. The nuts are accessible under the splash shield next to the frame rail.
19. Remove the top bolt from the lower front transaxle shock absorber, if equipped (V6 engine only).
20. Remove the left (driver) side front and rear cradle-to-body bolts.
21. Remove the left front wheel. Attach an axle shaft removing tool (G.M. part no. J-28468 or the equivalent) to a slide hammer. Place the tool behind the axle shaft cones and pull the cones out away from the transaxle. Remove the right shaft in the same manner. Set the shafts out of the way. Plug the openings in the transaxle to prevent fluid leakage and the entry of dirt.
22. Swing the partial engine cradle to the left (driver) side and wire it out of the way outboard of the fender well.
23. Remove the four torque converter and starter shield bolts. Remove the two transaxle extension bolts from the engine-to-transaxle bracket.
24. Attach a transaxle jack to the case.
25. Use a felt pen to matchmark the torque converter and flywheel. Remove the three torque converter-to-flywheel bolts.
26. Remove the transaxle-to-engine bolt near the starter. Remove the transaxle by sliding it to the left, away from the engine.

Installation is the reverse. As the transaxle is installed, slide the right axle shaft into the case. Install the cradle-to-body bolts before the stabilizer bar is installed. To aid in stabilizer bar installation, a pry hole has been provided in the engine cradle.

Suspension and Steering

FRONT SUSPENSION

The A-Bodies use a MacPherson strut front suspension design. A MacPherson strut combines the functions of a shock absorber and an upper suspension member (upper arm) into one unit. The strut is surrounded by a coil spring, which provides normal front suspension functions.

The strut bolts to the body shell at its upper end, and to the steering knuckle at the lower end. The strut pivots with the steering knuckle by means of a sealed mounting assembly at the upper end which contains a preloaded, non-adjustable bearing.

The steering knuckle is connected to the chassis at the lower end by a conventional lower control arm, and pivots in the arm in a preloaded ball joint of standard design. The knuckle is fastened to the ball joint stud by means of a castellated nut and cotter pin.

Advantages of the MacPherson strut design,

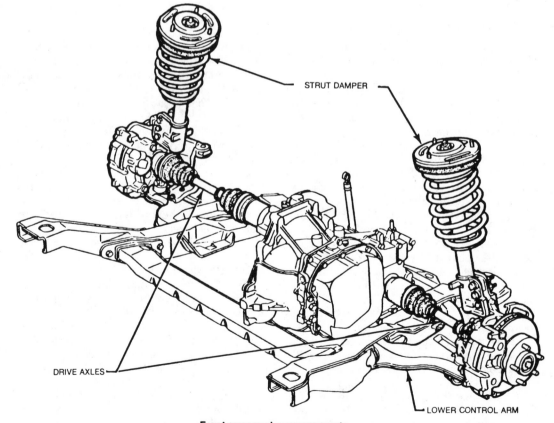

STRUT DAMPER

DRIVE AXLES

LOWER CONTROL ARM

Front suspension components

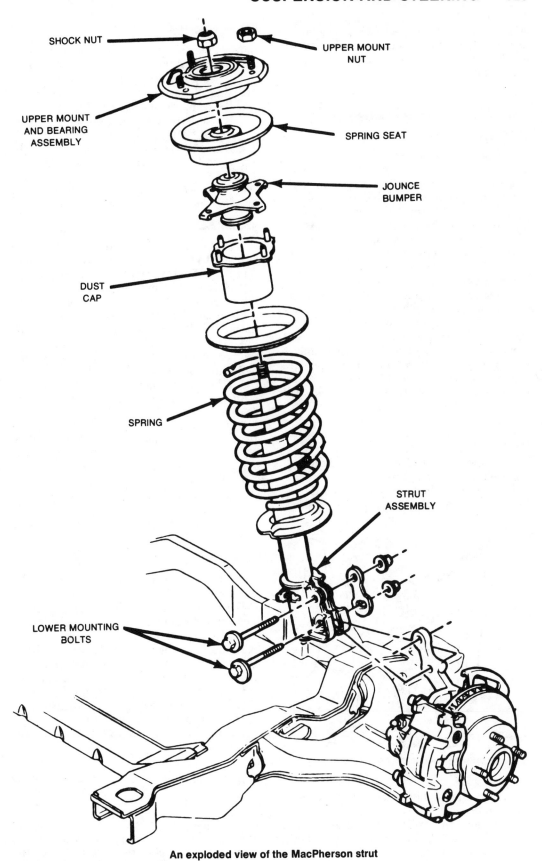

SHOCK NUT

UPPER MOUNT
NUT

UPPER MOUNT
AND BEARING
ASSEMBLY

SPRING SEAT

JOUNCE
BUMPER

DUST
CAP

SPRING

STRUT
ASSEMBLY

LOWER MOUNTING
BOLTS

An exploded view of the MacPherson strut

aside from its relative simplicity, include reduced weight and friction, minimal intrusion into the engine and passenger compartments, and ease of service.

Springs and Shock Absorbers
TESTING

The function of the shock absorber is to dampen harsh spring movement and provide a means of dissipating the motion of the wheels so that the shocks encountered by the wheels are not totally transmitted to the body and, therefore, to you and your passengers. As the wheel moves up and down, the shock absorber shortens and lengthens, thereby imposing a restraint on movement by its hydraulic action.

A good way to see if your shock absorbers are functioning correctly is to push one corner of the car until it is moving up and down for almost the full suspension travel, then release it and watch its recovery. If the car bounces slightly about one more time and then comes to a rest, the shock is alright. If the car continues to bounce excessively, the shocks will probably require replacement.

REMOVAL

1. Loosen the wheel nuts, raise the car, and remove the wheel and tire.
2. Remove the brake hose clip-to-strut bolt. Do not disconnect the hose from the caliper.

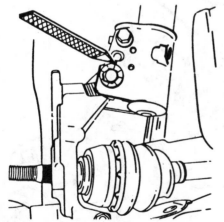

Mark the camber eccentric before removal

3. Mark the camber cam eccentric adjuster for assembly.
4. Remove the two lower strut-to-steering knuckle bolts and the three upper strut-to-body nuts. Remove the strut.

DISASSEMBLY

A MacPherson strut compressor tool, G.M. part J-26584 or the equivalent must be used.
1. Clamp the strut compressor in a vise.
2. Install the strut in the compressor. Install the compressor adapters, if used.
3. Compress the spring approximately ½ in. *Do not bottom the spring or the strut rod.*
4. Remove the strut shaft top nut and the top mount and bearing assembly from the strut.
5. Unscrew the compressor until all spring tension is relieved. Remove the spring.

ASSEMBLY

1. Place the strut into the compressor. Rotate the strut until the spindle mounting flange is facing out, away from the compressor.
2. Place the spring on the strut. Make sure it is properly seated on the strut bottom plate.
3. Install the strut spring assembly on the spring. Install the compressor adapters, if used.
4. Tighten the strut compressor until it just contacts the spring seat, or the adapters if a tool with adapters is being used.
5. Thread an alignment rod, G.M. tool J-26584-27 or the equivalent, onto the strut damper shaft, hand tight.
6. Compress the spring until approximately 1½ in. of the damper rod can be pulled up through the top spring seat. *Do not compress the spring until it bottoms.*
7. Remove the alignment rod and install the top mount and nut. Tighten the nut to 68 ft. lbs. (90 nm.).
8. Unscrew the compressor and remove the strut.

INSTALLATION

1. Install the strut to the body. Tighten the upper nuts hand tight.
2. Place a jack under the lower arm. Raise the arm and install the lower strut-to-knuckle bolts. Align the camber eccentric cam with the marks made during removal. Tighten the strut-to-knuckle bolts to 140 ft. lbs. (190 Nm.), and the strut-to-body nuts to 18 ft. lbs. (24 Nm.).
3. Install the brake hose clip on the strut.
4. Install the wheel and lower the car.
NOTE: *If a new strut damper has been installed, the front end will have to be realigned.*

Ball Joints
INSPECTION

The ball joints have built-in wear indicators. As long as the wear indicator (part of the grease nipple) extends below the ball joint seat, the

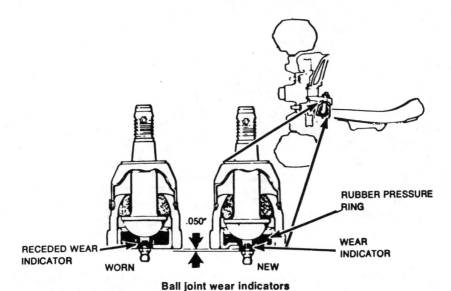

Ball joint wear indicators

RECEDED WEAR INDICATOR   WORN   NEW   RUBBER PRESSURE RING   WEAR INDICATOR   .050"

ball joint is OK. When the indicator recedes beneath the seat, replacement is necessary.

REPLACEMENT

Only one ball joint is used in each lower arm. The MacPherson strut design does not use an upper ball joint.

1. Loosen the wheel nuts, raise the car, and remove the wheel.

2. Use a ⅛ in. drill bit to drill a hole approximately ¼ in. deep in the center of each of the three ball joint rivets.

3. Use a ½ in. drill bit to drill off the rivet heads. Drill only enough to remove the rivet head.

4. Use a hammer and punch to remove the rivets. Drive them out from the bottom.

5. Loosen the ball joint pinch bolt in the steering knuckle.

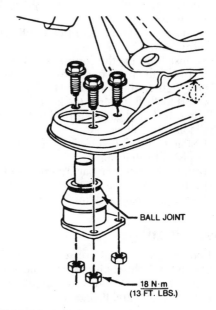

BALL JOINT

18 N·m (13 FT. LBS.)

Ball joint installation

6. Remove the ball joint.

7. Install the new ball joint in the control arm. Tighten the bolts supplied with the replacement joint to 8 ft. lbs.

8. Install the ball stud into the knuckle pinch bolt fitting. It should go in easily; if not, check the stud alignment. Install the pinch bolt from the rear to the front. Tighten to 45 ft. lbs. (60 Nm.).

9. Install the wheel and lower the car.

Control Arm

REMOVAL AND INSTALLATION

1. Loosen the wheel nuts, raise the car, and remove the wheel.

Drill out the ball joint rivets

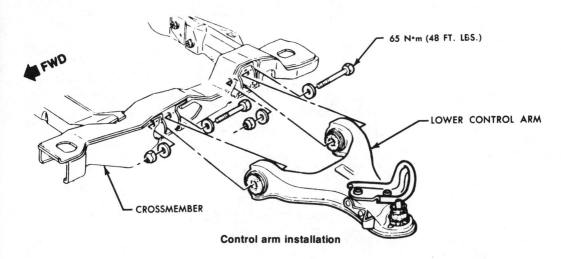

65 N•m (48 FT. LBS.)

FWD

LOWER CONTROL ARM

CROSSMEMBER

Control arm installation

2. Remove the stabilizer bar from the control arm.

3. Remove the ball joint pinch bolt in the steering knuckle.

4. Remove the control arm pivot bolts and the control arm.

5. To install, insert the control arm into its fittings. Install the pivot bolts from the rear to the front. Tighten the bolts to 50 ft. lbs.

6. Insert the ball stud into the knuckle pinch bolt fitting. It should go in easily; if not, check the ball joint stud alignment.

7. Install the pinch bolt from the rear to the front. Tighten to 40 ft. lbs.

8. Install the stabilizer bar clamp. Tighten to 35 ft. lbs. (45 Nm.).

9. Install the wheel and lower the car.

Wheel Bearings

The front wheel bearings are sealed, non-adjustable units which require no periodic attention. They are bolted to the steering knuckle by means of an integral flange.

You will need a special tool to pull the bearing free of the halfshaft, G.M. tool no. J-28733 or the equivalent. You should also use a halfshaft boot protector, G.M. tool no. J-28712 or the equivalent to protect the parts from damage.

1. Remove the wheel cover, loosen the hub nut, and raise and support the car. Remove the front wheel.

2. Install the boot cover, G.M. part no. J-28712 or the equivalent.

3. Remove and discard the hub nut. Be sure to use a new one on assembly, not the old one.

4. Remove the brake caliper and rotor:

   a. Remove the allen head caliper mounting bolts;

   b. Remove the caliper from the knuckle and suspend from a length of wire. Do not allow the caliper to hang from the brake hose. Pull the rotor from the knuckle.

5. Remove the three hub and bearing attaching bolts. If the old bearing is to be reused, match mark the bolts and holes for installa-

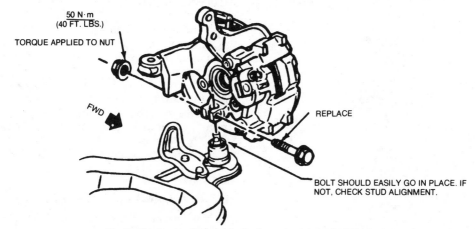

50 N·m
(40 FT. LBS.)

TORQUE APPLIED TO NUT

FWD

REPLACE

BOLT SHOULD EASILY GO IN PLACE. IF NOT, CHECK STUD ALIGNMENT.

The ball joint stud should slip into the knuckle fitting

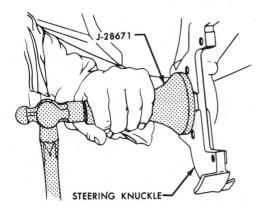

Use a seal driver when installing a new seal into the knuckle

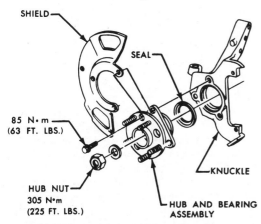

Exploded view of the hub and bearing attachment to the steering knuckle

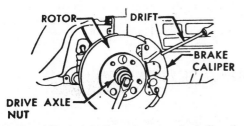

Insert a drift pin into the rotor when installing the hub nut

tion. The brake rotor splash shield will have to come off, too.

6. Attach a puller, G.M. part no. J-28733 or the equivalent, and remove the bearing. If corrosion is present, make sure the bearing is loose in the knuckle before using the puller.

7. Clean the mating surfaces of all dirt and corrosion. Check the knuckle bore and knuckle seal for damage. If a new bearing is to be installed, remove the old knuckle seal and install a new one. Grease the lips of the new seal before installation; install with a seal

driver made for the purpose, G.M. tool no. J-28671 or the equivalent.

8. Push the bearing onto the halfshaft. Install a new washer and hub nut.

9. Tighten the new hub nut on the halfshaft until the bearing is seated. If the rotor and hub start to rotate as the hub nut is tightened, insert a drift through the caliper and into the rotor cooling fins to prevent rotation. Do not apply full torque to the hub nut at this time—just seat the bearing.

10. Install the brake shield and the bearing retaining bolts. Tighten the bolts evenly to 63 ft. lbs. (85 Nm.).

11. Install the caliper and rotor. Be sure that the caliper hose isn't twisted. Install the caliper bolts and tighten to 21–35 ft. lbs. (28–47 Nm.).

12. Install the wheel. Lower the car. Tighten the hub nut to 225 ft. lbs. (305 Nm.).

Front End Alignment

Only camber and toe are adjustable on the A-Body cars; caster is preset and non-adjustable.

CAMBER

Camber is the inward or outward tilt from the vertical, measured in degrees, of the front wheels at the top. An outward tilt gives the wheel positive camber; an inward tilt is called negative camber. Proper camber is critical to assure even tire wear.

Camber angle is adjusted on the A-Bodies by loosening the cam and through bolts which attach the MacPherson strut to the steering knuckle and rotating the cam bolt to move the upper end of the knuckle in or out. The bolts must be tightened to 140 ft. lbs. (190 Nm.) afterwards. The cam bolt must be seated properly between the inner and outer guide surfaces on the strut flange. Measurement of the camber angle requires special alignment equipment; thus the adjustment of camber is not a do-it-yourself job, and not covered here.

TOE

Toe is the amount, measured in a fraction of a millimeter, that the wheels are closer together at one end than the other. Toe-in means that the front wheels are closer together at the front than the rear; toe-out means the rear of the front wheels are closer together than the front. A-Body cars are designed to have a slight amount of toe-in.

Toe is adjusted by turning the tie rods. It must be checked after camber has been adjusted, but it can be adjusted without disturbing the camber setting. You can make this adjustment without special equipment if you

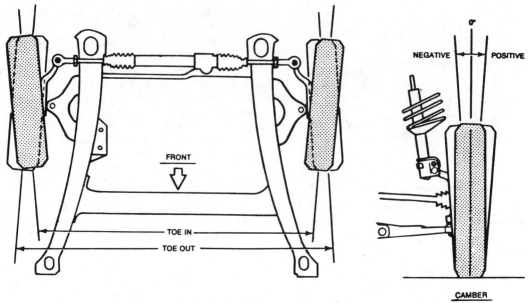

Wheel alignment: toe (left) and camber (right)

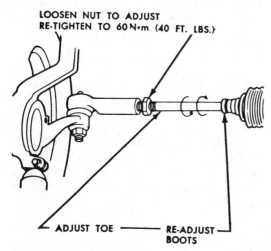

LOOSEN NUT TO ADJUST
RE-TIGHTEN TO 60 N·m (40 FT. LBS.)

ADJUST TOE ———— RE-ADJUST BOOTS

Toe adjustment is made at the tie rods

make very careful measurements. The wheels must be straight ahead.

1. Toe can be determined by measuring the distance between the centers of the tire treads, at the front of the tire and at the rear. If the tread pattern makes this impossible, you can measure between the edges of the wheel rims, but make sure to move the car forward and measure in a couple of places to avoid errors caused by bent rims or wheel runout.

2. If the measurement is not within specifications, loosen the nuts at the steering knuckle end of the tie rod, and remove the tie rod boot clamps. Rotate the tie rods to align the toe to specifications. Rotate the tie rods evenly, or the steering wheel will be crooked when you're done.

3. When the adjustment is correct, tighten the nuts to 45 ft. lbs. (60 Nm.). Adjust the boots and tighten the clamps.

REAR SUSPENSION

Rear suspension consists of a solid rear axle tube containing an integral, welded-in stabilizer bar, coil springs, shock absorbers, a lateral track bar, and trailing arms. The trailing arms (control arms) are welded to the axle, and pivot at the frame. Fore and aft movement is controlled by the trailing arms; lateral movement is controlled by the track bar. A perma-

Wheel Alignment Specifications

Year	Model	Caster* Range (deg)	Pref Setting (deg)	Camber Range (deg)	Pref Setting (deg)	Toe-In (in.)	Steering Axis (deg) inclination
'82–83	All	0–4P	2P	½N–½P	0	$^1/_{16}$ out–$^1/_{16}$ in	14.5

*Caster is not adjustable

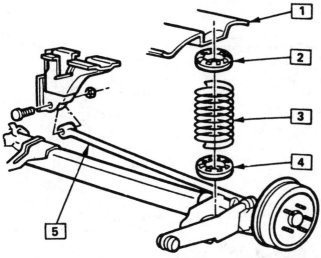

1. Underbody
2. Insulator upper
3. Spring
4. Lower insulator
5. Track bar

Rear suspension

nently lubricated and sealed hub and bearing assembly is bolted to each end of the axle tube; it is a non-adjustable unit which must be replaced as an assembly if defective.

Shock Absorbers

TESTING

Visually inspect the shock absorber. If there is evidence of leakage and the shock absorber is covered with oil, the shock is defective and should be replaced.

If there is no sign of excessive leakage (a small amount of weeping is normal) bounce the car at one corner by pressing down on the fender or bumper and releasing. When you have the car bouncing as much as you can, release the fender or bumper. The car should stop bouncing after the first rebound. If the bouncing continues past the center point of the bounce more than once, the shock absorbers are worn and should be replaced.

REMOVAL AND INSTALLATION

1. Open the hatch or trunk lid, remove the trim cover if present, and remove the upper shock absorber nut.
2. Raise and support the car at a convenient working height if you desire. It is not necessary to remove the weight of the car from the shock absorbers, however, so you can leave the car on the ground if you prefer.
3. If the car is equipped with superlift shock absorbers, disconnect the air line.
4. Remove the lower attaching bolt and remove the shock.
5. If new shock absorbers are being installed, repeatedly compress them while inverted and extend them in their normal upright position. This will purge them of air.

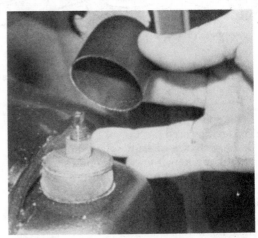

The upper shock absorber mounts are accessible in the trunk

6. Install the shocks in the reverse order of removal. Tighten the lower mount nut and bolt to 35 ft. lbs. (47 Nm.), the upper to 7 ft. lbs. (10 Nm.).

Springs

REMOVAL AND INSTALLATION

CAUTION: *The coil springs are under a considerable amount of tension. Be very careful when removing or installing them; they can exert enough force to cause very serious injuries.*

1. Raise and support the car on a hoist. Do not use twin-post hoist. The swing arc of the axle may cause it to slip from the hoist when the bolts are removed. If a suitable hoist is not available, raise and support the car on jackstands, and use a jack under the axle.

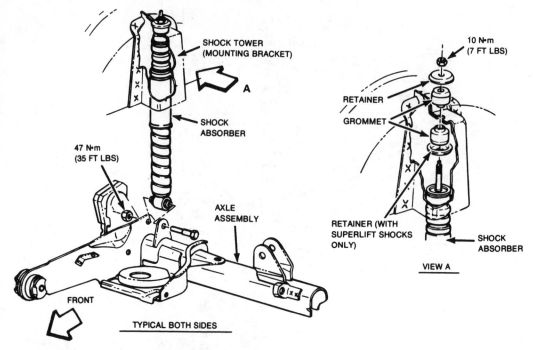

Shock absorber installation details

2. Support the axle with a jack that can be raised and lowered.

3. Remove the brake hose attaching brackets (right and left), allowing the hoses to hang freely. Do not disconnect the hoses.

4. Remove the track bar attaching bolts from the rear axle.

5. Remove both shock absorber lower attaching bolts from the axle.

6. Lower the axle. Remove the coil spring and insulator.

7. To install, position the spring and insulator on the axle. The leg on the upper coil of the spring must be parallel to the axle, facing the lefthand side of the car.

8. Install the shock absorber bolts. Tighten to 34 ft. lbs. (47 Nm.). Install the track bar, tightening to 33 ft. lbs. (45 Nm.). Install the

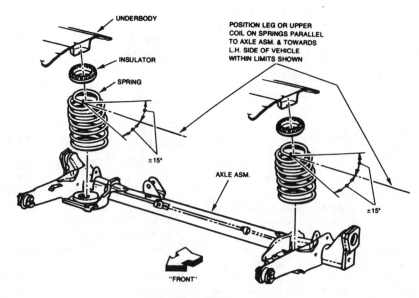

Spring installation

brake line brackets. Tighten to 8 ft. lbs. (11 Nm.).

Rear Hub and Bearing
REMOVAL AND INSTALLATION

1. Loosen the wheel lug nuts. Raise and support the car and remove the wheel.

2. Remove the brake drum. Removal procedures are covered in the next chapter, if needed.

NOTE: *Do not hammer on the brake drum to remove; damage to the bearing will result.*

3. Remove the four hub and bearing retaining bolts and remove the assembly from the axle.

4. Installation is the reverse. Hub and bearing bolt torque is 35 ft. lbs. (55 Nm.).

STEERING

The A-Body cars use an aluminum-housed Saginaw manual rack and pinion steering gear as standard equipment. The pinion is supported by and turns in a sealed ball bearing at the top and a pressed-in roller bearing at the bottom. The rack moves in bushings pressed into each end of the rack housing.

Wear compensation occurs through the action of an adjuster spring which forces the rack against the pinion teeth. This adjuster eliminates the need for periodic pinion preload adjustments. Preload is adjustable only at overhaul.

The inner tie rod assemblies are both threaded and staked to the rack. A special joint is used, allowing both rocking and rotating motion of the tie rods. The inner tie rod assemblies are lubricated for life and require no periodic attention.

Any service other than replacement of the outer tie rods or the boots requires removal of the unit from the car.

The optional power rack and pinion steering gear is an integral unit, and shares most features with the manual gear. A rotary control valve directs the hydraulic fluid to either side of the rack piston. The integral rack piston is attached to the rack and converts the hydraulic pressure into left or right linear mo-

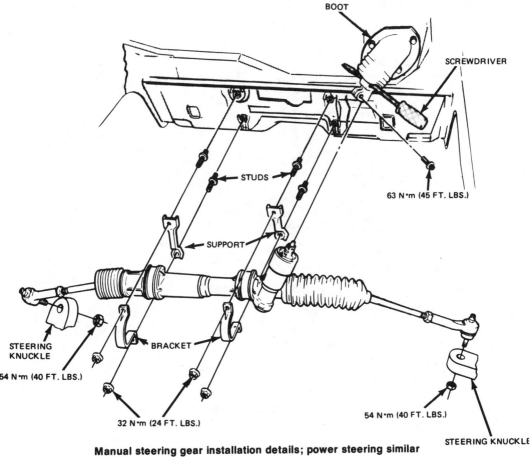

Manual steering gear installation details; power steering similar

tion. A vane-type constant displacement pump with integral reservoir provides hydraulic pressure. No in-car adjustments are necessary or possible on the system, except for periodic belt tension checks and adjustments for the pump.

Power Steering Pump
REMOVAL AND INSTALLATION
Gasoline Engines

All models use integral rack and pinion power steering. A pump delivers hydraulic pressure through two hoses to the steering gear itself.

1. Remove the hoses at the pump and tape the openings shut to prevent contamination. Position the disconnected lines in a raised position to prevent leakage.
2. Remove the pump belt.
3. On the four cylinder, remove the radiator hose clamp bolt. On the 6-173, disconnect the negative battery cable, disconnect the electrical connector at the blower motor, drain the cooling system, and remove the heater hose at the water pump. On the 6-183, remove the alternator.
4. Loosen the retaining bolts and any braces, and remove the pump.

5. Install the pump on the engine with the retaining bolts handtight.
6. Connect and tighten the hose fittings.
7. Refill the pump with fluid and bleed by turning the pulley counterclockwise (viewed from the front). Stop the bleeding when air bubbles no longer appear.
8. Install the pump belt on the pulley and adjust the tension.
9. Replace all other parts in reverse order of removal.

Diesel Engine

1. Remove the drive belt.
2. Siphon the fluid from the power steering reservoir.
3. Disconnect the hoses from the pump.
4. Remove the three bolts from the front of the pump through the access holes in the pulley.
5. Remove the two nuts holding the lower brace to the engine. Remove the brace.
6. Remove the pump.
7. Installation is the reverse of removal. Torque the brace nuts to 40 ft. lb.; the pump bolt to 40 ft. lb.

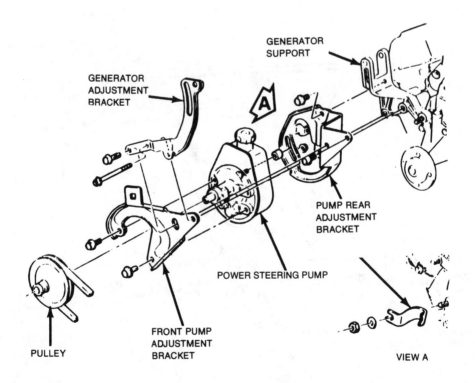

TORQUE ALL FASTENERS SHOWN
TO 50 N·m (35 FT. LBS.)

Power steering pump removal, 6-183

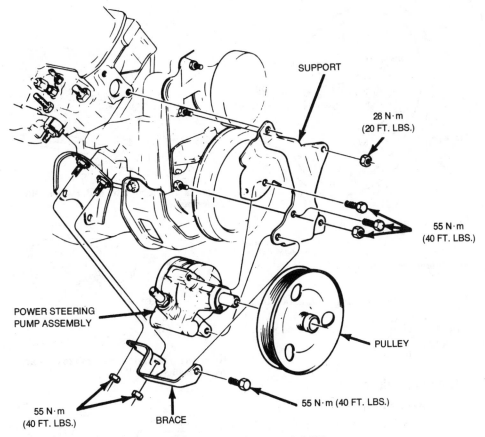

Power steering pump removal, 6-263

Bleeding Power Steering System

1. Fill the fluid reservoir.
2. Let the fluid stand undisturbed for two minutes, then crank the engine for about two seconds. Refill reservoir if necessary.
3. Repeat Steps 1 and 2 above until the fluid level remains constant after cranking the engine.
4. Raise the front of the car until the wheels are off the ground, then start the engine. Increase the engine speed to about 1,500 rpm.
5. Turn the wheels lightly against the stops to the left and right, checking the fluid level and refilling if necessary.

Steering Wheel
REMOVAL AND INSTALLATION

CAUTION: *Disconnect the battery ground cable before removing the steering wheel. When installing a steering wheel, always make sure that the turn signal lever is in the neutral position.*

1. Remove the trim retaining screws from behind the wheel. On wheels with a center cap, pull off the cap.
2. Lift the trim off and pull the horn wires from the turn signal cancelling cam.
3. Remove the retainer and the steering wheel nut.
4. Mark the wheel-to-shaft relationship, and then remove the wheel with a puller.
5. Install the wheel on the shaft aligning the previously made marks. Tighten the nut.

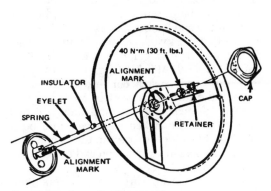

Sport steering wheel removal

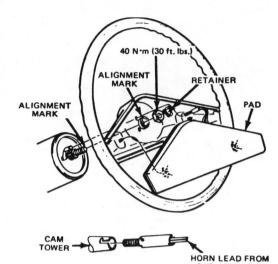

Standard steering wheel removal

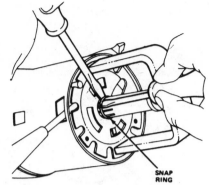

Depress the lockplate and remove the snapring

6. Insert the horn wires into the cancelling cam.

7. Install the center trim and reconnect the battery cable.

Turn Signal Switch

REMOVAL AND INSTALLATION

1. Remove the steering wheel as previously outlined. Remove the trim cover.

2. Loosen the cover screws. Pry the cover off with a screwdriver, and lift the cover off the shaft.

3. Position the U-shaped lockplate compressing tool on the end of the steering shaft and compress the lock plate by turning the shaft nut clockwise. Pry the wire snap-ring out of the shaft groove.

4. Remove the tool and lift the lock plate off the shaft.

5. Slip the cancelling cam, upper bearing preload spring, and thrust washer off the shaft.

6. Remove the turn signal lever. Push the flasher knob in and unscrew it. Remove the button retaining screw and remove the button, spring and knob.

7. Pull the switch connector out the mast jacket and tape the upper part to facilitate switch removal. Attach a long piece of wire to the turn signal switch connector. When installing the turn signal switch, feed this wire through the column first, and then use this wire to pull the switch connector into position. On tilt wheels, place the turn signal and shifter housing in low position and remove the harness cover.

8. Remove the three switch mounting screws. Remove the switch by pulling it

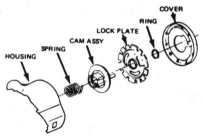

Remove these parts for access to the turn signal switch

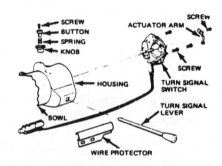

Turn signal switch

straight up while guiding the wiring harness cover through the column.

9. Install the replacement switch by working the connector and cover down through the housing and under the bracket. On tilt models, the connector is worked down through the housing, under the bracket, and then the cover is installed on the harness.

10. Install the sitch mounting screws and the connector on the mast jacket bracket. Install the column-to-dash trim plate.

11. Install the flasher knob and the turn signal lever.

12. With the turn signal lever in neutral and the flasher knob out, slide the thrust washer, upper bearing preload spring, and cancelling cam onto the shaft.

13. Position the lock plate on the shaft and

press it down until a new snapring can be inserted in the shaft groove. Always use a new snapring when assembling.

14. Install the cover and the steering wheel.

Ignition Switch
REMOVAL AND INSTALLATION

The switch is located inside the channel section of the brake pedal support and is completely inaccessible without first lowering the steering column. The switch is actuated by a rod and rack assembly. A gear on the end of the lock cylinder engages the toothed upper end of the rod.

1. Lower the steering column; be sure to properly support it.
2. Put the switch in the "Off-Unlocked" position. With the cylinder removed, the rod is in "Lock" when it is in the next to the uppermost detent. "Off-Unlocked" is two detents from the top.
3. Remove the two switch screws and remove the switch assembly.
4. Before installing, place the new switch in "Off-Unlocked" position and make sure the lock cylinder and actuating rod are in "Off-Unlocked" (third detent from the top) position.
5. Install the activating rod into the switch and assemble the switch on the column. Tighten the mounting screws. Use only the specified screws since overlength screws could impair the collapsibility of the column.
6. Reinstall the steering column.

Ignition Lock Cylinder
REMOVAL AND INSTALLATION

1. Place the lock in the Run position.
2. Remove the lock plate, turn signal switch and buzzer switch.

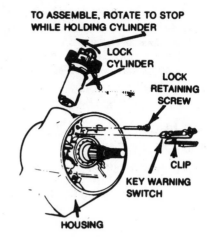

Ignition lock cylinder

3. Remove the screw and lock cylinder.
CAUTION: *If the screw is dropped on removal, it could fall into the column, requiring complete disassembly to retrieve the screw.*

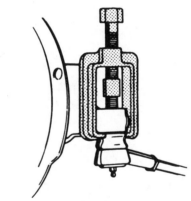

Separate the tie-rod end from the knuckle with a puller

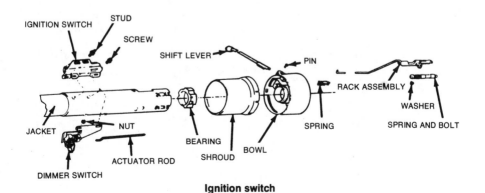

Ignition switch

4. Rotate the cylinder clockwise to align cylinder key with the keyway in the housing.

5. Push the lock all the way in.

6. Install the screw. Tighten the screw to 14 in. lb. for adjustable columns and 25 in. lb. for standard columns.

Tie Rod Ends

REMOVAL AND INSTALLATION

1. Loosen the jam nut on the steering rack (inner tie rod).

2. Remove the tie rod end nut. Separate the tie rod end from the steering knuckle using a puller.

3. Unscrew the tie rod end, counting the number of turns.

4. To install, screw the tie rod end onto the steering rack (inner tie-rod) the same number of turns as counted for removal. This will give approximately correct toe.

5. Install the tie rod end into the knuckle. Install the nut and tighten to 40 ft. lbs.

6. If the toe must be adjusted, use pliers to expand the boot clamp. Turn the inner tie rod to adjust. Replace the clamp.

7. Tighten the jam nut to 50 ft. lbs.

UNDERSTANDING THE BRAKE SYSTEM

Hydraulic System

A hydraulic system is used to actuate the brakes. The system transports the power required to force the frictional surfaces of the braking system together from the pedal to the individual braking units at each wheel. A hydraulic system is used for three reasons. First, fluid under pressure can be carried to all parts of the automobile by small hoses—some of which are flexible—without taking up a significant amount of room or posing routing problems. Second, liquid is noncompressible; a hydraulic system can transport force without modifying or reducing that force. Third, a great mechanical advantage can be given to the brake pedal end of the system, and the foot pressure required to actuate the brakes can be reduced by making the surface area of the master cylinder pistons smaller than that of any of the pistons in the wheel cylinders or calipers.

The master cylinder consists of a fluid reservoir and a double cylinder and piston assembly. Double type master cylinders are designed to separate the front and rear braking systems hydraulically in case of a leak.

Steel lines carry the brake fluid to a point on the vehicle's frame near each of the vehicle's wheels. The fluid is then carried to the slave cylinders by flexible tubes in order to allow for suspension and steering movements.

In drum brake systems, the slave cylinders are called wheel cylinders. Each wheel cylinder contains two pistons, one at either end, which push outward in opposite directions. In disc brake systems, the slave cylinders are part of the calipers. One or four cylinders are used to force the brake pads against the disc, but all cylinders contain one piston only. All slave cylinder pistons employ some type of seal, usually made of rubber, to minimize the leakage of fluid around the piston. A rubber dust boot seals the outer end of the cylinder against dust and dirt. The boot fits around the outer end of the piston on disc brake calipers, and around the brake actuating rod on wheel cylinders.

The hydraulic system operates as follows: When at rest, the entire system, from the pistons in the master cylinder to those in the wheel cylinders or calipers, is full of brake fluid. Upon application of the brake pedal, fluid trapped in front of the master cylinder pistons is forced through the lines to the slave cylinders. Here, it forces the pistons outward, in the case of drum brakes, and inward toward the disc, in the case of disc brakes. The motion of the pistons is opposed by return springs mounted outside the cylinders in drum brakes, and by internal springs or spring seals in disc brakes.

Upon release of the brake pedal, a spring located inside the master cylinder immediately returns the master cylinder pistons to the normal position. The pistons contain check valves and the master cylinder has compensating ports drilled in it. These are uncovered as the pistons reach their normal position. The piston check valves allow fluid to flow toward the wheel cylinders or calipers as the pistons withdraw. Then, as the return springs force the brake pads or shoes into the released position, the excess fluid returns to the master cylinder fluid reservoir through the compensating ports. It is during the time the pedal is in the released position that any fluid that has leaked out of the system will be replaced through the compensating ports.

Dual circuit master cylinders employ two pistons, located one behind the other, in the same cylinder. The primary piston is actuated by fluid trapped between the two pistons. If a leak develops in front of the secondary piston, it moves forward until it bottoms against the front of the master cylinder, and the fluid trapped between the pistons will operate the rear brakes. If the rear brakes develop a leak, the primary piston will move forward until direct contact with the secondary piston takes place, and it will force the secondary piston to actuate the front brakes. In either case, the brake pedal moves farther when the brakes are applied, and less braking power is available.

All dual-circuit systems use a distributor switch to warn the driver when only half of the brake system is operational. This switch is located in a valve body which is mounted on the master cylinder. A hydraulic piston receives pressure from both circuits, each circuit's pressure being applied to one end of the piston. When the pressures are in balance, the piston remains stationary. When one circuit has a leak, however, the greater pressure in that circuit during application of the brakes will push the piston to one side, closing the distributor switch and activating the brake warning light.

In disc brake systems, this valve body also contains a metering valve and, in some cases, a proportioning valve. The metering valve keeps pressure from traveling to the disc brakes on the front wheels until the brake shoes on the rear wheels have contacted the drums, ensuring that the front brakes will never be used alone. The proportioning valve throttles the pressure to the rear brakes so as to avoid rear wheel lock-up during very hard braking.

These valves may be tested by removing the lies to the front and rear brake systems and installing special brake pressure testing gauges. Front and rear system pressures are then compared as the pedal is gradually depressed. Specifications vary with the manufacturer and design of the brake system.

Brake system warning lights may be tested by depressing the brake pedal and holding it while opening one of the wheel cylinder bleeder screws. If this does not cause the light to go on, substitute a new lamp, make continuity checks, and, finally, replace the switch as necessary.

The hydraulic system may be checked for leaks by applying pressure to the pedal gradually and steadily. If the pedal sinks very slowly to the floor, the system has a leak. This is not to be confused with a springy or spongy feel due to the compression of air within the lines. If the system leaks, there will be a gradual change in the position of the pedal with a constant pressure.

Check for leaks along all lines and at wheel cylinders. If no external leaks are apparent, the problem is inside the master cylinder.

Disc Brakes

Instead of the traditional expanding brakes that press outward against a circular drum, disc brake systems utilize a cast iron disc with brake pads positioned on either side of it. Braking effect is achieved in a manner similar to the way you would squeeze a spinning phonograph record between your fingers. The disc (rotor) is a one-piece casting with cooling fins between the two braking surfaces. This enables air to circulate between the braking surfaces making them less sensitive to heat buildup and more resistant to fade. Dirt and water do not affect braking action since contaminants are thrown off by the centrifugal action of the rotor or scraped off by the pads. Also, the equal clamping action of the two brake pads tends to ensure uniform, straight-line stops. All disc brakes are self-adjusting.

Drum Brakes

Drum brakes employ two brake shoes mounted on a stationary backing plate. These shoes are positioned inside a circular cast iron drum which rotates with the wheel assembly. The shoes are held in place by springs; this allows them to slide toward the drums (when they are applied) while keeping the linings and drums in alignment. The shoes are actuated by a wheel cylinder which is mounted at the top of the backing plate. When the brakes are applied, hydraulic pressure forces the wheel cylinder's two actuating links outward. Since these links bear directly against the top of the brake shoes, the tops of the shoes are then forced outward against the inner side of the drum. This action forces the bottoms of the two shoes to contact the brake drum by rotating the entire assembly slightly (known as servo action). When pressure within the wheel cylinder is relaxed, return springs pull the shoes back away from the drum.

The drum brakes are designed to self-adjust during application when the car is moving in reverse. This motion causes both shoes to rotate very slightly with the drum, rocking an adjusting lever, thereby causing rotation of the adjusting screw by means of an actuating lever.

Power Brake Boosters

Power brakes operate just as standard brake systems except in the actuation of the master cylinder pistons. A vacuum diaphragm is located on the front of the master cylinder and assists the driver in applying the brakes, reducing both the effort and travel he must put into moving the brake pedal.

The vacuum diaphragm housing is connected to the intake manifold by a vacuum hose. A check valve is placed at the point where the hose enters the diaphragm housing, so that during periods of low manifold vacuum brake assist vacuum will not be lost.

Depressing the brake pedal closes off the vacuum source and allows atmospheric pressure to enter on one side of the diaphragm. This causes the master cylinder pistons to move and apply the brakes. When the brake pedal is released, vacuum is applied to both sides of the diaphragm, and return springs return the diaphragm and master cylinder pistons to the released position. If the vacuum fails, the brake pedal rod will butt against the end of the master cylinder actuating rod, and direct mechanical application will occur as the pedal is depressed.

The hydraulic and mechanical problems that apply to conventional brake systems also apply to power brakes, and should be checked for if the following tests do not reveal the problem.

Test for a system vacuum leak as described below:

1. Operate the engine at idle with the transaxle in Neutral without touching the brake pedal for at least one minute.

2. Turn off the engine, and wait one minute.

3. Test for the presence of assist vacuum by depressing the brake pedal and releasing it several times. Light application will produce less and less pedal travel, if vacuum was present. If there is no vacuum, air is leaking into the system somewhere.

Test for system operation as follows:

1. Pump the brake pedal (with engine off) until the supply vacuum is entirely gone.

2. Put a light, steady pressure on the pedal.

3. Start the engine, and operate it at idle with the transaxle in Neutral. If the system is operating, the brake pedal should fall toward the floor if constant pressure is maintained on the pedal.

Power brake systems may be tested for hydraulic leaks just as ordinary systems are tested, except that the engine should be idling with the transaxle in Neutral throughout the test.

BRAKE SYSTEM

The A-Body cars have a diagonally-split hydraulic system. This differs from conventional practice in that the left front and right rear brakes are on one hydraulic circuit, and the right front and left rear are on the other.

A diagonally-split system necessitates the use of a special master cylinder design. The A-Body master cylinder incorporates the functions of a standard tandem master cylinder, plus a warning light switch and proportioning valves. Additionally, the master cylinder is designed with a quick take-up feature which provides a large volume of fluid to the brakes at low pressure when the brakes are initially applied. The low pressure fluid acts to quickly fill the large displacement requirements of the system.

The front disc brakes are single piston sliding caliper units. Fluid pressure acts equally against the piston and the bottom of the piston bore in the caliper. This forces the piston outward until the pad contacts the rotor. The force on the caliper bore forces the caliper to slide over, carrying the other pad into contact with the other side of the rotor. The disc brakes are self-adjusting.

Rear drum brakes are conventional duo-servo units. A dual piston wheel cylinder, mounted to the top of the backing plate, actuates both brake shoes. Wheel cylinder force to the shoes is supplemented by the tendency of the shoes to wrap into the drum (servo action). An actuating link, pivot and lever serve to automatically engage the adjuster as the brakes are applied when the car is moving in reverse. Provisions for manual adjustment are also provided. The rear brakes also serve as the parking brakes; linkage is mechanical.

Vacuum boost is an option. The booster is a conventional tandem vacuum unit.

Adjustment
DISC BRAKES

The front disc brakes are self-adjusting. No adjustments are either necessary or possible.

DRUM BRAKES

The drum brakes are designed to self-adjust when applied with the car moving in reverse. However, they can also be adjusted manually. This manual adjustment should also be performed whenever the linings are replaced.

1. Use a punch to knock out the stamped area on the brake drum. If this is done with the drum installed on the car, the drum must then be removed to clean out all metal pieces. After adjustments are complete, obtain a hole cover from your dealer (Part no. 4874119 or the equivalent) to prevent entry of dirt and water into the brakes.

2. Use an adjusting tool especially made for the purpose to turn the brake adjusting screw star wheel. Expand the shoes until the drum can just barely be turned by hand.

3. Back off the adjusting screw a few notches. If the shoes still are dragging lightly,

back off the adjusting screw one or two additional notches. If the brakes still drag, the parking brake adjustment is incorrect or the parking brake is applied. Fix and start over.

4. Install the hole cover into the drum.

5. Check the parking brake adjustment.

On some models, no marked area or stamped area is present on the drum. In this case, a hole must be drilled in the backing plate:

1. All backing plates have two round flat areas in the lower half through which the parking brake cable is installed. Drill a ½ in. hole into the round flat area on the backing plate opposite the parking brake cable. This will allow access to the star wheel.

2. After drilling the hole, remove the drum and remove all metal particles. Install a hole plug (Part no. 4874119 or the equivalent) to prevent the entry of water or dirt.

HYDRAULIC SYSTEM

Master Cylinder

REMOVAL AND INSTALLATION

1. If your car does not have power brakes, disconnect the master cylinder pushrod at the brake pedal inside the car. The pushrod is retained to the brake pedal by a clip; there is a washer under the clip, and a spring washer on the other side of the pushrod.

2. Unplug the electrical connector from the master cylinder.

3. Place a number of cloths or a container under the mastery cylinder to catch the brake fluid. Disconnect the brake tubes from the master cylinder; use a flare nut wrench if one

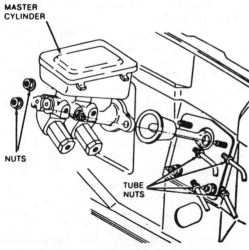

MASTER CYLINDER

NUTS

TUBE NUTS

Master cylinder removal; power brakes similar

is available. Tape over the open ends of the tubes.

NOTE: *Brake fluid eats paint. Wipe up any spilled fluid immediately, then flush the area with clear water.*

4. Remove the two nuts attaching the master cylinder to the booster or firewall.

5. Remove the master cylinder.

6. To install, attach the master cylinder to the firewall or the booster with the nuts. Torque to 22–30 ft. lbs. (30–45 Nm.).

7. Reconnect the pushrod to the brake pedal with non-power brakes.

8. Remove the tape from the lines and connect to the master cylinder. Torque to 10–15 ft. lbs. (13–20 Nm.). Connect the electrical lead.

9. Bleed the brakes.

OVERHAUL

This is a tedious, time-consuming job. You can save yourself a lot of trouble by buying a rebuilt master cylinder from your dealer or parts supply house. The small difference in price between a rebuilding kit and a rebuilt part usually makes it more economical, in terms of time and work, to buy the rebuilt part.

1. Remove the master cylinder.

2. Remove the reservoir cover and drain the fluid.

3. Remove the pushrod and rubber boot on non-power models.

4. Unbolt the proportioners and failure warning switch from the side of the master cylinder body. Discard the O-rings found under the proportioners. Use new ones on installation. There may or may not be an O-ring under the original equipment failure warning switch. If there is, discard it. In either case, use an O-ring upon assembly.

5. Clamp the master cylinder body in a vise, taking care not to crush it. Depress the primary piston with a wooden dowel and remove the lock ring with a pair of snap-ring pliers.

6. The primary and secondary pistons can be removed by applying compressed air into one of the outlets at the end of the cylinder and plugging the other three outlets. The primary piston must be replaced as an assembly if the seals are bad. The secondary piston seals are replaceable. Install these new seals with the lips facing outwards.

7. Inspect the bore for corrosion. If any corrosion is evident, the master cylinder body must be replaced. Do not attempt to polish the bore with crocus cloth, sandpaper, or anything else. The body is aluminum; polishing the bore won't work.

8. To remove the failure warning switch

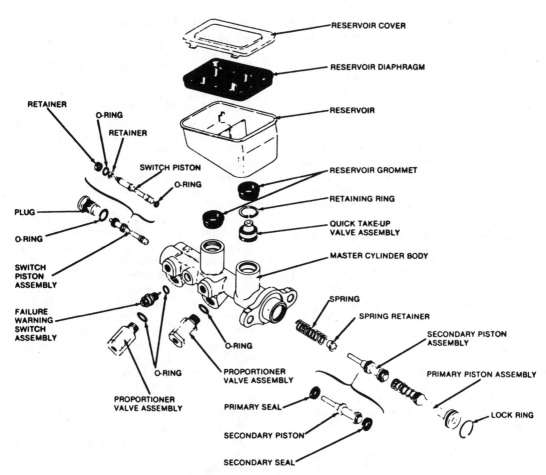

Exploded view of the master cylinder

piston assembly, remove the allen head plug from the end of the bore and withdraw the assembly with a pair of needlenose pliers. The switch piston assembly seals are replaceable.

9. The reservoir can be removed from the master cylinder body if necessary. Clamp the body in a vise by its mounting flange. Use a pry bar to remove the reservoir. If the reservoir is removed, remove the reservoir grommets and discard them. The quick takeup valves under the grommets are accessible after the retaining snap-rings are removed. Use snap-ring pliers; no other tool will work.

10. Clean all parts in denatured alcohol and allow to air dry. Do not use anything else to clean, and do not wipe dry with a rag, which will leave bits of lint behind. Inspect all parts for corrosion or wear. Generally, it is best to replace *all* rubber parts whenever the master cylinder is disassembled, and replace any metal part which shows any sign whatsoever of wear or corrosion.

11. Lubricate all parts with clean brake fluid before assembly.

12. Install the quick take-up valves into the master cylinder body and secure with the snap-rings. Make sure the snapr-ings are properly seated in their grooves. Lubricate the new reservoir grommets with clean brake fluid and press them into the master cylinder.

13. Install the reservoir into the grommets by placing the reservoir on its lid and pressing the master cylinder body down onto it with a rocking motion.

14. Lubricate the switch piston assembly with clean brake fluid. Install new O-rings and retainers on the piston. Install the piston assembly into the master cylinder and secure with the plug, using a new O-ring on the plug. Torque is 40–140 in. lbs. (5–16 Nm.).

15. Assemble the new secondary piston seals onto the piston. Lubricate the parts with clean brake fluid, then install the spring, spring retainer and secondary piston into the cylinder. Install the primary piston, depress, and install the lock ring.

16. Install new O-rings on the proportioners and the failure warning switch. Install the pro-

portioners and torque to 18–30 ft. lbs. (25–40 Nm.). Install the failure warning switch and torque to 15–50 in. lbs. (2–6 Nm.).

17. Clamp the master cylinder body upright into a vise by one of the mounting flanges. Fill the reservoir with fresh brake fluid. Pump the piston with a dowel until fluid squirts from the outlet ports. Continue pumping until the expelled fluid is free of air bubbles.

18. Install the master cylinder, and bleed the brakes. Check the brake system for proper operation. Do not move the car until a "hard" brake pedal is obtained and the brake system has been thoroughly checked for soundness.

Proportioning Valves and Failure Warning Switch

These parts are installed in the master cylinder body. No separate proportioning or metering valve is used. Replacement of these parts requires disassembly of the master cylinder.

Bleeding

The purpose of bleeding the brakes is to expel air trapped in the hydraulic system. The system must be bled whenever the pedal feels spongy, indicating that compressible air has entered the system. It must also be bled whenever the system has been opened or repaired. You will need a helper for this job.

CAUTION: *Never reuse brake fluid which has been bled from the brake system.*

1. The sequence for bleeding is right rear, left front, left rear and right front. If the car has power brakes, remove the vacuum by applying the brakes several times. Do not run the engine while bleeding the brakes.

2. Clean all the bleeder screws. You may want to give each one a shot of penetrating solvent to loosen it up; seizure is a common

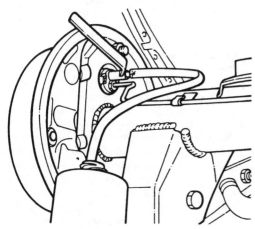

Bleeding the brakes

problem with bleeder screws, which then break off, sometimes requiring replacement of the part to which they are attached.

3. Fill the master cylinder with DOT 3 brake fluid.

NOTE: *Brake fluid absorbs moisture from the air. Don't leave the master cylinder or the fluid container uncovered any longer than necessary. Be careful handling the fluid—it eats paint.*

Check the level of the fluid often when bleeding, and refill the reservoirs as necessary. Don't let them run dry, or you will have to repeat the process.

4. Attach a length of clear vinyl tubing to the bleeder screw on the wheel cylinder. Insert the other end of the tube into a clear, clean jar half filled with brake fluid.

5. Have your assistant slowly depress the brake pedal. As this is done, open the bleeder screw ⅓–½ of a turn, and allow the fluid to run through the tube. Then close the bleeder screw before the pedal reaches the end of its travel. Have your assistant slowly release the pedal. Repeat this process until no air bubbles appear in the expelled fluid.

6. Repeat the procedure on the other three brakes, checking the level of fluid in the master cylinder reservoir often.

After you're done, there should be no sponginess in the brake pedal feel. If there is, either there is still air in the line, in which case the process should be repeated, or there is a leak somewhere, which of course must be corrected before the car is moved.

FRONT DISC BRAKES

Pads

INSPECTION

The pad thickness should be inspected every time that the tires are removed for rotation. The outer pad can be checked by looking in at each end, which is the point at which the highest rate of wear occurs. The inner pad can be checked by looking down through the inspection hole in the top of the caliper. If the thickness of the pad is worn to within 0.030 in. (0.76 mm) of the rivet at either end of the pad, all the pads should be replaced. This is the factory-recommended measurement; your state's automobile inspection laws may not agree with this.

NOTE: *Always replace all pads on both front wheels at the same time. Failure to do so will result in uneven braking action and premature wear.*

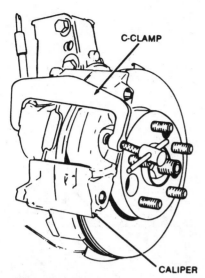

Install a C-clamp to retract the disc brake pads

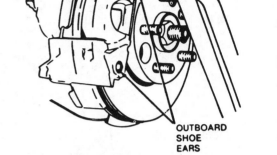

Bend the outboard pad ears into place with a large pair of slip joint pliers

REMOVAL AND INSTALLATION

1. Siphon ⅔ of the brake fluid from the master cylinder reservoir. Loosen the wheel lug nuts and raise the car. Remove the wheel.

2. Position a C-clamp across the caliper so that it presses on the pads and tighten it until the caliper piston bottoms in its bore.

NOTE: *If you haven't removed some brake fluid from the master cylinder, it will overflow when the piston is retracted.*

3. Remove the C-clamp.

4. Remove the allen head caliper mounting bolts. Inspect the bolts for corrosion, and replace as necessary.

5. Remove the caliper from the steering knuckle and suspend it from the body of the car with a length of wire. Do not allow the caliper to hang by its hose.

6. Remove the pad retaining springs and remove the pads from the caliper.

7. Remove the plastic sleeves and the rubber bushings from the mounting bolt holes.

8. Install new sleeves and bushings. Lubricate the sleeves with a light coating of silicone grease before installation. These parts must always be replaced when the pads are replaced. The parts are usually included in the pad replacement kits.

9. Install the outboard pad into the caliper.

10. Install the retainer spring on the inboard pad. A new spring should be included in the pad replacement kit.

11. Install the new inboard pad into the caliper. The retention lugs fit into the piston.

12. Use a large pair of slip joint pliers to bend the outer pad ears down over the caliper.

13. Install the caliper onto the steering knuckle. Tighten the mounting bolts to 21–35 ft. lbs. (28–47 Nm.). Install the wheel and lower the car. Fill the master cylinder to its proper level with fresh brake fluid meeting DOT 3 specifications. Since the brake hose wasn't disconnected, it isn't really necessary to bleed the brakes, although most mechanics do this as a matter of course.

Caliper

REMOVAL AND INSTALLATION

1. Follow Steps 1, 2 and 3 of the pad replacement procedure.

2. Before removing the caliper mounting bolts, remove the bolt holding the brake hose to the caliper.

3. Remove the allen head caliper mounting bolts. Inspect them for corrosion and replace them if necessary.

4. Installation is the reverse. Mounting bolt torque is 21–35 ft. lbs. (28–47 Nm.) for the caliper. The brake hose fitting should be tightened to 18–30 ft. lbs. (24–40 Nm.).

OVERHAUL

1. Remove the caliper.

2. Remove the pads.

3. Place some cloths or a slat of wood in front of the piston. Remove the piston by applying compressed air to the fluid inlet fitting. Use just enough air pressure to ease the piston from the bore.

CAUTION: *Do not try to catch the piston with your fingers, which can result in serious injury.*

4. Remove the piston boot with a screw-

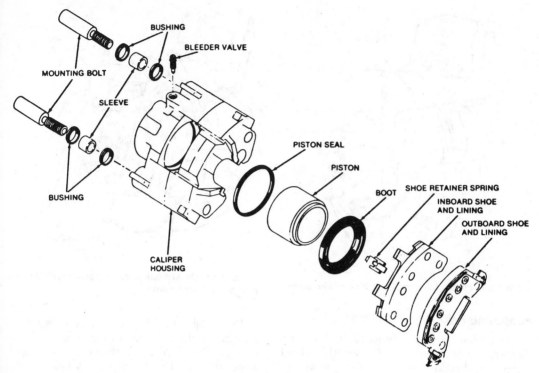

Exploded view of the disc brake caliper

driver, working carefully so that the piston bore is not scratched.

5. Remove the bleeder screw.

6. Inspect the piston for scoring, nicks, corrosion, wear, etc., and damaged or worn chrome plating. Replace the piston if any defects are found.

7. Remove the piston seal from the caliper bore groove using a piece of pointed wood or plastic. Do not use a screwdriver, which will damage the bore. Inspect the caliper bore for nicks, corrosion, and so on. Very light wear can be cleaned up with crocus cloth. Use finger pressure to rub the crocus cloth around

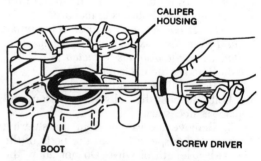

Remove the piston boot with a screwdriver

the circumference of the bore—do not slide it in and out. More extensive wear or corrosion warrants replacement of the part.

8. Clean any parts which are to be reused in denatured alcohol. Dry them with compressed air or allow to air dry. Don't wipe the parts dry with a cloth, which will leave behind bits of lint.

9. Lubricate the new seal, provided in the repair kit, with clean brake fluid. Install the seal in its groove, making sure it is fully seated and not twisted.

10. Install the new dust boot on the piston. Lubricate the bore of the caliper with clean brake fluid and insert the piston into its bore. Position the boot in the caliper housing and seat with a seal driver of the appropriate size, or G.M. tool no. J-29077.

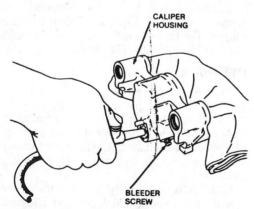

Use air pressure to remove the piston from the bore

11. Install the bleeder screw, tightening to 80–140 ft. lbs. (9–16 Nm.). Do not over-tighten.

12. Install the pads, install the caliper, and bleed the brakes.

Disc (Rotor)
REMOVAL AND INSTALLATION

1. Remove the caliper.
2. Remove the rotor.
3. Installation is the reverse.

INSPECTION

1. Check the rotor surface for wear or scoring. Deep scoring, grooves or rust pitting can be removed by refacing, a job to be referred to your local machine shop or garage. Minimum thickness is stamped on the rotor (0.965 in., or 24.47 mm). If the rotor will be thinner than this after refinishing, it must be replaced.

2. Check the rotor parallelism; it must vary less than 0.0005 in. (0.013 mm) measured at four or more points around the circumference. Make all measurements at the same distance in from the edge of the rotor. Refinish the rotor if it fails to meet this specification.

3. Measure the disc runout with a dial indicator. If runout exceeds 0.005 in. (0.127 mm), and the wheel bearings are OK (if runout is being measured with the disc on the car), the rotor must be refaced or replaced as necessary.

REAR DRUM BRAKES

Brake Drums
REMOVAL AND INSTALLATION

1. Loosen the wheel lug nuts. Raise and support the car. Mark the relationship of the wheel to the axle and remove the wheel.

2. Mark the relationship of the drum to the axle and remove the drum. If it cannot be slipped off easily, check to see that the parking brake is fully released. If so, the brke shoes are probably locked against the drum. See the "Adjustment" section earlier in this chapter for details on how to back off the adjuster.

3. Installation is the reverse. Be sure to align the matchmarks made during removal. Lug nut torque is 102 ft. lbs. (140 Nm.).

INSPECTION

1. After removing the brake drum, wipe out the accumulated dust with a damp cloth.
WARNING: *Do not blow the brake dust out of the drums with compressed air or lung-power. Brake linings contain asbestos, a*

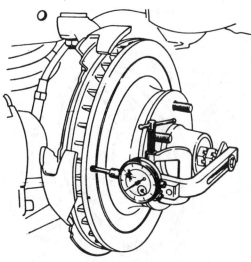
Check the rotor runout with a dial indicator

known cancer causing substance. Dispose of the cloth used to clean the parts after use.

2. Inspect the drums for cracks, deep grooves, roughness, scoring, or out-of-roundness. Replace any drum which is cracked; do not try to weld it up.

3. Smooth any slight scores by polishing the friction surface with fine emery cloth. Heavy or extensive scoring will cause excessive lining wear and should be removed from the drum through resurfacing, a job to be referred to your local machine shop or garage. The maximum finished diameter of the drums is 7.894 in. (200.64 mm). The drum must be replaced if the diameter is 7.924 in. (201.40 mm) or greater.

Brake Shoes
INSPECTION

After removing the brake drum, inspect the brake shoes. If the lining is worn down to within 1/32 in. (0.76 mm) of a rivet, the shoes must be replaced.
NOTE: *This figure may disagree with your state's automobile inspection laws.*

If the brake lining is soaked with brake fluid or grease, it must be replaced. If this is the case, the brake drum should be sanded with crocus cloth to remove all traces of brake fluid, and the wheel cylinders should be rebuilt. Clean all grit from the friction surface of the drum before replacing it.

If the lining is chipped, cracked, or otherwise damaged, it must be replaced with a new lining.
NOTE: *Always replace the brake linings in sets of two on both ends of the axle. Never*

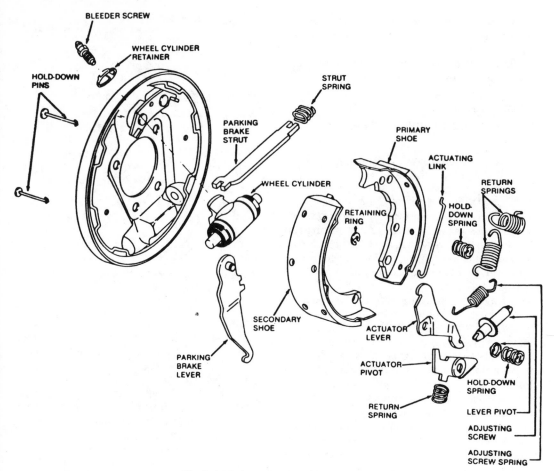

Exploded view of the drum brake

replace just one shoe, or both shoes on one side.

Check the condition of the shoes, retracting springs, and hold-down springs for signs of overheating. If the shoes or springs have a slight blue color, this indicates overheating and replacement of the shoes and springs is recommended. The wheel cylinders should be rebuilt as a precaution against future problems.

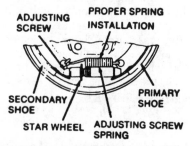

Proper spring installation is with the coils over the adjuster, not the star wheel

REMOVAL AND INSTALLATION

1. Loosen the lug nuts on the wheel to be serviced, raise and support the car, and remove the wheel and brake drum.

NOTE: *It is not really necessary to remove the hub and wheel bearing assembly from the axle, but it does make the job easier. If you can work with the hub and bearing assembly in place, skip down to Step 3.*

2. Remove the four hub and bearing assembly retaining bolts and remove the assembly from the axle.

3. Remove the return springs from the shoes with a pair of needle nose pliers. There are also special brake spring pliers for this job.

4. Remove the hold down springs by gripping them with a pair of pliers, then pressing down and turning 90°. There are special tools to grab and turn these parts, but pliers work fairly well.

5. Remove the shoe hold-down pins from behind the brake backing plate. They will sim-

ply slide out once the hold-down spring tension is relieved.

6. Lift up the actuator lever for the self-adjusting mechanism and remove the actuating link. Remove the actuator lever, pivot, and the pivot return spring.

7. Spread the shoes apart to clear the wheel cylinder pistons and remove the parking brake strut and spring.

8. If the hub and bearing assembly is still in place, spread the shoes far enough apart to clear it.

9. Disconnect the parking brake cable from the lever. Remove the shoes, still connected by their adjusting screw spring, from the car.

10. With the shoes removed, note the position of the adjusting spring and remove the spring and adjusting screw.

11. Remove the C-clip from the parking brake lever and remove the lever from the secondary shoe.

12. Use a damp cloth to remove all dirt and dust from the backing plate and brake parts.

13. Check the wheel cylinders by carefully pulling the lower edges of the wheel cylinder boots away from the cylinders. If there is excessive leakage, the inside of the cylinder will be moist with fluid. If leakage exists, a wheel cylinder overhaul is in order. Do not delay, because brake failure could result.

NOTE: *A small amount of fluid will be present to act as a lubricant for the wheel cylinder pistons. Fluid spilling from the boot center hole, after the piston is removed, indicates cup leakage and the necessity for cylinder overhaul.*

14. Check the backing plate attaching bolts to make sure that they are tight. Use fine emery cloth to clean all rust and dirt from the shoe contact surfaces on the plate.

15. Lubricate the fulcrum end of the parking brake lever with brake grease specially made for the purpose. Install the lever on the secondary shoe and secure with the C-clip.

16. Install the adjusting screw and spring on the shoes, connecting them together. The coils of the spring must *not* be over the star wheel on the adjuster. The left and right hand springs are *not* interchangeable. Do not mix them up.

17. Lubricate the shoe contact surfaces on the backing plate with the brake grease. Be certain when you are using this stuff that none of it actually gets on the linings or drums. Apply the same grease to the point where the parking brake cable contacts the plate. Use the grease sparingly.

18. Spread the shoe assemblies apart and connect the parking brake cable. Install the shoes on the backing plate, engaging the shoes

at the top temporarily with the wheel cylinder pistons. Make sure that the star wheel on the adjuster is lined up with the adjusting hole in the backing plate, if the hole is back there.

19. Spread the shoes apart slightly and install the parking brake strut and spring. Make sure that the end of the strut without the spring engages the parking brake lever. The end with the spring engages the primary shoe (the one with the shorter lining).

20. Install the actuator pivot, lever and return spring. Install the actuating link in the shoe retainer. Lift up the actuator lever and hook the link into the lever.

21. Install the hold-down pins through the back of the plate, install the lever pivots and hold-down springs. Install the shoe return springs with a pair of pliers. Be very careful not to stretch or otherwise distort these springs.

22. Take a look at everything. Make sure the linings are in the right place, the self-adjusting mechanism is correctly installed, and the parking brake parts are all hooked up. If in doubt, remove the other wheel and take a look at that one for comparison.

23. Measure the width of the linings, then measure the inside width of the drum. Adjust the linings by means of the adjuster so that the drum will fit onto the linings.

24. Install the hub and bearing assembly onto the axle if removed. Tighten the retaining bolts to 35 ft. lbs. (55 Nm.).

25. Install the drum and wheel. Adjust the brakes. Be sure to install a rubber hole cover in the knock-out hole after the adjustment is complete. Adjust the parking brake.

26. Lower the car and check the pedal for any sponginess or lack of a "hard" feel. Check the braking action and the parking brake. The brakes must not be applied severely immediately after installation. They should be used moderately for the first 200 miles of city driving or 1000 miles of highway driving, to allow the linings to conform to the shape of the drum.

Wheel Cylinders
REMOVAL AND INSTALLATION

1. Loosen the wheel lug nuts, raise and support the car, and remove the wheel. Remove the drum and brake shoes. Leave the hub and wheel bearing assembly in place.

2. Remove any dirt from around the brake line fitting. Disconnect the brake line.

3. Remove the wheel cylinder retainer by using two awls or punches with a tip diameter of 1/8 in. or less. Insert the awls or punches into the access slots between the wheel cylinder pilot and retainer locking tabs. Bend both

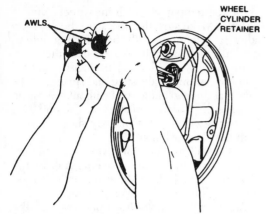

Remove the wheel cylinder retainer from the backing plate with a pair of awls or punches

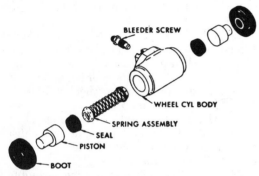

Exploded view of the wheel cylinder

tabs away simultaneously. Remove the wheel cylinder from the backing plate.

4. To install, position the wheel cylinder against the backing plate and hold it in place with a wooden block between the wheel cylinder and the hub and bearing assembly.

5. Install a new retainer over the wheel cylinder abutment on the rear of the backing plate by pressing it into place with a 1⅛ in. 12-point socket and an extension.

6. Install a new bleeder screw into the wheel cylinder. Install the brake line and tighten to 10–15 ft. lbs. (13–20 Nm.).

7. The rest of installation is the reverse of removal. After the drum is installed, bleed the brakes.

OVERHAUL

As is the case with master cylinders, overhaul kits are available for the wheel cylinders. And, as is the case with master cylinders, it is usually more profitable to simply buy new or rebuilt wheel cylinders rather than rebuilding them. When rebuilding wheel cylinders, avoid getting any contaminants in the system. Always install new high-quality brake fluid; the

use of improper fluid will swell and deteriorate the rubber parts.

1. Remove the wheel cylinders.

2. Remove the rubber boots from the cylinder ends. Discard the boots.

3. Remove and discard the pistons and cups.

4. Wash the cylinder and metal parts in denatured alcohol.

CAUTION: *Never use mineral-based solvents to clean the brake parts.*

5. Allow the parts to air dry and inspect the cylinder bore for corrosion or wear. Light corrosion can be cleaned up with crocus cloth; use finger pressure and rotate the cloth around the circumference of the bore. Do not move the cloth in and out. Any deep corrosion or pitting or wear warrants replacement of the parts.

6. Rinse the parts and allow to dry. Do not dry with a rag, which will leave bits of lint behind.

7. Lubricate the cylinder bore with clean brake fluid. Insert the spring assembly.

8. Install new cups. Do not lubricate prior to assembly.

9. Install the new pistons.

10. Press the new boots onto the cylinders by hand. Do not lubricate prior to assembly.

11. Install the wheel cylinders. Bleed the brakes after installation of the drum.

Vacuum Booster
REMOVAL AND INSTALLATION

1. Remove the master cylinder from the booster. It is not necessary to disconnect the lines from the master cylinder. Just move the cylinder aside.

2. Disconnect the vacuum booster pushrod from the brake pedal inside the car. It is retained by a bolt. A spring washer lives under the bolt head, and a flat washer goes on the

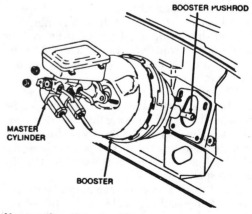

Vacuum booster mounting

other side of the pushrod eye, next to the pedal arm.

3. Remove the four attaching nuts from inside the car. Remove the booster.

4. Install the booster on the firewall. Tighten the mounting nuts to 22–33 ft. lbs. (30–45 Nm.).

5. Connect the pushrod to the brake pedal.

6. Install the master cylinder. Mounting torque is 25 ft. lbs. (40 Nm.).

OVERHAUL

This job is not difficult, but requires a number of special tools which are expensive, especially if they're to be used only once. Generally, it's better to leave this job to your dealer, or buy a rebuilt vacuum booster and install it yourself.

PARKING BRAKE

ADJUSTMENT

1. Raise and support the car with both rear wheels off the ground.

2. Depress the parking brake pedal exactly two ratchet clicks.

3. Loosen the equalizer locknut, then tighten the adjusting nut until the left rear wheel can just be turned backward using two hands, but is locked in forward rotation.

4. Tighten the locknut.

5. Release the parking brake. Rotate the rear wheels—there should be no drag.

6. Lower the car.

Cable

REMOVAL AND INSTALLATION

Front Cable

1. Depress the parking brake pedal.

2. Clamp a pair of locking pliers on the upper cable where it enters the casing.

3. Pull the brake release, and remove the cable from the control assembly.

4. Release the locking tabs on the casing and remove the casing from the control assembly.

5. Unhook the parking brake cable from the parking brake lever.

6. Pull the cable casing from the backing plate after the retaining legs have been released.

7. Remove the equalizer retaining bolt. Remove the nut attaching the cable to the pivot. Remove the cable casing from the cable guide bracket behind the equalizer by releasing the retaining legs.

8. Unhook the cable from the connector that attaches to the left cable.

9. Installation is the reverse. Apply white grease to all parts in sliding contact. Adjust the parking brake after installation.

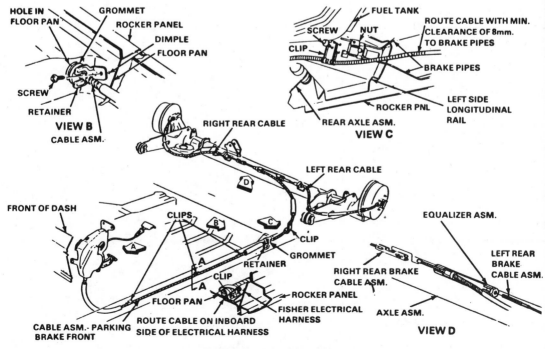

Parking brake cable routing

Brake Specifications

Model	Lug Nut Torque (ft/lb)	Master Cylinder Bore	Brake Disc		Brake Drum			Minimum Lining Thickness	
			Minimum Thickness	Maximum Run-Out	Diameter	Max Machine O/S	Max Wear Limit	Front	Rear
All	103	0.874	0.965②	0.005	7.884	7.905	7.935	①	①

① Minimum lining thickness is to $^1/_{32}$ of rivet

NOTE: *Minimum lining thickness is as recommended by the manufacturer. Because of variations in state inspection regulations, the minimum allowable thickness may be different than recommended by the manufacturer.*

Left Rear Cable

1. Perform Steps 1–7 of the right rear cable procedure.

2. Remove the cable casing from the rear axle.

3. Disconnect the cable at the connector at the center of the axle.

4. Installation is the reverse. Lubricate all parts in sliding contact with white waterproof grease, and adjust the parking brake after installation.

5. Push the grommet and the cable through the firewall into the engine compartment.

6. Remove the cable from its guide bracket on the firewall.

7. Remove the cable from the rear cable guide. Unhook the cable from the equalizer lever.

8. Installation is the reverse. Coat all areas in sliding contact with white waterproof grease. Adjust the parking brake after cable installation.

Right Rear Cable

1. Raise and support the car. Remove the wheel and the brake drum.

2. Insert a screwdriver between the brake shoe and the top part of the adjuster bracket. Push the bracket to the front and release the top adjuster bracket rod.

3. Remove the rear hold-down spring and remove the actuator lever and return spring.

4. Remove the adjuster screw spring.

5. Remove the top rear brake shoe return spring.

Troubleshooting

9

This section is designed to aid in the quick, accurate diagnosis of automotive problems. While automotive repairs can be made by many people, accurate troubleshooting is a rare skill for the amateur and professional alike.

In its simplest state, troubleshooting is an exercise in logic. It is essential to realize that an automobile is really composed of a series of systems. Some of these systems are interrelated; others are not. Automobiles operate within a framework of logical rules and physical laws, and the key to troubleshooting is a good understanding of all the automotive systems.

This section breaks the car or truck down into its component systems, allowing the problem to be isolated. The charts and diagnostic road maps list the most common problems and the most probable causes of trouble. Obviously it would be impossible to list every possible problem that could happen along with every possible cause, but it will locate MOST problems and eliminate a lot of unnecessary guesswork. The systematic format will locate problems within a given system, but, because many automotive systems are interrelated, the solution to your particular problem may be found in a number of systems on the car or truck.

USING THE TROUBLESHOOTING CHARTS

This book contains all of the specific information that the average do-it-yourself mechanic needs to repair and maintain his or her car or truck. The troubleshooting charts are designed to be used in conjunction with the specific procedures and information in the text. For instance, troubleshooting a point-type ignition system is fairly standard for all models, but you may be directed to the text to find procedures for troubleshooting an individual type of electronic ignition. You will also have to refer to the specification charts throughout the book for specifications applicable to your car or truck.

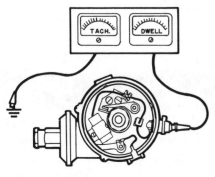

Tach-dwell hooked-up to distributor

TOOLS AND EQUIPMENT

The tools illustrated in Chapter 1 (plus two more diagnostic pieces) will be adequate to troubleshoot most problems. The two other tools needed are a voltmeter and an ohmmeter. These can be purchased separately or in combination, known as a VOM meter.

In the event that other tools are required, they will be noted in the procedures.

Troubleshooting Engine Problems
See Chapters 2, 3, 4 for more information and service procedures.

Index to Systems

System	To Test	Group
Battery	Engine need not be running	1
Starting system	Engine need not be running	2
Primary electrical system	Engine need not be running	3
Secondary electrical system	Engine need not be running	4
Fuel system	Engine need not be running	5
Engine compression	Engine need not be running	6
Engine vacuum	Engine must be running	7
Secondary electrical system	Engine must be running	8
Valve train	Engine must be running	9
Exhaust system	Engine must be running	10
Cooling system	Engine must be running	11
Engine lubrication	Engine must be running	12

Index to Problems

Problem: Symptom	Begin at Specific Diagnosis, Number ___
Engine Won't Start:	
Starter doesn't turn	1.1, 2.1
Starter turns, engine doesn't	2.1
Starter turns engine very slowly	1.1, 2.4
Starter turns engine normally	3.1, 4.1
Starter turns engine very quickly	6.1
Engine fires intermittently	4.1
Engine fires consistently	5.1, 6.1
Engine Runs Poorly:	
Hard starting	3.1, 4.1, 5.1, 8.1
Rough idle	4.1, 5.1, 8.1
Stalling	3.1, 4.1, 5.1, 8.1
Engine dies at high speeds	4.1, 5.1
Hesitation (on acceleration from standing stop)	5.1, 8.1
Poor pickup	4.1, 5.1, 8.1
Lack of power	3.1, 4.1, 5.1, 8.1
Backfire through the carburetor	4.1, 8.1, 9.1
Backfire through the exhaust	4.1, 8.1, 9.1
Blue exhaust gases	6.1, 7.1
Black exhaust gases	5.1
Running on (after the ignition is shut off)	3.1, 8.1
Susceptible to moisture	4.1
Engine misfires under load	4.1, 7.1, 8.4, 9.1
Engine misfires at speed	4.1, 8.4
Engine misfires at idle	3.1, 4.1, 5.1, 7.1, 8.4

Sample Section

Test and Procedure	Results and Indications	Proceed to
4.1—Check for spark: Hold each spark plug wire approximately ¼″ from ground with gloves or a heavy, dry rag. Crank the engine and observe the spark.	→ If no spark is evident:	→**4.2**
	→ If spark is good in some cases:	→**4.3**
	→ If spark is good in all cases:	→**4.6**

Specific Diagnosis

This section is arranged so that following each test, instructions are given to proceed to another, until a problem is diagnosed.

Section 1—Battery

Test and Procedure	Results and Indications	Proceed to
1.1—Inspect the battery visually for case condition (corrosion, cracks) and water level.	If case is cracked, replace battery:	**1.4**
	If the case is intact, remove corrosion with a solution of baking soda and water (**CAUTION**: *do not get the solution into the battery*), and fill with water:	**1.2**

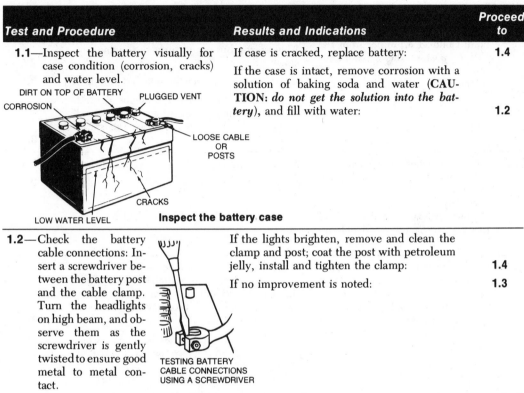

Inspect the battery case

1.2—Check the battery cable connections: Insert a screwdriver between the battery post and the cable clamp. Turn the headlights on high beam, and observe them as the screwdriver is gently twisted to ensure good metal to metal contact.	If the lights brighten, remove and clean the clamp and post; coat the post with petroleum jelly, install and tighten the clamp:	**1.4**
	If no improvement is noted:	**1.3**

TESTING BATTERY CABLE CONNECTIONS USING A SCREWDRIVER

1.3—Test the state of charge of the battery using an individual cell tester or hydrometer.	If indicated, charge the battery. **NOTE:** *If no obvious reason exists for the low state of charge (i.e., battery age, prolonged storage), proceed to:*	**1.4**

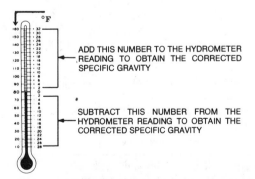

ADD THIS NUMBER TO THE HYDROMETER READING TO OBTAIN THE CORRECTED SPECIFIC GRAVITY

SUBTRACT THIS NUMBER FROM THE HYDROMETER READING TO OBTAIN THE CORRECTED SPECIFIC GRAVITY

Specific Gravity (@ 80° F.)

Minimum		Battery Charge
1.260	....	100% Charged
1.230	....	75% Charged
1.200	....	50% Charged
1.170	....	25% Charged
1.140	....	Very Little Power Left
1.110	....	Completely Discharged

The effects of temperature on battery specific gravity (left) and amount of battery charge in relation to specific gravity (right)

1.4—Visually inspect battery cables for cracking, bad connection to ground, or bad connection to starter.	If necessary, tighten connections or replace the cables:	**2.1**

Section 2—Starting System
See Chapter 3 for service procedures

Test and Procedure	Results and Indications	Proceed to
Note: Tests in Group 2 are performed with coil high tension lead disconnected to prevent accidental starting.		
2.1—Test the starter motor and solenoid: Connect a jumper from the battery post of the solenoid (or relay) to the starter post of the solenoid (or relay).	If starter turns the engine normally:	2.2
	If the starter buzzes, or turns the engine very slowly:	2.4
	If no response, replace the solenoid (or relay).	3.1
	If the starter turns, but the engine doesn't, ensure that the flywheel ring gear is intact. If the gear is undamaged, replace the starter drive.	3.1
2.2—Determine whether ignition override switches are functioning properly (clutch start switch, neutral safety switch), by connecting a jumper across the switch(es), and turning the ignition switch to "start".	If starter operates, adjust or replace switch:	3.1
	If the starter doesn't operate:	2.3
2.3—Check the ignition switch "start" position: Connect a 12V test lamp or voltmeter between the starter post of the solenoid (or relay) and ground. Turn the ignition switch to the "start" position, and jiggle the key.	If the lamp doesn't light or the meter needle doesn't move when the switch is turned, check the ignition switch for loose connections, cracked insulation, or broken wires. Repair or replace as necessary:	3.1
	If the lamp flickers or needle moves when the key is jiggled, replace the ignition switch.	3.3

Checking the ignition switch "start" position

STARTER RELAY
(IF EQUIPPED)

2.4—Remove and bench test the starter, according to specifications in the engine electrical section.	If the starter does not meet specifications, repair or replace as needed:	3.1
	If the starter is operating properly:	2.5
2.5—Determine whether the engine can turn freely: Remove the spark plugs, and check for water in the cylinders. Check for water on the dipstick, or oil in the radiator. Attempt to turn the engine using an 18″ flex drive and socket on the crankshaft pulley nut or bolt.	If the engine will turn freely only with the spark plugs out, and hydrostatic lock (water in the cylinders) is ruled out, check valve timing:	9.2
	If engine will not turn freely, and it is known that the clutch and transmission are free, the engine must be disassembled for further evaluation:	Chapter 3

Section 3—Primary Electrical System

Test and Procedure	Results and Indications	Proceed to
3.1—Check the ignition switch "on" position: Connect a jumper wire between the distributor side of the coil and ground, and a 12V test lamp between the switch side of the coil and ground. Remove the high tension lead from the coil. Turn the ignition switch on and jiggle the key.	If the lamp lights:	**3.2**
	If the lamp flickers when the key is jiggled, replace the ignition switch:	**3.3**
	If the lamp doesn't light, check for loose or open connections. If none are found, remove the ignition switch and check for continuity. If the switch is faulty, replace it:	**3.3**

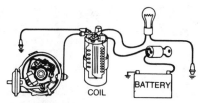

Checking the ignition switch "on" position

3.2—Check the ballast resistor or resistance wire for an open circuit, using an ohmmeter. See Chapter 3 for specific tests.	Replace the resistor or resistance wire if the resistance is zero. **NOTE:** *Some ignition systems have no ballast resistor.*	**3.3**

 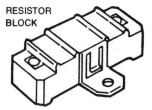

RESISTOR BLOCK

CALIBRATED RESISTANCE LEAD

Two types of resistors

3.3—On point-type ignition systems, visually inspect the breaker points for burning, pitting or excessive wear. Gray coloring of the point contact surfaces is normal. Rotate the crankshaft until the contact heel rests on a high point of the distributor cam and adjust the point gap to specifications. On electronic ignition models, remove the distributor cap and visually inspect the armature. Ensure that the armature pin is in place, and that the armature is on tight and rotates when the engine is cranked. Make sure there are no cracks, chips or rounded edges on the armature.	If the breaker points are intact, clean the contact surfaces with fine emery cloth, and adjust the point gap to specifications. If the points are worn, replace them. On electronic systems, replace any parts which appear defective. If condition persists:	**3.4**

Test and Procedure	Results and Indications	Proceed to
3.4—On point-type ignition systems, connect a dwell-meter between the distributor primary lead and ground. Crank the engine and observe the point dwell angle. On electronic ignition systems, conduct a stator (magnetic pickup assembly) test. See Chapter 3.	On point-type systems, adjust the dwell angle if necessary. **NOTE:** *Increasing the point gap decreases the dwell angle and vice-versa.*	**3.6**
	If the dwell meter shows little or no reading;	**3.5**
	On electronic ignition systems, if the stator is bad, replace the stator. If the stator is good, proceed to the other tests in Chapter 3.	

WIDE GAP

NARROW GAP

CLOSE　　　　　OPEN

NORMAL DWELL

SMALL DWELL

INSUFFICIENT DWELL

LARGE DWELL

EXCESSIVE DWELL

Dwell is a function of point gap

3.5—On the point-type ignition systems, check the condenser for short: connect an ohmeter across the condenser body and the pigtail lead.	If any reading other than infinite is noted, replace the condenser	**3.6**

OHMMETER

Checking the condenser for short

3.6—Test the coil primary resistance: On point-type ignition systems, connect an ohmmeter across the coil primary terminals, and read the resistance on the low scale. Note whether an external ballast resistor or resistance wire is used. On electronic ignition systems, test the coil primary resistance as in Chapter 3.	Point-type ignition coils utilizing ballast resistors or resistance wires should have approximately 1.0 ohms resistance. Coils with internal resistors should have approximately 4.0 ohms resistance. If values far from the above are noted, replace the coil.	**4.1**

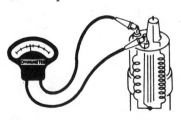

Check the coil primary resistance

Section 4—Secondary Electrical System
See Chapters 2–3 for service procedures

Test and Procedure	Results and Indications	Proceed to
4.1—Check for spark: Hold each spark plug wire approximately ¼" from ground with gloves or a heavy, dry rag. Crank the engine, and observe the spark.	If no spark is evident:	**4.2**
	If spark is good in some cylinders:	**4.3**
	If spark is good in all cylinders:	**4.6**

Check for spark at the plugs

4.2—Check for spark at the coil high tension lead: Remove the coil high tension lead from the distributor and position it approximately ¼" from ground. Crank the engine and observe spark. **CAUTION:** *This test should not be performed on engines equipped with electronic ignition.*	If the spark is good and consistent:	**4.3**
	If the spark is good but intermittent, test the primary electrical system starting at 3.3:	**3.3**
	If the spark is weak or non-existent, replace the coil high tension lead, clean and tighten all connections and retest. If no improvement is noted:	**4.4**
4.3—Visually inspect the distributor cap and rotor for burned or corroded contacts, cracks, carbon tracks, or moisture. Also check the fit of the rotor on the distributor shaft (where applicable).	If moisture is present, dry thoroughly, and retest per 4.1:	**4.1**
	If burned or excessively corroded contacts, cracks, or carbon tracks are noted, replace the defective part(s) and retest per 4.1:	**4.1**
	If the rotor and cap appear intact, or are only slightly corroded, clean the contacts thoroughly (including the cap towers and spark plug wire ends) and retest per 4.1:	
	If the spark is good in all cases:	**4.6**
	If the spark is poor in all cases:	**4.5**

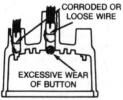
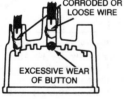

CORRODED OR LOOSE WIRE

EXCESSIVE WEAR OF BUTTON

HIGH RESISTANCE CARBON

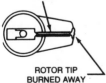

ROTOR TIP BURNED AWAY

Inspect the distributor cap and rotor

Test and Procedure	Results and Indications	Proceed to
4.4—Check the coil secondary resistance: On point-type systems connect an ohmmeter across the distributor side of the coil and the coil tower. Read the resistance on the high scale of the ohmmeter. On electronic ignition systems, see Chapter 3 for specific tests.	The resistance of a satisfactory coil should be between 4,000 and 10,000 ohms. If resistance is considerably higher (i.e., 40,000 ohms) replace the coil and retest per 4.1. **NOTE:** *This does not apply to high performance coils.*	

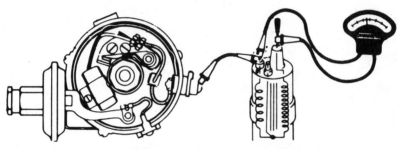

Testing the coil secondary resistance

4.5—Visually inspect the spark plug wires for cracking or brittleness. Ensure that no two wires are positioned so as to cause induction firing (adjacent and parallel). Remove each wire, one by one, and check resistance with an ohmmeter.	Replace any cracked or brittle wires. If any of the wires are defective, replace the entire set. Replace any wires with excessive resistance (over $8000\,\Omega$ per foot for suppression wire), and separate any wires that might cause induction firing.	**4.6**

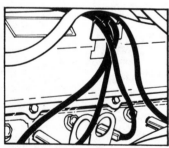

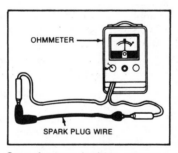

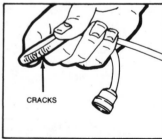

Misfiring can be the result of spark plug leads to adjacent, consecutively firing cylinders running parallel and too close together	**On point-type ignition systems, check the spark plug wires as shown. On electronic ignitions, do not remove the wire from the distributor cap terminal; instead, test through the cap**	**Spark plug wires can be checked visually by bending them in a loop over your finger. This will reveal any cracks, burned or broken insulation. Any wire with cracked insulation should be replaced**

4.6—Remove the spark plugs, noting the cylinders from which they were removed, and evaluate according to the color photos in the middle of this book.	See following.	**See following.**

CHILTON'S
AUTO BODY
REPAIR TIPS

**Tools and Materials • Step-by-Step Illustrated Procedures
How To Repair Dents, Scratches and Rust Holes
Spray Painting and Refinishing Tips**

With a little practice, basic body repair procedures can be mastered by any do-it-yourself mechanic. The step-by-step repairs shown here can be applied to almost any type of auto body repair.

TOOLS & MATERIALS

You may already have basic tools, such as hammers and electric drills. Other tools unique to body repair — body hammers, grinding attachments, sanding blocks, dent puller, half-round plastic file and plastic spreaders — are relatively inexpensive and can be obtained wherever auto parts or auto body repair parts are sold. Portable air compressors and paint spray guns can be purchased or rented.

Auto Body Repair Kits

The best and most often used products are available to the do-it-yourselfer in kit form, from major manufacturers of auto body repair products. The same manufacturers also merchandise the individual products for use by pros.

Kits are available to make a wide variety of repairs, including holes, dents and scratches and fiberglass, and offer the advantage of buying the materials you'll need for the job. There is little waste or chance of materials going bad from not being used. Many kits may also contain basic body-working tools such as body files, sanding blocks and spreaders. Check the contents of the kit before buying your tools.

BODY REPAIR TIPS

Safety

Many of the products associated with auto body repair and refinishing contain toxic chemicals. Read all labels before opening containers and store them in a safe place and manner.
- Wear eye protection (safety goggles) when using power tools or when performing any operation that involves the removal of any type of material.
- Wear lung protection (disposable mask or respirator) when grinding, sanding or painting.

Sanding

1 Sand off paint before using a dent puller. When using a non-adhesive sanding disc, cover the back of the disc with an overlapping layer or two of masking tape and trim the edges. The disc will last considerably longer.

2 Use the circular motion of the sanding disc to grind *into* the edge of the repair. Grinding or sanding away from the jagged edge will only tear the sandpaper.

3 Use the palm of your hand flat on the panel to detect high and low spots. Do not use your fingertips. Slide your hand slowly back and forth.

WORKING WITH BODY FILLER

Mixing The Filler

Cleanliness and proper mixing and application are extremely important. Use a clean piece of plastic or glass or a disposable artist's palette to mix body filler.

1 Allow plenty of time and follow directions. No useful purpose will be served by adding more hardener to make it cure (set-up) faster. Less hardener means more curing time, but the mixture dries harder; more hardener means less curing time but a softer mixture.

2 Both the hardener and the filler should be thoroughly kneaded or stirred before mixing. Hardener should be a solid paste and dispense like thin toothpaste. Body filler should be smooth, and free of lumps or thick spots.

Getting the proper amount of hardener in the filler is the trickiest part of preparing the filler. Use the same amount of hardener in cold or warm weather. For contour filler (thick coats), a bead of hardener twice the diameter of the filler is about right. There's about a 15% margin on either side, but, if in doubt use less hardener.

3 Mix the body filler and hardener by wiping across the mixing surface, picking the mixture up and wiping it again. Colder weather requires longer mixing times. Do not mix in a circular motion; this will trap air bubbles which will become holes in the cured filler.

Applying The Filler

1 For best results, filler should not be applied over ¼" thick.

Apply the filler in several coats. Build it up to above the level of the repair surface so that it can be sanded or grated down.

The first coat of filler must be pressed on with a firm wiping motion.

Apply the filler in one direction only. Working the filler back and forth will either pull it off the metal or trap air bubbles.

REPAIRING DENTS

Before you start, take a few minutes to study the damaged area. Try to visualize the shape of the panel before it was damaged. If the damage is on the left fender, look at the right fender and use it as a guide. If there is access to the panel from behind, you can reshape it with a body hammer. If not, you'll have to use a dent puller. Go slowly and work the metal a little at a time. Get the panel as straight as possible before applying filler.

1 This dent is typical of one that can be pulled out or hammered out from behind. Remove the headlight cover, headlight assembly and turn signal housing.

2 Drill a series of holes ½ the size of the end of the dent puller along the stress line. Make some trial pulls and assess the results. If necessary, drill more holes and try again. Do not hurry.

3 If possible, use a body hammer and block to shape the metal back to its original contours. Get the metal back as close to its original shape as possible. Don't depend on body filler to fill dents.

4 Using an 80-grit grinding disc on an electric drill, grind the paint from the surrounding area down to bare metal. Use a new grinding pad to prevent heat buildup that will warp metal.

5 The area should look like this when you're finished grinding. Knock the drill holes in and tape over small openings to keep plastic filler out.

6 Mix the body filler (see Body Repair Tips). Spread the body filler evenly over the entire area (see Body Repair Tips). Be sure to cover the area completely.

7 Let the body filler dry until the surface can just be scratched with your fingernail. Knock the high spots from the body filler with a body file ("Cheesegrater"). Check frequently with the palm of your hand for high and low spots.

8 Check to be sure that trim pieces that will be installed later will fit exactly. Sand the area with 40-grit paper.

9 If you wind up with low spots, you may have to apply another layer of filler.

10 Knock the high spots off with 40-grit paper. When you are satisfied with the contours of the repair, apply a thin coat of filler to cover pin holes and scratches.

11 Block sand the area with 40-grit paper to a smooth finish. Pay particular attention to body lines and ridges that must be well-defined.

12 Sand the area with 400 paper and then finish with a scuff pad. The finished repair is ready for priming and painting (see Painting Tips).

Materials and photos courtesy of Ritt Jones Auto Body, Prospect Park, PA.

REPAIRING RUST HOLES

There are many ways to repair rust holes. The fiberglass cloth kit shown here is one of the most cost efficient for the owner because it provides a strong repair that resists cracking and moisture and is relatively easy to use. It can be used on large and small holes (with or without backing) and can be applied over contoured areas. Remember, however, that short of replacing an entire panel, no repair is a guarantee that the rust will not return.

1 Remove any trim that will be in the way. Clean away all loose debris. Cut away all the rusted metal. But be sure to leave enough metal to retain the contour or body shape.

2 Grind away all traces of rust with a 24-grit grinding disc. Be sure to grind back 3-4 inches from the edge of the hole down to bare metal and be sure all traces of paint, primer and rust are removed.

3 Block sand the area with 80 or 100 grit sandpaper to get a clear, shiny surface and feathered paint edge. Tap the edges of the hole inward with a ball peen hammer.

4 If you are going to use release film, cut a piece about 2-3″ larger than the area you have sanded. Place the film over the repair and mark the sanded area on the film. Avoid any unnecessary wrinkling of the film.

5 Cut 2 pieces of fiberglass matte to match the shape of the repair. One piece should be about 1″ smaller than the sanded area and the second piece should be 1″ smaller than the first. Mix enough filler and hardener to saturate the fiberglass material (see Body Repair Tips).

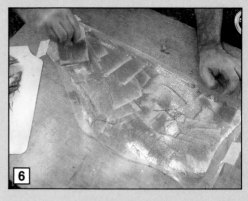

6 Lay the release sheet on a flat surface and spread an even layer of filler, large enough to cover the repair. Lay the smaller piece of fiberglass cloth in the center of the sheet and spread another layer of filler over the fiberglass cloth. Repeat the operation for the larger piece of cloth.

7 Place the repair material over the repair area, with the release film facing outward. Use a spreader and work from the center outward to smooth the material, following the body contours. Be sure to remove all air bubbles.

8 Wait until the repair has dried tack-free and peel off the release sheet. The ideal working temperature is 60°-90° F. Cooler or warmer temperatures or high humidity may require additional curing time. Wait longer, if in doubt.

9 Sand and feather-edge the entire area. The initial sanding can be done with a sanding disc on an electric drill if care is used. Finish the sanding with a block sander. Low spots can be filled with body filler; this may require several applications.

10 When the filler can just be scratched with a fingernail, knock the high spots down with a body file and smooth the entire area with 80-grit. Feather the filled areas into the surrounding areas.

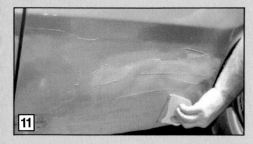

11 When the area is sanded smooth, mix some topcoat and hardener and apply it directly with a spreader. This will give a smooth finish and prevent the glass matte from showing through the paint.

12 Block sand the topcoat smooth with finishing sandpaper (200 grit), and 400 grit. The repair is ready for masking, priming and painting (see Painting Tips).

Materials and photos courtesy Marson Corporation, Chelsea, Massachusetts

PAINTING TIPS

Preparation

1 SANDING — Use a 400 or 600 grit wet or dry sandpaper. Wet-sand the area with a 1/4 sheet of sandpaper soaked in clean water. Keep the paper wet while sanding. Sand the area until the repaired area tapers into the original finish.

2 CLEANING — Wash the area to be painted thoroughly with water and a clean rag. Rinse it thoroughly and wipe the surface dry until you're sure it's completely free of dirt, dust, fingerprints, wax, detergent or other foreign matter.

3 MASKING — Protect any areas you don't want to overspray by covering them with masking tape and newspaper. Be careful not get fingerprints on the area to be painted.

4 PRIMING — All exposed metal should be primed before painting. Primer protects the metal and provides an excellent surface for paint adhesion. When the primer is dry, wet-sand the area again with 600 grit wet-sandpaper. Clean the area again after sanding.

Painting Techniques

Paint applied from either a spray gun or a spray can (for small areas) will provide good results. Experiment on an old piece of metal to get the right combination before you begin painting.

SPRAYING VISCOSITY (SPRAY GUN ONLY) — Paint should be thinned to spraying viscosity according to the directions on the can. Use only the recommended thinner or reducer and the same amount of reduction regardless of temperature.

AIR PRESSURE (SPRAY GUN ONLY) — This is extremely important. Be sure you are using the proper recommended pressure.

TEMPERATURE — The surface to be painted should be approximately the same temperature as the surrounding air. Applying warm paint to a cold surface, or vice versa, will completely upset the paint characteristics.

THICKNESS — Spray with smooth strokes. In general, the thicker the coat of paint, the longer the drying time. Apply several thin coats about 30 seconds apart. The paint should remain wet long enough to flow out and no longer; heavier coats will only produce sags or wrinkles. Spray a light (fog) coat, followed by heavier color coats.

DISTANCE — The ideal spraying distance is 8″-12″ from the gun or can to the surface. Shorter distances will produce ripples, while greater distances will result in orange peel, dry film and poor color match and loss of material due to overspray.

OVERLAPPING — The gun or can should be kept at right angles to the surface at all times. Work to a wet edge at an even speed, using a 50% overlap and direct the center of the spray at the lower or nearest edge of the previous stroke.

RUBBING OUT (BLENDING) FRESH PAINT — Let the paint dry thoroughly. Runs or imperfections can be sanded out, primed and repainted.

Don't be in too big a hurry to remove the masking. This only produces paint ridges. When the finish has dried for at least a week, apply a small amount of fine grade rubbing compound with a clean, wet cloth. Use lots of water and blend the new paint with the surrounding area.

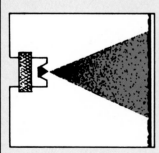

WRONG

Thin coat. Stroke too fast, not enough overlap, gun too far away.

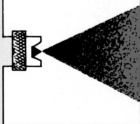

CORRECT

Medium coat. Proper distance, good stroke, proper overlap.

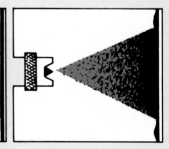

WRONG

Heavy coat. Stroke too slow, too much overlap, gun too close.

Test and Procedure	Results and Indications	Proceed to

4.7—Examine the location of all the plugs.

The following diagrams illustrate some of the conditions that the location of plugs will reveal.

4.8

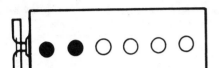

Two adjacent plugs are fouled in a 6-cylinder engine, 4-cylinder engine or either bank of a V-8. This is probably due to a blown head gasket between the two cylinders

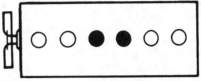

The two center plugs in a 6-cylinder engine are fouled. Raw fuel may be "boiled" out of the carburetor into the intake manifold after the engine is shut-off. Stop-start driving can also foul the center plugs, due to overly rich mixture. Proper float level, a new float needle and seat or use of an insulating spacer may help this problem

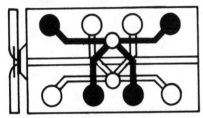

An unbalanced carburetor is indicated. Following the fuel flow on this particular design shows that the cylinders fed by the right-hand barrel are fouled from overly rich mixture, while the cylinders fed by the left-hand barrel are normal

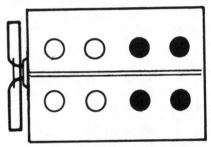

If the four rear plugs are overheated, a cooling system problem is suggested. A thorough cleaning of the cooling system may restore coolant circulation and cure the problem

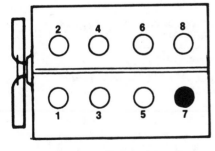

Finding one plug overheated may indicate an intake manifold leak near the affected cylinder. If the overheated plug is the second of two adjacent, consecutively firing plugs, it could be the result of ignition cross-firing. Separating the leads to these two plugs will eliminate cross-fire

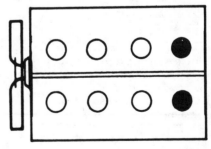

Occasionally, the two rear plugs in large, lightly used V-8's will become oil fouled. High oil consumption and smoky exhaust may also be noticed. It is probably due to plugged oil drain holes in the rear of the cylinder head, causing oil to be sucked in around the valve stems. This usually occurs in the rear cylinders first, because the engine slants that way

Test and Procedure	Results and Indications	Proceed to
4.8—Determine the static ignition timing. Using the crankshaft pulley timing marks as a guide, locate top dead center on the compression stroke of the number one cylinder.	The rotor should be pointing toward the No. 1 tower in the distributor cap, and, on electronic ignitions, the armature spoke for that cylinder should be lined up with the stator.	4.8
4.9—Check coil polarity: Connect a voltmeter negative lead to the coil high tension lead, and the positive lead to ground (**NOTE:** *Reverse the hook-up for positive ground systems*). Crank the engine momentarily. **Checking coil polarity**	If the voltmeter reads up-scale, the polarity is correct: If the voltmeter reads down-scale, reverse the coil polarity (switch the primary leads):	5.1 5.1

Section 5—Fuel System
See Chapter 4 for service procedures

Test and Procedure	Results and Indications	Proceed to
5.1—Determine that the air filter is functioning efficiently: Hold paper elements up to a strong light, and attempt to see light through the filter.	Clean permanent air filters in solvent (or manufacturer's recommendation), and allow to dry. Replace paper elements through which light cannot be seen:	5.2
5.2—Determine whether a flooding condition exists: Flooding is identified by a strong gasoline odor, and excessive gasoline present in the throttle bore(s) of the carburetor.	If flooding is not evident: If flooding is evident, permit the gasoline to dry for a few moments and restart. If flooding doesn't recur: If flooding is persistent:	5.3 5.7 5.5

If the engine floods repeatedly, check the choke butterfly flap

5.3—Check that fuel is reaching the carburetor: Detach the fuel line at the carburetor inlet. Hold the end of the line in a cup (not styrofoam), and crank the engine.	If fuel flows smoothly: If fuel doesn't flow (**NOTE:** *Make sure that there is fuel in the tank*), or flows erratically:	5.7 5.4

Check the fuel pump by disconnecting the output line (fuel pump-to-carburetor) at the carburetor and operating the starter briefly

Test and Procedure	Results and Indications	Proceed to
5.4—Test the fuel pump: Disconnect all fuel lines from the fuel pump. Hold a finger over the input fitting, crank the engine (with electric pump, turn the ignition or pump on); and feel for suction.	If suction is evident, blow out the fuel line to the tank with low pressure compressed air until bubbling is heard from the fuel filler neck. Also blow out the carburetor fuel line (both ends disconnected):	**5.7**
	If no suction is evident, replace or repair the fuel pump: NOTE: *Repeated oil fouling of the spark plugs, or a no-start condition, could be the result of a ruptured vacuum booster pump diaphragm, through which oil or gasoline is being drawn into the intake manifold (where applicable).*	**5.7**
5.5—Occasionally, small specks of dirt will clog the small jets and orifices in the carburetor. With the engine cold, hold a flat piece of wood or similar material over the carburetor, where possible, and crank the engine.	If the engine starts, but runs roughly the engine is probably not run enough. If the engine won't start:	**5.9**
5.6—Check the needle and seat: Tap the carburetor in the area of the needle and seat.	If flooding stops, a gasoline additive (e.g., Gumout) will often cure the problem:	**5.7**
	If flooding continues, check the fuel pump for excessive pressure at the carburetor (according to specifications). If the pressure is normal, the needle and seat must be removed and checked, and/or the float level adjusted:	**5.7**
5.7—Test the accelerator pump by looking into the throttle bores while operating the throttle.	If the accelerator pump appears to be operating normally:	**5.8**
	If the accelerator pump is not operating, the pump must be reconditioned. Where possible, service the pump with the carburetor(s) installed on the engine. If necessary, remove the carburetor. Prior to removal:	**5.8**

Check for gas at the carburetor by looking down the carburetor throat while someone moves the accelerator

5.8—Determine whether the carburetor main fuel system is functioning: Spray a commercial starting fluid into the carburetor while attempting to start the engine.	If the engine starts, runs for a few seconds, and dies:	**5.9**
	If the engine doesn't start:	**6.1**

Test and Procedure	Results and Indications	Proceed to
5.9—Uncommon fuel system malfunctions: See below:	If the problem is solved:	**6.1**
	If the problem remains, remove and recondition the carburetor.	

Condition	Indication	Test	Prevailing Weather Conditions	Remedy
Vapor lock	Engine will not restart shortly after running.	Cool the components of the fuel system until the engine starts. Vapor lock can be cured faster by draping a wet cloth over a mechanical fuel pump.	Hot to very hot	Ensure that the exhaust manifold heat control valve is operating. Check with the vehicle manufacturer for the recommended solution to vapor lock on the model in question.
Carburetor icing	Engine will not idle, stalls at low speeds.	Visually inspect the throttle plate area of the throttle bores for frost.	High humidity, 32–40° F.	Ensure that the exhaust manifold heat control valve is operating, and that the intake manifold heat riser is not blocked.
Water in the fuel	Engine sputters and stalls; may not start.	Pump a small amount of fuel into a glass jar. Allow to stand, and inspect for droplets or a layer of water.	High humidity, extreme temperature changes.	For droplets, use one or two cans of commercial gas line anti-freeze. For a layer of water, the tank must be drained, and the fuel lines blown out with compressed air.

Section 6—Engine Compression
See Chapter 3 for service procedures

		Proceed to
6.1—Test engine compression: Remove all spark plugs. Block the throttle wide open. Insert a compression gauge into a spark plug port, crank the engine to obtain the maximum reading, and record.	If compression is within limits on all cylinders:	**7.1**
	If gauge reading is extremely low on all cylinders:	**6.2**
	If gauge reading is low on one or two cylinders: (If gauge readings are identical and low on two or more adjacent cylinders, the head gasket must be replaced.)	**6.2**

Checking compression

		Proceed to
6.2—Test engine compression (wet): Squirt approximately 30 cc. of engine oil into each cylinder, and retest per 6.1.	If the readings improve, worn or cracked rings or broken pistons are indicated:	**See Chapter 3**
	If the readings do not improve, burned or excessively carboned valves or a jumped timing chain are indicated:	**7.1**
	NOTE: *A jumped timing chain is often indicated by difficult cranking.*	

Section 7—Engine Vacuum
See Chapter 3 for service procedures

Test and Procedure	Results and Indications	Proceed to
7.1—Attach a vacuum gauge to the intake manifold beyond the throttle plate. Start the engine, and observe the action of the needle over the range of engine speeds.	See below.	**See below**

INDICATION: normal engine in good condition

Proceed to: 8.1

Normal engine
Gauge reading: steady, from 17–22 in./Hg.

INDICATION: sticking valves or ignition miss

Proceed to: 9.1, 8.3

Sticking valves
Gauge reading: intermittent fluctuation at idle

INDICATION: late ignition or valve timing, low compression, stuck throttle valve, leaking carburetor or manifold gasket

Proceed to: 6.1

Incorrect valve timing
Gauge reading: low (10–15 in./Hg) but steady

INDICATION: improper carburetor adjustment or minor intake leak.

Proceed to: 7.2

Carburetor requires adjustment
Gauge reading: drifting needle

INDICATION: ignition miss, blown cylinder head gasket, leaking valve or weak valve spring

Proceed to: 8.3, 6.1

Blown head gasket
Gauge reading: needle fluctuates as engine speed increases

INDICATION: burnt valve or faulty valve clearance. Needle will fall when defective valve operates

Proceed to: 9.1

Burnt or leaking valves
Gauge reading: steady needle, but drops regularly

INDICATION: choked muffler, excessive back pressure in system

Proceed to: 10.1

Clogged exhaust system
Gauge reading: gradual drop in reading at idle

INDICATION: worn valve guides

Proceed to: 9.1

Worn valve guides
Gauge reading: needle vibrates excessively at idle, but steadies as engine speed increases

White pointer = steady gauge hand   Black pointer = fluctuating gauge hand

Test and Procedure	Results and Indications	Proceed to
7.2—Attach a vacuum gauge per 7.1, and test for an intake manifold leak. Squirt a small amount of oil around the intake manifold gaskets, carburetor gaskets, plugs and fittings. Observe the action of the vacuum gauge.	If the reading improves, replace the indicated gasket, or seal the indicated fitting or plug:	**8.1**
	If the reading remains low:	**7.3**
7.3—Test all vacuum hoses and accessories for leaks as described in 7.2. Also check the carburetor body (dashpots, automatic choke mechanism, throttle shafts) for leaks in the same manner.	If the reading improves, service or replace the offending part(s):	**8.1**
	If the reading remains low:	**6.1**

Section 8—Secondary Electrical System
See Chapter 2 for service procedures

Test and Procedure	Results and Indications	Proceed to
8.1—Remove the distributor cap and check to make sure that the rotor turns when the engine is cranked. Visually inspect the distributor components.	Clean, tighten or replace any components which appear defective.	**8.2**
8.2—Connect a timing light (per manufacturer's recommendation) and check the dynamic ignition timing. Disconnect and plug the vacuum hose(s) to the distributor if specified, start the engine, and observe the timing marks at the specified engine speed.	If the timing is not correct, adjust to specifications by rotating the distributor in the engine: (Advance timing by rotating distributor opposite normal direction of rotor rotation, retard timing by rotating distributor in same direction as rotor rotation.)	**8.3**
8.3—Check the operation of the distributor advance mechanism(s): To test the mechanical advance, disconnect the vacuum lines from the distributor advance unit and observe the timing marks with a timing light as the engine speed is increased from idle. If the mark moves smoothly, without hesitation, it may be assumed that the mechanical advance is functioning properly. To test vacuum advance and/or retard systems, alternately crimp and release the vacuum line, and observe the timing mark for movement. If movement is noted, the system is operating.	If the systems are functioning:	**8.4**
	If the systems are not functioning, remove the distributor, and test on a distributor tester:	**8.4**
8.4—Locate an ignition miss: With the engine running, remove each spark plug wire, one at a time, until one is found that doesn't cause the engine to roughen and slow down.	When the missing cylinder is identified:	**4.1**

Section 9—Valve Train
See Chapter 3 for service procedures

Test and Procedure	Results and Indications	Proceed to
9.1—Evaluate the valve train: Remove the valve cover, and ensure that the valves are adjusted to specifications. A mechanic's stethoscope may be used to aid in the diagnosis of the valve train. By pushing the probe on or near push rods or rockers, valve noise often can be isolated. A timing light also may be used to diagnose valve problems. Connect the light according to manufacturer's recommendations, and start the engine. Vary the firing moment of the light by increasing the engine speed (and therefore the ignition advance), and moving the trigger from cylinder to cylinder. Observe the movement of each valve.	Sticking valves or erratic valve train motion can be observed with the timing light. The cylinder head must be disassembled for repairs.	**See Chapter 3**
9.2—Check the valve timing: Locate top dead center of the No. 1 piston, and install a degree wheel or tape on the crankshaft pulley or damper with zero corresponding to an index mark on the engine. Rotate the crankshaft in its direction of rotation, and observe the opening of the No. 1 cylinder intake valve. The opening should correspond with the correct mark on the degree wheel according to specifications.	If the timing is not correct, the timing cover must be removed for further investigation.	**See Chapter 3**

Section 10—Exhaust System

Test and Procedure	Results and Indications	Proceed to
10.1—Determine whether the exhaust manifold heat control valve is operating: Operate the valve by hand to determine whether it is free to move. If the valve is free, run the engine to operating temperature and observe the action of the valve, to ensure that it is opening.	If the valve sticks, spray it with a suitable solvent, open and close the valve to free it, and retest. If the valve functions properly: If the valve does not free, or does not operate, replace the valve:	 **10.2** **10.2**
10.2—Ensure that there are no exhaust restrictions: Visually inspect the exhaust system for kinks, dents, or crushing. Also note that gases are flowing freely from the tailpipe at all engine speeds, indicating no restriction in the muffler or resonator.	Replace any damaged portion of the system:	**11.1**

Section 11—Cooling System
See Chapter 3 for service procedures

Test and Procedure	Results and Indications	Proceed to
11.1—Visually inspect the fan belt for glazing, cracks, and fraying, and replace if necessary. Tighten the belt so that the longest span has approximately ½″ play at its midpoint under thumb pressure (see Chapter 1).	Replace or tighten the fan belt as necessary:	**11.2**

Checking belt tension

Test and Procedure	Results and Indications	Proceed to
11.2—Check the fluid level of the cooling system.	If full or slightly low, fill as necessary:	**11.5**
	If extremely low:	**11.3**
11.3—Visually inspect the external portions of the cooling system (radiator, radiator hoses, thermostat elbow, water pump seals, heater hoses, etc.) for leaks. If none are found, pressurize the cooling system to 14–15 psi.	If cooling system holds the pressure:	**11.5**
	If cooling system loses pressure rapidly, reinspect external parts of the system for leaks under pressure. If none are found, check dipstick for coolant in crankcase. If no coolant is present, but pressure loss continues:	**11.4**
	If coolant is evident in crankcase, remove cylinder head(s), and check gasket(s). If gaskets are intact, block and cylinder head(s) should be checked for cracks or holes.	
	If the gasket(s) is blown, replace, and purge the crankcase of coolant:	**12.6**
	NOTE: *Occasionally, due to atmospheric and driving conditions, condensation of water can occur in the crankcase. This causes the oil to appear milky white. To remedy, run the engine until hot, and change the oil and oil filter.*	
11.4—Check for combustion leaks into the cooling system: Pressurize the cooling system as above. Start the engine, and observe the pressure gauge. If the needle fluctuates, remove each spark plug wire, one at a time, noting which cylinder(s) reduce or eliminate the fluctuation.	Cylinders which reduce or eliminate the fluctuation, when the spark plug wire is removed, are leaking into the cooling system. Replace the head gasket on the affected cylinder bank(s).	

Pressurizing the cooling system

Test and Procedure	Results and Indications	Proceed to
11.5—Check the radiator pressure cap: Attach a radiator pressure tester to the radiator cap (wet the seal prior to installation). Quickly pump up the pressure, noting the point at which the cap releases.	If the cap releases within ± 1 psi of the specified rating, it is operating properly:	**11.6**
	If the cap releases at more than ± 1 psi of the specified rating, it should be replaced:	**11.6**

Checking radiator pressure cap

Test and Procedure	Results and Indications	Proceed to
11.6—Test the thermostat: Start the engine cold, remove the radiator cap, and insert a thermometer into the radiator. Allow the engine to idle. After a short while, there will be a sudden, rapid increase in coolant temperature. The temperature at which this sharp rise stops is the thermostat opening temperature.	If the thermostat opens at or about the specified temperature:	**11.7**
	If the temperature doesn't increase: (If the temperature increases slowly and gradually, replace the thermostat.)	**11.7**
11.7—Check the water pump: Remove the thermostat elbow and the thermostat, disconnect the coil high tension lead (to prevent starting), and crank the engine momentarily.	If coolant flows, replace the thermostat and retest per 11.6:	**11.6**
	If coolant doesn't flow, reverse flush the cooling system to alleviate any blockage that might exist. If system is not blocked, and coolant will not flow, replace the water pump.	

Section 12—Lubrication
See Chapter 3 for service procedures

Test and Procedure	Results and Indications	Proceed to
12.1—Check the oil pressure gauge or warning light: If the gauge shows low pressure, or the light is on for no obvious reason, remove the oil pressure sender. Install an accurate oil pressure gauge and run the engine momentarily.	If oil pressure builds normally, run engine for a few moments to determine that it is functioning normally, and replace the sender.	—
	If the pressure remains low:	**12.2**
	If the pressure surges:	**12.3**
	If the oil pressure is zero:	**12.3**
12.2—Visually inspect the oil: If the oil is watery or very thin, milky, or foamy, replace the oil and oil filter.	If the oil is normal:	**12.3**
	If after replacing oil the pressure remains low:	**12.3**
	If after replacing oil the pressure becomes normal:	—

Test and Procedure	Results and Indications	Proceed to
12.3—Inspect the oil pressure relief valve and spring, to ensure that it is not sticking or stuck. Remove and thoroughly clean the valve, spring, and the valve body.	If the oil pressure improves: If no improvement is noted:	— **12.4**
12.4—Check to ensure that the oil pump is not cavitating (sucking air instead of oil): See that the crankcase is neither over nor underfull, and that the pickup in the sump is in the proper position and free from sludge.	Fill or drain the crankcase to the proper capacity, and clean the pickup screen in solvent if necessary. If no improvement is noted:	**12.5**
12.5—Inspect the oil pump drive and the oil pump:	If the pump drive or the oil pump appear to be defective, service as necessary and retest per 12.1: If the pump drive and pump appear to be operating normally, the engine should be disassembled to determine where blockage exists:	**12.1** **See Chapter 3**
12.6—Purge the engine of ethylene glycol coolant: Completely drain the crankcase and the oil filter. Obtain a commercial butyl cellosolve base solvent, designated for this purpose, and follow the instructions precisely. Following this, install a new oil filter and refill the crankcase with the proper weight oil. The next oil and filter change should follow shortly thereafter (1000 miles).		

TROUBLESHOOTING EMISSION CONTROL SYSTEMS

See Chapter 4 for procedures applicable to individual emission control systems used on specific combinations of engine/transmission/model.

TROUBLESHOOTING THE CARBURETOR
See Chapter 4 for service procedures

Carburetor problems cannot be effectively isolated unless all other engine systems (particularly ignition and emission) are functioning properly and the engine is properly tuned.

Condition	Possible Cause
Engine cranks, but does not start	1. Improper starting procedure 2. No fuel in tank 3. Clogged fuel line or filter 4. Defective fuel pump 5. Choke valve not closing properly 6. Engine flooded 7. Choke valve not unloading 8. Throttle linkage not making full travel 9. Stuck needle or float 10. Leaking float needle or seat 11. Improper float adjustment
Engine stalls	1. Improperly adjusted idle speed or mixture **Engine hot** 2. Improperly adjusted dashpot 3. Defective or improperly adjusted solenoid 4. Incorrect fuel level in fuel bowl 5. Fuel pump pressure too high 6. Leaking float needle seat 7. Secondary throttle valve stuck open 8. Air or fuel leaks 9. Idle air bleeds plugged or missing 10. Idle passages plugged **Engine Cold** 11. Incorrectly adjusted choke 12. Improperly adjusted fast idle speed 13. Air leaks 14. Plugged idle or idle air passages 15. Stuck choke valve or binding linkage 16. Stuck secondary throttle valves 17. Engine flooding—high fuel level 18. Leaking or misaligned float
Engine hesitates on acceleration	1. Clogged fuel filter 2. Leaking fuel pump diaphragm 3. Low fuel pump pressure 4. Secondary throttle valves stuck, bent or misadjusted 5. Sticking or binding air valve 6. Defective accelerator pump 7. Vacuum leaks 8. Clogged air filter 9. Incorrect choke adjustment (engine cold)
Engine feels sluggish or flat on acceleration	1. Improperly adjusted idle speed or mixture 2. Clogged fuel filter 3. Defective accelerator pump 4. Dirty, plugged or incorrect main metering jets 5. Bent or sticking main metering rods 6. Sticking throttle valves 7. Stuck heat riser 8. Binding or stuck air valve 9. Dirty, plugged or incorrect secondary jets 10. Bent or sticking secondary metering rods. 11. Throttle body or manifold heat passages plugged 12. Improperly adjusted choke or choke vacuum break.
Carburetor floods	1. Defective fuel pump. Pressure too high. 2. Stuck choke valve 3. Dirty, worn or damaged float or needle valve/seat 4. Incorrect float/fuel level 5. Leaking float bowl

Condition	Possible Cause
Engine idles roughly and stalls	1. Incorrect idle speed 2. Clogged fuel filter 3. Dirt in fuel system or carburetor 4. Loose carburetor screws or attaching bolts 5. Broken carburetor gaskets 6. Air leaks 7. Dirty carburetor 8. Worn idle mixture needles 9. Throttle valves stuck open 10. Incorrectly adjusted float or fuel level 11. Clogged air filter
Engine runs unevenly or surges	1. Defective fuel pump 2. Dirty or clogged fuel filter 3. Plugged, loose or incorrect main metering jets or rods 4. Air leaks 5. Bent or sticking main metering rods 6. Stuck power piston 7. Incorrect float adjustment 8. Incorrect idle speed or mixture 9. Dirty or plugged idle system passages 10. Hard, brittle or broken gaskets 11. Loose attaching or mounting screws 12. Stuck or misaligned secondary throttle valves
Poor fuel economy	1. Poor driving habits 2. Stuck choke valve 3. Binding choke linkage 4. Stuck heat riser 5. Incorrect idle mixture 6. Defective accelerator pump 7. Air leaks 8. Plugged, loose or incorrect main metering jets 9. Improperly adjusted float or fuel level 10. Bent, misaligned or fuel-clogged float 11. Leaking float needle seat 12. Fuel leak 13. Accelerator pump discharge ball not seating properly 14. Incorrect main jets
Engine lacks high speed performance or power	1. Incorrect throttle linkage adjustment 2. Stuck or binding power piston 3. Defective accelerator pump 4. Air leaks 5. Incorrect float setting or fuel level 6. Dirty, plugged, worn or incorrect main metering jets or rods 7. Binding or sticking air valve 8. Brittle or cracked gaskets 9. Bent, incorrect or improperly adjusted secondary metering rods 10. Clogged fuel filter 11. Clogged air filter 12. Defective fuel pump

TROUBLESHOOTING FUEL INJECTION PROBLEMS

Each fuel injection system has its own unique components and test procedures, for which it is impossible to generalize. Refer to Chapter 4 of this Repair & Tune-Up Guide for specific test and repair procedures, if the vehicle is equipped with fuel injection.

TROUBLESHOOTING ELECTRICAL PROBLEMS

See Chapter 5 for service procedures

For any electrical system to operate, it must make a complete circuit. This simply means that the power flow from the battery must make a complete circle. When an electrical component is operating, power flows from the battery to the component, passes through the component causing it to perform its function (lighting a light bulb), and then returns to the battery through the ground of the circuit. This ground is usually (but not always) the metal part of the car or truck on which the electrical component is mounted.

Perhaps the easiest way to visualize this is to think of connecting a light bulb with two wires attached to it to the battery. If one of the two wires attached to the light bulb were attached to the negative post of the battery and the other were attached to the positive post of the battery, you would have a complete circuit. Current from the battery would flow to the light bulb, causing it to light, and return to the negative post of the battery.

The normal automotive circuit differs from this simple example in two ways. First, instead of having a return wire from the bulb to the battery, the light bulb returns the current to the battery through the chassis of the vehicle. Since the negative battery cable is attached to the chassis and the chassis is made of electrically conductive metal, the chassis of the vehicle can serve as a ground wire to complete the circuit. Secondly, most automotive circuits contain switches to turn components on and off as required.

Every complete circuit from a power source must include a component which is using the power from the power source. If you were to disconnect the light bulb from the wires and touch the two wires together (don't do this) the power supply wire to the component would be grounded before the normal ground connection for the circuit.

Because grounding a wire from a power source makes a complete circuit—less the required component to use the power—this phenomenon is called a short circuit. Common causes are: broken insulation (exposing the metal wire to a metal part of the car or truck), or a shorted switch.

Some electrical components which require a large amount of current to operate also have a relay in their circuit. Since these circuits carry a large amount of current, the thickness of the wire in the circuit (gauge size) is also greater. If this large wire were connected from the component to the control switch on the instrument panel, and then back to the component, a voltage drop would occur in the circuit. To prevent this potential drop in voltage, an electromagnetic switch (relay) is used. The large wires in the circuit are connected from the battery to one side of the relay, and from the opposite side of the relay to the component. The relay is normally open, preventing current from passing through the circuit. An additional, smaller, wire is connected from the relay to the control switch for the circuit. When the control switch is turned on, it grounds the smaller wire from the relay and completes the circuit. This closes the relay and allows current to flow from the battery to the component. The horn, headlight, and starter circuits are three which use relays.

It is possible for larger surges of current to pass through the electrical system of your car or truck. If this surge of current were to reach an electrical component, it could burn it out. To prevent this, fuses, circuit breakers or fusible links are connected into the current supply wires of most of the major electrical systems. When an electrical current of excessive power passes through the component's fuse, the fuse blows out and breaks the circuit, saving the component from destruction.

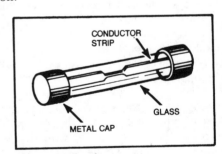

Typical automotive fuse

A circuit breaker is basically a self-repairing fuse. The circuit breaker opens the circuit the same way a fuse does. However, when either the short is removed from the circuit or the surge subsides, the circuit breaker resets itself and does not have to be replaced as a fuse does.

A fuse link is a wire that acts as a fuse. It is normally connected between the starter relay and the main wiring harness. This connection is usually under the hood. The fuse link (if installed) protects all the

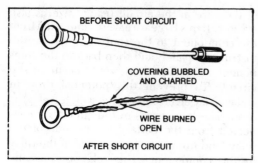

Most fusible links show a charred, melted insulation when they burn out

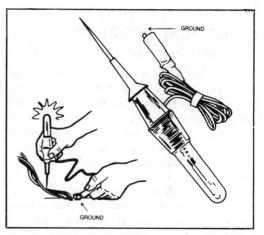

The test light will show the presence of current when touched to a hot wire and grounded at the other end

chassis electrical components, and is the probable cause of trouble when none of the electrical components function, unless the battery is disconnected or dead.

Electrical problems generally fall into one of three areas:

1. The component that is not functioning is not receiving current.

2. The component itself is not functioning.

3. The component is not properly grounded.

The electrical system can be checked with a test light and a jumper wire. A test light is a device that looks like a pointed screwdriver with a wire attached to it and has a light bulb in its handle. A jumper wire is a piece of insulated wire with an alligator clip attached to each end.

If a component is not working, you must follow a systematic plan to determine which of the three causes is the villain.

1. Turn on the switch that controls the inoperable component.

2. Disconnect the power supply wire from the component.

3. Attach the ground wire on the test light to a good metal ground.

4. Touch the probe end of the test light to the end of the power supply wire that was disconnected from the component. If the component is receiving current, the test light will go on.

NOTE: *Some components work only when the ignition switch is turned on.*

If the test light does not go on, then the problem is in the circuit between the battery and the component. This includes all the switches, fuses, and relays in the system. Follow the wire that runs back to the battery. The problem is an open circuit between the

battery and the component. If the fuse is blown and, when replaced, immediately blows again, there is a short circuit in the system which must be located and repaired. If there is a switch in the system, bypass it with a jumper wire. This is done by connecting one end of the jumper wire to the power supply wire into the switch and the other end of the jumper wire to the wire coming out of the switch. If the test light lights with the jumper wire installed, the switch or whatever was bypassed is defective.

NOTE: *Never substitute the jumper wire for the component, since it is required to use the power from the power source.*

5. If the bulb in the test light goes on, then the current is getting to the component that is not working. This eliminates the first of the three possible causes. Connect the power supply wire and connect a jumper wire from the component to a good metal ground. Do this with the switch which controls the component turned on, and also the ignition switch turned on if it is required for the component to work. If the component works with the jumper wire installed, then it has a bad ground. This is usually caused by the metal area on which the component mounts to the chassis being coated with some type of foreign matter.

6. If neither test located the source of the trouble, then the component itself is defective. Remember that for any electrical system to work, all connections must be clean and tight.

Troubleshooting Basic Turn Signal and Flasher Problems
See Chapter 5 for service procedures

Most problems in the turn signals or flasher system can be reduced to defective flashers or bulbs, which are easily replaced. Occasionally, the turn signal switch will prove defective.

F = Front   R = Rear   ● = Lights off   ○ = Lights on

Condition		Possible Cause
Turn signals light, but do not flash	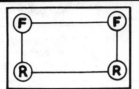	Defective flasher
No turn signals light on either side	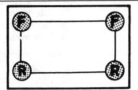	Blown fuse. Replace if defective. Defective flasher. Check by substitution. Open circuit, short circuit or poor ground.
Both turn signals on one side don't work	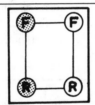	Bad bulbs. Bad ground in both (or either) housings.
One turn signal light on one side doesn't work	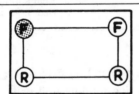	Defective bulb. Corrosion in socket. Clean contacts. Poor ground at socket.
Turn signal flashes too fast or too slowly	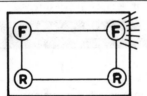	Check any bulb on the side flashing too fast. A heavy-duty bulb is probably installed in place of a regular bulb. Check the bulb flashing too slowly. A standard bulb was probably installed in place of a heavy-duty bulb. Loose connections or corrosion at the bulb socket.
Indicator lights don't work in either direction		Check if the turn signals are working. Check the dash indicator lights. Check the flasher by substitution.
One indicator light doesn't light	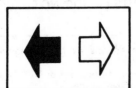	On systems with one dash indicator: See if the lights work on the same side. Often the filaments have been reversed in systems combining stoplights with tail-lights and turn signals. Check the flasher by substitution. On systems with two indicators: Check the bulbs on the same side. Check the indicator light bulb. Check the flasher by substitution.

Troubleshooting Lighting Problems
See Chapter 5 for service procedures

Condition	Possible Cause
One or more lights don't work, but others do	1. Defective bulb(s) 2. Blown fuse(s) 3. Dirty fuse clips or light sockets 4. Poor ground circuit
Lights burn out quickly	1. Incorrect voltage regulator setting or defective regulator 2. Poor battery/alternator connections
Lights go dim	1. Low/discharged battery 2. Alternator not charging 3. Corroded sockets or connections 4. Low voltage output
Lights flicker	1. Loose connection 2. Poor ground. (Run ground wire from light housing to frame) 3. Circuit breaker operating (short circuit)
Lights "flare"—Some flare is normal on acceleration—If excessive, see "Lights Burn Out Quickly"	High voltage setting
Lights glare—approaching drivers are blinded	1. Lights adjusted too high 2. Rear springs or shocks sagging 3. Rear tires soft

Troubleshooting Dash Gauge Problems

Most problems can be traced to a defective sending unit or faulty wiring. Occasionally, the gauge itself is at fault. See Chapter 5 for service procedures.

Condition	Possible Cause
COOLANT TEMPERATURE GAUGE	
Gauge reads erratically or not at all	1. Loose or dirty connections 2. Defective sending unit. 3. Defective gauge. To test a bi-metal gauge, remove the wire from the sending unit. Ground the wire for an instant. If the gauge registers, replace the sending unit. To test a magnetic gauge, disconnect the wire at the sending unit. With ignition ON gauge should register COLD. Ground the wire; gauge should register HOT.
AMMETER GAUGE—TURN HEADLIGHTS ON (DO NOT START ENGINE). NOTE REACTION	
Ammeter shows charge Ammeter shows discharge Ammeter does not move	1. Connections reversed on gauge 2. Ammeter is OK 3. Loose connections or faulty wiring 4. Defective gauge

Condition	Possible Cause

OIL PRESSURE GAUGE

Condition	Possible Cause
Gauge does not register or is inaccurate	1. On mechanical gauge, Bourdon tube may be bent or kinked. 2. Low oil pressure. Remove sending unit. Idle the engine briefly. If no oil flows from sending unit hole, problem is in engine. 3. Defective gauge. Remove the wire from the sending unit and ground it for an instant with the ignition ON. A good gauge will go to the top of the scale. 4. Defective wiring. Check the wiring to the gauge. If it's OK and the gauge doesn't register when grounded, replace the gauge. 5. Defective sending unit.

ALL GAUGES

Condition	Possible Cause
All gauges do not operate All gauges read low or erratically All gauges pegged	1. Blown fuse 2. Defective instrument regulator 3. Defective or dirty instrument voltage regulator 4. Loss of ground between instrument voltage regulator and frame 5. Defective instrument regulator

WARNING LIGHTS

Condition	Possible Cause
Light(s) do not come on when ignition is ON, but engine is not started Light comes on with engine running	1. Defective bulb 2. Defective wire 3. Defective sending unit. Disconnect the wire from the sending unit and ground it. Replace the sending unit if the light comes on with the ignition ON. 4. Problem in individual system 5. Defective sending unit

Troubleshooting Clutch Problems

It is false economy to replace individual clutch components. The pressure plate, clutch plate and throwout bearing should be replaced as a set, and the flywheel face inspected, whenever the clutch is overhauled. See Chapter 6 for service procedures.

Condition	Possible Cause
Clutch chatter	1. Grease on driven plate (disc) facing 2. Binding clutch linkage or cable 3. Loose, damaged facings on driven plate (disc) 4. Engine mounts loose 5. Incorrect height adjustment of pressure plate release levers 6. Clutch housing or housing to transmission adapter misalignment 7. Loose driven plate hub
Clutch grabbing	1. Oil, grease on driven plate (disc) facing 2. Broken pressure plate 3. Warped or binding driven plate. Driven plate binding on clutch shaft
Clutch slips	1. Lack of lubrication in clutch linkage or cable (linkage or cable binds, causes incomplete engagement) 2. Incorrect pedal, or linkage adjustment 3. Broken pressure plate springs 4. Weak pressure plate springs 5. Grease on driven plate facings (disc)

Troubleshooting Clutch Problems (cont.)

Condition	Possible Cause
Incomplete clutch release	1. Incorrect pedal or linkage adjustment or linkage or cable binding 2. Incorrect height adjustment on pressure plate release levers 3. Loose, broken facings on driven plate (disc) 4. Bent, dished, warped driven plate caused by overheating
Grinding, whirring grating noise when pedal is depressed	1. Worn or defective throwout bearing 2. Starter drive teeth contacting flywheel ring gear teeth. Look for milled or polished teeth on ring gear.
Squeal, howl, trumpeting noise when pedal is being released (occurs during first inch to inch and one-half of pedal travel)	Pilot bushing worn or lack of lubricant. If bushing appears OK, polish bushing with emery cloth, soak lube wick in oil, lube bushing with oil, apply film of chassis grease to clutch shaft pilot hub, reassemble. NOTE: Bushing wear may be due to misalignment of clutch housing or housing to transmission adapter
Vibration or clutch pedal pulsation with clutch disengaged (pedal fully depressed)	1. Worn or defective engine transmission mounts 2. Flywheel run out. (Flywheel run out at face not to exceed 0.005") 3. Damaged or defective clutch components

Troubleshooting Manual Transmission Problems
See Chapter 6 for service procedures

Condition	Possible Cause
Transmission jumps out of gear	1. Misalignment of transmission case or clutch housing. 2. Worn pilot bearing in crankshaft. 3. Bent transmission shaft. 4. Worn high speed sliding gear. 5. Worn teeth or end-play in clutch shaft. 6. Insufficient spring tension on shifter rail plunger. 7. Bent or loose shifter fork. 8. Gears not engaging completely. 9. Loose or worn bearings on clutch shaft or mainshaft. 10. Worn gear teeth. 11. Worn or damaged detent balls.
Transmission sticks in gear	1. Clutch not releasing fully. 2. Burred or battered teeth on clutch shaft, or sliding sleeve. 3. Burred or battered transmission mainshaft. 4. Frozen synchronizing clutch. 5. Stuck shifter rail plunger. 6. Gearshift lever twisting and binding shifter rail. 7. Battered teeth on high speed sliding gear or on sleeve. 8. Improper lubrication, or lack of lubrication. 9. Corroded transmission parts. 10. Defective mainshaft pilot bearing. 11. Locked gear bearings will give same effect as stuck in gear.
Transmission gears will not synchronize	1. Binding pilot bearing on mainshaft, will synchronize in high gear only. 2. Clutch not releasing fully. 3. Detent spring weak or broken. 4. Weak or broken springs under balls in sliding gear sleeve. 5. Binding bearing on clutch shaft, or binding countershaft. 6. Binding pilot bearing in crankshaft. 7. Badly worn gear teeth. 8. Improper lubrication. 9. Constant mesh gear not turning freely on transmission mainshaft. Will synchronize in that gear only.

Condition	Possible Cause
Gears spinning when shifting into gear from neutral	1. Clutch not releasing fully. 2. In some cases an extremely light lubricant in transmission will cause gears to continue to spin for a short time after clutch is released. 3. Binding pilot bearing in crankshaft.
Transmission noisy in all gears	1. Insufficient lubricant, or improper lubricant. 2. Worn countergear bearings. 3. Worn or damaged main drive gear or countergear. 4. Damaged main drive gear or mainshaft bearings. 5. Worn or damaged countergear anti-lash plate.
Transmission noisy in neutral only	1. Damaged main drive gear bearing. 2. Damaged or loose mainshaft pilot bearing. 3. Worn or damaged countergear anti-lash plate. 4. Worn countergear bearings.
Transmission noisy in one gear only	1. Damaged or worn constant mesh gears. 2. Worn or damaged countergear bearings. 3. Damaged or worn synchronizer.
Transmission noisy in reverse only	1. Worn or damaged reverse idler gear or idler bushing. 2. Worn or damaged mainshaft reverse gear. 3. Worn or damaged reverse countergear. 4. Damaged shift mechanism.

TROUBLESHOOTING AUTOMATIC TRANSMISSION PROBLEMS

Keeping alert to changes in the operating characteristics of the transmission (changing shift points, noises, etc.) can prevent small problems from becoming large ones. If the problem cannot be traced to loose bolts, fluid level, misadjusted linkage, clogged filters or similar problems, you should probably seek professional service.

Transmission Fluid Indications

The appearance and odor of the transmission fluid can give valuable clues to the overall condition of the transmission. Always note the appearance of the fluid when you check the fluid level or change the fluid. Rub a small amount of fluid between your fingers to feel for grit and smell the fluid on the dipstick.

If the fluid appears:	It indicates:
Clear and red colored	Normal operation
Discolored (extremely dark red or brownish) or smells burned	Band or clutch pack failure, usually caused by an overheated transmission. Hauling very heavy loads with insufficient power or failure to change the fluid often result in overheating. Do not confuse this appearance with newer fluids that have a darker red color and a strong odor (though not a burned odor).
Foamy or aerated (light in color and full of bubbles)	1. The level is too high (gear train is churning oil) 2. An internal air leak (air is mixing with the fluid). Have the transmission checked professionally.
Solid residue in the fluid	Defective bands, clutch pack or bearings. Bits of band material or metal abrasives are clinging to the dipstick. Have the transmission checked professionally.
Varnish coating on the dipstick	The transmission fluid is overheating

TROUBLESHOOTING DRIVE AXLE PROBLEMS

First, determine when the noise is most noticeable.

Drive Noise: Produced under vehicle acceleration.

Coast Noise: Produced while coasting with a closed throttle.

Float Noise: Occurs while maintaining constant speed (just enough to keep speed constant) on a level road.

External Noise Elimination

It is advisable to make a thorough road test to determine whether the noise originates in the rear axle or whether it originates from the tires, engine, transmission, wheel bearings or road surface. Noise originating from other places cannot be corrected by servicing the rear axle.

ROAD NOISE

Brick or rough surfaced concrete roads produce noises that seem to come from the rear axle. Road noise is usually identical in Drive or Coast and driving on a different type of road will tell whether the road is the problem.

TIRE NOISE

Tire noise can be mistaken as rear axle noise, even though the tires on the front are at fault. Snow tread and mud tread tires or tires worn unevenly will frequently cause vibrations which seem to originate elsewhere; *temporarily, and for test purposes only,* inflate the tires to 40–50 lbs. This will significantly alter the noise produced by the tires, but will not alter noise from the rear axle. Noises from the rear axle will normally cease at speeds below 30 mph on coast, while tire noise will continue at lower tone as speed is decreased. The rear axle noise will usually change from drive conditions to coast conditions, while tire noise will not. Do not forget to lower the tire pressure to normal after the test is complete.

ENGINE/TRANSMISSION NOISE

Determine at what speed the noise is most pronounced, then stop in a quiet place. With the transmission in Neutral, run the engine through speeds corresponding to road speeds where the noise was noticed. Noises produced with the vehicle standing still are coming from the engine or transmission.

FRONT WHEEL BEARINGS

Front wheel bearing noises, sometimes confused with rear axle noises, will not change when comparing drive and coast conditions. While holding the speed steady, lightly apply the footbrake. This will often cause wheel bearing noise to lessen, as some of the weight is taken off the bearing. Front wheel bearings are easily checked by jacking up the wheels and spinning the wheels. Shaking the wheels will also determine if the wheel bearings are excessively loose.

REAR AXLE NOISES

Eliminating other possible sources can narrow the cause to the rear axle, which normally produces noise from worn gears or bearings. Gear noises tend to peak in a narrow speed range, while bearing noises will usually vary in pitch with engine speeds.

Noise Diagnosis

The Noise Is:	Most Probably Produced By:
1. Identical under Drive or Coast	Road surface, tires or front wheel bearings
2. Different depending on road surface	Road surface or tires
3. Lower as speed is lowered	Tires
4. Similar when standing or moving	Engine or transmission
5. A vibration	Unbalanced tires, rear wheel bearing, unbalanced driveshaft or worn U-joint
6. A knock or click about every two tire revolutions	Rear wheel bearing
7. Most pronounced on turns	Damaged differential gears
8. A steady low-pitched whirring or scraping, starting at low speeds	Damaged or worn pinion bearing
9. A chattering vibration on turns	Wrong differential lubricant or worn clutch plates (limited slip rear axle)
10. Noticed only in Drive, Coast or Float conditions	Worn ring gear and/or pinion gear

Troubleshooting Steering & Suspension Problems

Condition	Possible Cause
Hard steering (wheel is hard to turn)	1. Improper tire pressure 2. Loose or glazed pump drive belt 3. Low or incorrect fluid 4. Loose, bent or poorly lubricated front end parts 5. Improper front end alignment (excessive caster) 6. Bind in steering column or linkage 7. Kinked hydraulic hose 8. Air in hydraulic system 9. Low pump output or leaks in system 10. Obstruction in lines 11. Pump valves sticking or out of adjustment 12. Incorrect wheel alignment
Loose steering (too much play in steering wheel)	1. Loose wheel bearings 2. Faulty shocks 3. Worn linkage or suspension components 4. Loose steering gear mounting or linkage points 5. Steering mechanism worn or improperly adjusted 6. Valve spool improperly adjusted 7. Worn ball joints, tie-rod ends, etc.
Veers or wanders (pulls to one side with hands off steering wheel)	1. Improper tire pressure 2. Improper front end alignment 3. Dragging or improperly adjusted brakes 4. Bent frame 5. Improper rear end alignment 6. Faulty shocks or springs 7. Loose or bent front end components 8. Play in Pitman arm 9. Steering gear mountings loose 10. Loose wheel bearings 11. Binding Pitman arm 12. Spool valve sticking or improperly adjusted 13. Worn ball joints
Wheel oscillation or vibration transmitted through steering wheel	1. Low or uneven tire pressure 2. Loose wheel bearings 3. Improper front end alignment 4. Bent spindle 5. Worn, bent or broken front end components 6. Tires out of round or out of balance 7. Excessive lateral runout in disc brake rotor 8. Loose or bent shock absorber or strut
Noises (see also "Troubleshooting Drive Axle Problems")	1. Loose belts 2. Low fluid, air in system 3. Foreign matter in system 4. Improper lubrication 5. Interference or chafing in linkage 6. Steering gear mountings loose 7. Incorrect adjustment or wear in gear box 8. Faulty valves or wear in pump 9. Kinked hydraulic lines 10. Worn wheel bearings
Poor return of steering	1. Over-inflated tires 2. Improperly aligned front end (excessive caster) 3. Binding in steering column 4. No lubrication in front end 5. Steering gear adjusted too tight
Uneven tire wear (see "How To Read Tire Wear")	1. Incorrect tire pressure 2. Improperly aligned front end 3. Tires out-of-balance 4. Bent or worn suspension parts

HOW TO READ TIRE WEAR

The way your tires wear is a good indicator of other parts of the suspension. Abnormal wear patterns are often caused by the need for simple tire maintenance, or for front end alignment.

Excessive wear at the center of the tread indicates that the air pressure in the tire is consistently too high. The tire is riding on the center of the tread and wearing it prematurely. Occasionally, this wear pattern can result from outrageously wide tires on narrow rims. The cure for this is to replace either the tires or the wheels.

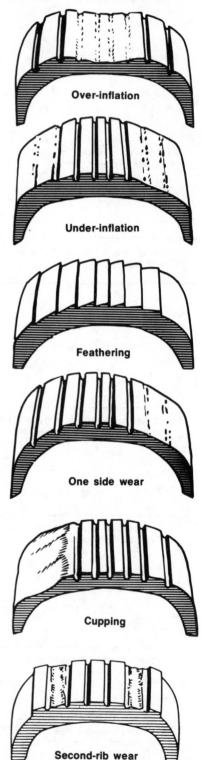

Over-inflation

This type of wear usually results from consistent under-inflation. When a tire is under-inflated, there is too much contact with the road by the outer treads, which wear prematurely. When this type of wear occurs, and the tire pressure is known to be consistently correct, a bent or worn steering component or the need for wheel alignment could be indicated.

Under-inflation

Feathering is a condition when the edge of each tread rib develops a slightly rounded edge on one side and a sharp edge on the other. By running your hand over the tire, you can usually feel the sharper edges before you'll be able to see them. The most common causes of feathering are incorrect toe-in setting or deteriorated bushings in the front suspension.

Feathering

When an inner or outer rib wears faster than the rest of the tire, the need for wheel alignment is indicated. There is excessive camber in the front suspension, causing the wheel to lean too much putting excessive load on one side of the tire. Misalignment could also be due to sagging springs, worn ball joints, or worn control arm bushings. Be sure the vehicle is loaded the way it's normally driven when you have the wheels aligned.

One side wear

Cups or scalloped dips appearing around the edge of the tread almost always indicate worn (sometimes bent) suspension parts. Adjustment of wheel alignment alone will seldom cure the problem. Any worn component that connects the wheel to the suspension can cause this type of wear. Occasionally, wheels that are out of balance will wear like this, but wheel imbalance usually shows up as bald spots between the outside edges and center of the tread.

Cupping

Second-rib wear is usually found only in radial tires, and appears where the steel belts end in relation to the tread. It can be kept to a minimum by paying careful attention to tire pressure and frequently rotating the tires. This is often considered normal wear but excessive amounts indicate that the tires are too wide for the wheels.

Second-rib wear

Troubleshooting Disc Brake Problems

Condition	Possible Cause
Noise—groan—brake noise emanating when slowly releasing brakes (creep-groan)	Not detrimental to function of disc brakes—no corrective action required. (This noise may be eliminated by slightly increasing or decreasing brake pedal efforts.)
Rattle—brake noise or rattle emanating at low speeds on rough roads, (front wheels only).	1. Shoe anti-rattle spring missing or not properly positioned. 2. Excessive clearance between shoe and caliper. 3. Soft or broken caliper seals. 4. Deformed or misaligned disc. 5. Loose caliper.
Scraping	1. Mounting bolts too long. 2. Loose wheel bearings. 3. Bent, loose, or misaligned splash shield.
Front brakes heat up during driving and fail to release	1. Operator riding brake pedal. 2. Stop light switch improperly adjusted. 3. Sticking pedal linkage. 4. Frozen or seized piston. 5. Residual pressure valve in master cylinder. 6. Power brake malfunction. 7. Proportioning valve malfunction.
Leaky brake caliper	1. Damaged or worn caliper piston seal. 2. Scores or corrosion on surface of cylinder bore.
Grabbing or uneven brake action—Brakes pull to one side	1. Causes listed under "Brakes Pull". 2. Power brake malfunction. 3. Low fluid level in master cylinder. 4. Air in hydraulic system. 5. Brake fluid, oil or grease on linings. 6. Unmatched linings. 7. Distorted brake pads. 8. Frozen or seized pistons. 9. Incorrect tire pressure. 10. Front end out of alignment. 11. Broken rear spring. 12. Brake caliper pistons sticking. 13. Restricted hose or line. 14. Caliper not in proper alignment to braking disc. 15. Stuck or malfunctioning metering valve. 16. Soft or broken caliper seals. 17. Loose caliper.
Brake pedal can be depressed without braking effect	1. Air in hydraulic system or improper bleeding procedure. 2. Leak past primary cup in master cylinder. 3. Leak in system. 4. Rear brakes out of adjustment. 5. Bleeder screw open.
Excessive pedal travel	1. Air, leak, or insufficient fluid in system or caliper. 2. Warped or excessively tapered shoe and lining assembly. 3. Excessive disc runout. 4. Rear brake adjustment required. 5. Loose wheel bearing adjustment. 6. Damaged caliper piston seal. 7. Improper brake fluid (boil). 8. Power brake malfunction. 9. Weak or soft hoses.

Troubleshooting Disc Brake Problems (cont.)

Condition	Possible Cause
Brake roughness or chatter (pedal pumping)	1. Excessive thickness variation of braking disc. 2. Excessive lateral runout of braking disc. 3. Rear brake drums out-of-round. 4. Excessive front bearing clearance.
Excessive pedal effort	1. Brake fluid, oil or grease on linings. 2. Incorrect lining. 3. Frozen or seized pistons. 4. Power brake malfunction. 5. Kinked or collapsed hose or line. 6. Stuck metering valve. 7. Scored caliper or master cylinder bore. 8. Seized caliper pistons.
Brake pedal fades (pedal travel increases with foot on brake)	1. Rough master cylinder or caliper bore. 2. Loose or broken hydraulic lines/connections. 3. Air in hydraulic system. 4. Fluid level low. 5. Weak or soft hoses. 6. Inferior quality brake shoes or fluid. 7. Worn master cylinder piston cups or seals.

Troubleshooting Drum Brakes

Condition	Possible Cause
Pedal goes to floor	1. Fluid low in reservoir. 2. Air in hydraulic system. 3. Improperly adjusted brake. 4. Leaking wheel cylinders. 5. Loose or broken brake lines. 6. Leaking or worn master cylinder. 7. Excessively worn brake lining.
Spongy brake pedal	1. Air in hydraulic system. 2. Improper brake fluid (low boiling point). 3. Excessively worn or cracked brake drums. 4. Broken pedal pivot bushing.
Brakes pulling	1. Contaminated lining. 2. Front end out of alignment. 3. Incorrect brake adjustment. 4. Unmatched brake lining. 5. Brake drums out of round. 6. Brake shoes distorted. 7. Restricted brake hose or line. 8. Broken rear spring. 9. Worn brake linings. 10. Uneven lining wear. 11. Glazed brake lining. 12. Excessive brake lining dust. 13. Heat spotted brake drums. 14. Weak brake return springs. 15. Faulty automatic adjusters. 16. Low or incorrect tire pressure.

Condition	Possible Cause
Squealing brakes	1. Glazed brake lining. 2. Saturated brake lining. 3. Weak or broken brake shoe retaining spring. 4. Broken or weak brake shoe return spring. 5. Incorrect brake lining. 6. Distorted brake shoes. 7. Bent support plate. 8. Dust in brakes or scored brake drums. 9. Linings worn below limit. 10. Uneven brake lining wear. 11. Heat spotted brake drums.
Chirping brakes	1. Out of round drum or eccentric axle flange pilot.
Dragging brakes	1. Incorrect wheel or parking brake adjustment. 2. Parking brakes engaged or improperly adjusted. 3. Weak or broken brake shoe return spring. 4. Brake pedal binding. 5. Master cylinder cup sticking. 6. Obstructed master cylinder relief port. 7. Saturated brake lining. 8. Bent or out of round brake drum. 9. Contaminated or improper brake fluid. 10. Sticking wheel cylinder pistons. 11. Driver riding brake pedal. 12. Defective proportioning valve. 13. Insufficient brake shoe lubricant.
Hard pedal	1. Brake booster inoperative. 2. Incorrect brake lining. 3. Restricted brake line or hose. 4. Frozen brake pedal linkage. 5. Stuck wheel cylinder. 6. Binding pedal linkage. 7. Faulty proportioning valve.
Wheel locks	1. Contaminated brake lining. 2. Loose or torn brake lining. 3. Wheel cylinder cups sticking. 4. Incorrect wheel bearing adjustment. 5. Faulty proportioning valve.
Brakes fade (high speed)	1. Incorrect lining. 2. Overheated brake drums. 3. Incorrect brake fluid (low boiling temperature). 4. Saturated brake lining. 5. Leak in hydraulic system. 6. Faulty automatic adjusters.
Pedal pulsates	1. Bent or out of round brake drum.
Brake chatter and shoe knock	1. Out of round brake drum. 2. Loose support plate. 3. Bent support plate. 4. Distorted brake shoes. 5. Machine grooves in contact face of brake drum (Shoe Knock). 6. Contaminated brake lining. 7. Missing or loose components. 8. Incorrect lining material. 9. Out-of-round brake drums. 10. Heat spotted or scored brake drums. 11. Out-of-balance wheels.

Troubleshooting Drum Brakes (cont.)

Condition	Possible Cause
Brakes do not self adjust	1. Adjuster screw frozen in thread. 2. Adjuster screw corroded at thrust washer. 3. Adjuster lever does not engage star wheel. 4. Adjuster installed on wrong wheel.
Brake light glows	1. Leak in the hydraulic system. 2. Air in the system. 3. Improperly adjusted master cylinder pushrod. 4. Uneven lining wear. 5. Failure to center combination valve or proportioning valve.

Mechanic's Data

General Conversion Table

Multiply By	To Convert	To	
	LENGTH		
2.54	Inches	Centimeters	.3937
25.4	Inches	Millimeters	.03937
30.48	Feet	Centimeters	.0328
.304	Feet	Meters	3.28
.914	Yards	Meters	1.094
1.609	Miles	Kilometers	.621
	VOLUME		
.473	Pints	Liters	2.11
.946	Quarts	Liters	1.06
3.785	Gallons	Liters	.264
.016	Cubic inches	Liters	61.02
16.39	Cubic inches	Cubic cms.	.061
28.3	Cubic feet	Liters	.0353
	MASS (Weight)		
28.35	Ounces	Grams	.035
.4536	Pounds	Kilograms	2.20
—	**To obtain**	**From**	**Multiply by**

Multiply By	To Convert	To	
	AREA		
.645	Square inches	Square cms.	.155
.836	Square yds.	Square meters	1.196
	FORCE		
4.448	Pounds	Newtons	.225
.138	Ft./lbs.	Kilogram/meters	7.23
1.36	Ft./lbs.	Newton-meters	.737
.112	In./lbs.	Newton-meters	8.844
	PRESSURE		
.068	Psi	Atmospheres	14.7
6.89	Psi	Kilopascals	.145
	OTHER		
1.104	Horsepower (DIN)	Horsepower (SAE)	.9861
.746	Horsepower (SAE)	Kilowatts (KW)	1.34
1.60	Mph	Km/h	.625
.425	Mpg	Km/1	2.35
—	**To obtain**	**From**	**Multiply by**

Tap Drill Sizes

National Coarse or U.S.S.

Screw & Tap Size	Threads Per Inch	Use Drill Number
No. 5	40	39
No. 6	32	36
No. 8	32	29
No. 10	24	25
No. 12	24	17
1/4	20	8
5/16	18	F
3/8	16	5/16
7/16	14	U
1/2	13	27/64
9/16	12	31/64
5/8	11	17/32
3/4	10	21/32
7/8	9	49/64

National Coarse or U.S.S.

Screw & Tap Size	Threads Per Inch	Use Drill Number
1	8	7/8
1 1/8	7	63/64
1 1/4	7	1 7/64
1 1/2	6	1 11/32

National Fine or S.A.E.

Screw & Tap Size	Threads Per Inch	Use Drill Number
No. 5	44	37
No. 6	40	33
No. 8	36	29
No. 10	32	21

National Fine or S.A.E.

Screw & Tap Size	Threads Per Inch	Use Drill Number
No. 12	28	15
1/4	28	3
6/16	24	1
3/8	24	Q
7/16	20	W
1/2	20	29/64
9/16	18	33/64
5/8	18	37/64
3/4	16	11/16
7/8	14	13/16
1 1/8	12	1 3/64
1 1/4	12	1 11/64
1 1/2	12	1 27/64

Drill Sizes In Decimal Equivalents

Inch	Decimal	Wire	mm
1/64	.0156		.39
	.0157		.4
	.0160	78	
	.0165		.42
	.0173		.44
	.0177		.45
	.0180	77	
	.0181		.46
	.0189		.48
	.0197		.5
	.0200	76	
	.0210	75	
	.0217		.55
	.0225	74	
	.0236		.6
	.0240	73	
	.0250	72	
	.0256		.65
	.0260	71	
	.0276		.7
	.0280	70	
	.0292	69	
	.0295		.75
	.0310	68	
1/32	.0312		.79
	.0315		.8
	.0320	67	
	.0330	66	
	.0335		.85
	.0350	65	
	.0354		.9
	.0360	64	
	.0370	63	
	.0374		.95
	.0380	62	
	.0390	61	
	.0394		1.0
	.0400	60	
	.0410	59	
	.0413		1.05
	.0420	58	
	.0430	57	
	.0433		1.1
	.0453		1.15
3/64	.0465	56	
	.0469		1.19
	.0472		1.2
	.0492		1.25
	.0512		1.3
	.0520	55	
	.0531		1.35
	.0550	54	
	.0551		1.4
	.0571		1.45
	.0591		1.5
	.0595	53	
	.0610		1.55
1/16	.0625		1.59
	.0630		1.6
	.0635	52	
	.0650		1.65
	.0669		1.7
	.0670	51	
	.0689		1.75
	.0700	50	
	.0709		1.8
	.0728		1.85

Inch	Decimal	Wire	mm
	.0730	49	
	.0748		1.9
	.0760	48	
	.0768		1.95
5/64	.0781		1.98
	.0785	47	
	.0787		2.0
	.0807		2.05
	.0810	46	
	.0820	45	
	.0827		2.1
	.0846		2.15
	.0860	44	
	.0866		2.2
	.0886		2.25
	.0890	43	
	.0906		2.3
	.0925		2.35
	.0935	42	
3/32	.0938		2.38
	.0945		2.4
	.0960	41	
	.0965		2.45
	.0980	40	
	.0981		2.5
	.0995	39	
	.1015	38	
	.1024		2.6
	.1040	37	
	.1063		2.7
	.1065	36	
	.1083		2.75
7/64	.1094		2.77
	.1100	35	
	.1102		2.8
	.1110	34	
	.1130	33	
	.1142		2.9
	.1160	32	
	.1181		3.0
	.1200	31	
	.1220		3.1
1/8	.1250		3.17
	.1260		3.2
	.1280		3.25
	.1285	30	
	.1299		3.3
	.1339		3.4
	.1360	29	
	.1378		3.5
	.1405	28	
9/64	.1406		3.57
	.1417		3.6
	.1440	27	
	.1457		3.7
	.1470	26	
	.1476		3.75
	.1495	25	
	.1496		3.8
	.1520	24	
	.1535		3.9
	.1540	23	
5/32	.1562		3.96
	.1570	22	
	.1575		4.0
	.1590	21	
	.1610	20	

Inch	Decimal	Wire & Letter	mm
	.1614		4.1
	.1654		4.2
	.1660	19	
	.1673		4.25
	.1693		4.3
	.1695	18	
11/64	.1719		4.36
	.1730	17	
	.1732		4.4
	.1770	16	
	.1772		4.5
	.1800	15	
	.1811		4.6
	.1820	14	
	.1850	13	
	.1850		4.7
	.1870		4.75
3/16	.1875		4.76
	.1890		4.8
	.1890	12	
	.1910	11	
	.1929		4.9
	.1935	10	
	.1960	9	
	.1969		5.0
	.1990	8	
	.2008		5.1
	.2010	7	
13/64	.2031		5.16
	.2040	6	
	.2047		5.2
	.2055	5	
	.2067		5.25
	.2087		5.3
	.2090	4	
	.2126		5.4
	.2130	3	
7/32	.2188		5.5
	.2205		5.6
	.2210	2	
	.2244		5.7
	.2264		5.75
	.2280	1	
	.2283		5.8
	.2323		5.9
	.2340	A	
15/64	.2344		5.95
	.2362		6.0
	.2380	B	
	.2402		6.1
	.2420	C	
	.2441		6.2
	.2460	D	
	.2461		6.25
	.2480		6.3
1/4	.2500	E	
	.2520		6.
	.2559		6.5
	.2570	F	
	.2598		6.6
	.2610	G	
	.2638		6.7
17/64	.2656		6.74
	.2657		6.75
	.2660	H	
	.2677		6.8

Inch	Decimal	Letter	mm
	.2717		6.9
	.2720	I	
	.2756		7.0
	.2770	J	
	.2795		7.1
	.2810	K	
9/32	.2812		7.14
	.2835		7.2
	.2854		7.25
	.2874		7.3
	.2900	L	
	.2913		7.4
	.2950	M	
	.2953		7.5
19/64	.2969		7.54
	.2992		7.6
	.3020	N	
	.3031		7.7
	.3051		7.75
	.3071		7.8
	.3110		7.9
5/16	.3125		7.93
	.3150		8.0
	.3160	O	
	.3189		8.1
	.3228		8.2
	.3230	P	
	.3248		8.25
	.3268		8.3
21/64	.3281		8.33
	.3307		8.4
	.3320	Q	
	.3346		8.5
	.3386		8.6
	.3390	R	
	.3425		8.7
11/32	.3438		8.73
	.3445		8.75
	.3465		8.8
	.3480	S	
	.3504		8.9
	.3543		9.0
	.3580	T	
	.3583		9.1
23/64	.3594		9.12
	.3622		9.2
	.3642		9.25
	.3661		9.3
	.3680	U	
	.3701		9.4
	.3740		9.5
3/8	.3750		9.52
	.3770	V	
	.3780		9.6
	.3819		9.7
	.3839		9.75
	.3858		9.8
	.3860	W	
	.3898		9.9
25/64	.3906		9.92
	.3937		10.0
	.3970	X	
	.4040	Y	
13/32	.4062		10.31
	.4130	Z	
	.4134		10.5
27/64	.4219		10.71

Inch	Decimal	mm
	.4331	11.0
7/16	.4375	11.11
	.4528	11.5
29/64	.4531	11.51
15/32	.4688	11.90
	.4724	12.0
31/64	.4844	12.30
	.4921	12.5
1/2	.5000	12.70
	.5118	13.0
33/64	.5156	13.09
17/32	.5312	13.49
	.5315	13.5
35/64	.5469	13.89
	.5512	14.0
9/16	.5625	14.28
	.5709	14.5
37/64	.5781	14.68
	.5906	15.0
19/32	.5938	15.08
39/64	.6094	15.47
	.6102	15.5
5/8	.6250	15.87
	.6299	16.0
41/64	.6406	16.27
	.6496	16.5
21/32	.6562	16.66
	.6693	17.0
43/64	.6719	17.06
11/16	.6875	17.46
	.6890	17.5
45/64	.7031	17.85
	.7087	18.0
23/32	.7188	18.25
	.7283	18.5
47/64	.7344	18.65
	.7480	19.0
3/4	.7500	19.05
49/64	.7656	19.44
	.7677	19.5
25/32	.7812	19.84
	.7874	20.0
51/64	.7969	20.24
	.8071	20.5
13/16	.8125	20.63
	.8268	21.0
53/64	.8281	21.03
27/32	.8438	21.43
	.8465	21.5
55/64	.8594	21.82
	.8661	22.0
7/8	.8750	22.22
	.8858	22.5
57/64	.8906	22.62
	.9055	23.0
29/32	.9062	23.01
59/64	.9219	23.41
	.9252	23.5
15/16	.9375	23.81
	.9449	24.0
61/64	.9531	24.2
	.9646	24.5
31/32	.9688	24.6
	.9843	25.0
63/64	.9844	25.0
1	1.0000	25.4

Index

Chilton's Repair & Tune-Up Guides

The complete line covers domestic cars, imports, trucks, vans, RV's and 4-wheel drive vehicles.

CODE	TITLE	CODE	TITLE
#7199	AMC 75-82; all models	#6935	GM Sub-compact 71-81 inc. Vega,
#7165	Alliance 1983		Monza, Astre, Sunbird, Starfire & Skyhawk
#7323	Aries 81-82	#6937	Granada 75-80
#7032	Arrow Pick-Up 79-81	#5905	GTO 68-73
#7193	Aspen 76-80	#5821	GTX 68-73
#5902	Audi 70-73	#7204	Honda 73-82
#7028	Audi 4000/5000 77-81	#7191	Horizon 78-82
#6337	Audi Fox 73-75	#5912	International Scout 67-73
#5807	Barracuda 65-72	#7136	Jeep CJ 1945-81
#7203	Blazer 69-82	#6739	Jeep Wagoneer, Commando, Cherokee 66-79
#5576	BMW 59-70	#6962	Jetta 1980
#6844	BMW 70-79	#7203	Jimmy 69-82
#7027	Bobcat	#7059	J-2000 1982
#7307	Buick Century/Regal 75-83	#7165	Le Car 76-83
#7045	Camaro 67-81	#7323	Le Baron 1982
#6695	Capri 70-77	#5905	Le Mans 68-73
#7195	Capri 79-82	#7055	Lynx 81-82 inc. EXP & LN-7
#7059	Cavalier 1982	#6634	Maverick 70-77
#5807	Challenger 65-72	#7198	Mazda 71-82
#7037	Challenger (Import) 71-81	#7031	Mazda RX-7 79-81
#7041	Champ 78-81	#6065	Mercedes-Benz 59-70
#6316	Charger/Coronet 71-75	#5907	Mercedes-Benz 68-73
#7162	Chevette 76-82 inc. diesel	#6809	Mercedes-Benz 74-79
#7313	Chevrolet 68-83 all full size models	#7128	Mercury 68-71 all full sized models
#7167	Chevrolet/GMC Pick-Ups 70-82	#7194	Mercury Mid-Size 71-82 inc. Continental,
#7169	Chevrolet/GMC Vans 67-82		Cougar, XR-7 & Montego
#7310	Chevrolet S-10/GMC S-15 Pick-Ups 82-83	#7173	MG 61-80
#7051	Chevy Luv 72-81 inc. 4wd	#6973	Monarch 75-80
#7056	Chevy Mid-Size 64-82 inc. El Camino,	#6542	Mustang 65-73
	Chevelle, Laguna, Malibu & Monte Carlo	#6812	Mustang II 74-78
#6841	Chevy II 62-79	#7195	Mustang 79-82
#7059	Cimarron 1982	#6841	Nova 69-79
#7049	Citation 80-81	#7049	Omega 81-82
#7037	Colt 71-81	#7191	Omni 78-82
#6634	Comet 70-77	#6575	Opel 71-75
#7194	Continental 1982	#5982	Peugeot 70-74
#6691	Corvair 60-69 inc. Turbo	#7049	Phoenix 81-82
#6576	Corvette 53-62	#7027	Pinto 71-80
#7192	Corvette 63-82	#8552	Plymouth 68-76 full sized models
#7190	Cutlass 70-82	#7168	Plymouth Vans 67-82
#6324	Dart 68-76	#5822	Porsche 69-73
#6962	Dasher 74-80	#7048	Porsche 924 & 928 77-81 inc. Turbo
#5790	Datsun 61-72	#6962	Rabbit 75-80
#7196	Datsun F10, 310, Nissan Stanza 77-82	#7323	Reliant 81-82
#7170	Datsun 200SX, 510, 610, 710, 810 73-82	#7165	Renault 75-83
#7197	Datsun 1200, 210/Nissan Sentra 73-82	#5821	Roadrunner 68-73
#7172	Datsun Z & ZX 70-82	#5988	Saab 69-75
#7050	Datsun Pick-Ups 70-81 inc. 4wd	#7041	Sapporo 78-81
#6324	Demon 68-76	#5821	Satellite 68-73
#6554	Dodge 68-77 all full sized models	#6962	Scirocco 75-80
#7323	Dodge 400 1982	#7059	Skyhawk 1982
#6486	Dodge Charger 67-70	#7049	Skylark 80-81
#7168	Dodge Vans 67-82	#7208	Subaru 70-82
#6326	Duster 68-76	#5905	Tempest 68-73
#7055	Escort 81-82 inc. EXP & LN-7	#6320	Torino 62-75
#6320	Fairlane 62-75	#5795	Toyota 66-70
#7312	Fairmont 78-83	#7043	Toyota Celica & Supra 71-81
#7042	Fiat 69-81	#7036	Toyota Corolla, Carina, Tercel, Starlet 70-81
#6846	Fiesta 78-80	#7044	Toyota Corona, Cressida, Crown, Mark II 70-81
#7046	Firebird 67-81	#7035	Toyota Pick-Ups 70-81
#7059	Firenza 1982	#5910	Triumph 69-73
#7128	Ford 68-81 all full sized models	#7162	T-1000 1982
#7140	Ford Bronco 66-81	#6326	Valiant 68-76
#6983	Ford Courier 72-80	#5796	Volkswagen 49-71
#7194	Ford Mid-Size 71-82 inc. Torino, Gran	#6837	Volkswagen 70-81
	Torino, Ranchero, Elite, LTD II & Thunder-	#7193	Volaré 76-80
	bird	#6529	Volvo 56-69
#7166	Ford Pick-Ups 65-82 inc. 4wd	#7040	Volvo 70-80
#7171	Ford Vans 61-82	#7312	Zephyr 78-83
#7165	Fuego 82-83		

Chilton's Repair & Tune-Up Guides are available at your local retailer or by mailing a check or money order for **$10.95** plus **$1.00** to cover postage and handling to:

Chilton Book Company
Dept. DM
Radnor, PA 19089

NOTE: When ordering be sure to include your name & address, book code & title.